ELDER ABUSE

ELDER ABUSE
Forensic, Legal and Medical Aspects

Edited by
AMY CARNEY

ELSEVIER

ACADEMIC PRESS
An imprint of Elsevier

Academic Press is an imprint of Elsevier
125 London Wall, London EC2Y 5AS, United Kingdom
525 B Street, Suite 1650, San Diego, CA 92101, United States
50 Hampshire Street, 5th Floor, Cambridge, MA 02139, United States
The Boulevard, Langford Lane, Kidlington, Oxford OX5 1GB, United Kingdom

Notices
Knowledge and best practice in this field are constantly changing. As new research and experience broaden our understanding, changes in research methods, professional practices, or medical treatment may become necessary.

Practitioners and researchers must always rely on their own experience and knowledge in evaluating and using any information, methods, compounds, or experiments described herein. In using such information or methods they should be mindful of their own safety and the safety of others, including parties for whom they have a professional responsibility.

To the fullest extent of the law, neither the Publisher nor the authors, contributors, or editors, assume any liability for any injury and/or damage to persons or property as a matter of products liability, negligence or otherwise, or from any use or operation of any methods, products, instructions, or ideas contained in the material herein.

Library of Congress Cataloging-in-Publication Data
A catalog record for this book is available from the Library of Congress

British Library Cataloguing-in-Publication Data
A catalogue record for this book is available from the British Library

ISBN: 978-0-12-815779-4

For information on all Academic Press publications visit our website at https://www.elsevier.com/books-and-journals

Publisher: Stacy Masucci
Acquisition Editor: Elizabeth Brown
Editorial Project Manager: Ana Claudia Garcia
Production Project Manager: Mohana Natarajan
Cover Designer: Matthew Limbert

Typeset by TNQ Technologies

CONTENTS

List of Contributors xi

Foreword xiii

Acknowledgments... xv

Introduction.. xvii

Chapter 1 Epidemiology of Elder Abuse and Neglect **1**

Elder Abuse: Danger for an Aging Population.................... 1

Demographics: The Impact of an Aging Population 11

Forensic, Medical, and Legal Implications 15

Case Study 15

References 16

Chapter 2 Identification of Elder Abuse **19**

Risk and Vulnerability 19

Observable Injury versus Suspected Abuse 30

Documenting Elder Abuse... 34

Cultural Awareness 38

Intervention and Advocacy... 44

Identification of Elder Abuse 49

Case Study 50

References 51

Further Reading 54

Chapter 3 Dementia and Memory Disorders in Abuse in the Elderly **55**

Introduction 56

Case 1.. 57

Case 2 57

The First Evaluation: Is It Neurodegeneration or Other Illness? 58

Case 1 Review 59

Case 2 Review 60

Elder Maltreatment, Memory Disorders, and Dementia 60

Case 1 Resolution 61

Case 2 Resolution 61

Elder Maltreatment and Alzheimer's Dementia 61

Case 3 63

Vascular Dementia 64

Case 4 65

Case 5 66

Frontotemporal Dementia 67

Case 6 68

Dementia with Lewy Bodies 69

Case 7 70

Mixed Dementia and Overlapping Presentations 71

Stages of Dementia and Risk for Abuse 71

Mild Stage 71

Case 8 72

Moderate Stage 73

Nurse Case 9 73

Severe Stage 75

Case 10 75

Care Transitions 76

Assisted Living Facilities 76

Nursing Homes 77

Case 11 78

Conclusion 79

References 80

Further Reading 83

Chapter 4 Interpersonal Violence and the Elderly 85

The Elderly and Interpersonal Violence 85

Risk Factors 86

Elder Abuse and Violence: The Role of Relationships 90

Case Study 1 92

Case Study 2 94

Case Study 3 97

Unintentional Elder Abuse and Violence 99

Prevention and Advocacy 100

References 103

Chapter 5 Wound Identification and Physical Abuse 107

Introduction 108

Definitions 109

The Integument 109

Skin Anatomical Structures and Aging Influence 110

Impact of Aging on Integument 111

Trauma and Older Age 112

Skin Injury and Overlapping Phases of Healing 114

Healing Phases 119

Definitions of Injury Terms 121

Field Triage Decision Schema 127

Intentional Injury in Older Persons 129

Case Presentations 131

Summary 134

References 135

Chapter 6 Sexual Assault And Rape of the Older Person 139

Introduction 140

Definitions 141

Aging and the Genitalia 141

Case 1... 142

Sexuality and the Older Person 143

Case 2... 145

Offenders With Paraphilias That Include Older Persons................... 146

Case 3... 148

Sexually Transmitted Diseases.. 149

Case 4... 149

Sex, Rape, and Genital Injury.. 150

Sexual Assault, Sexuality, and Dementia.. 152

Case 5... 152

Case 6... 154

Overcoming Trauma 155

Case 7... 156

Conclusion... 157

References... 158

Further Reading 162

Chapter 7 Psychological Abuse **163**

Psychological Abuse: Elder Harm Without Visible Injury.................. 163

The Need for Both Forensic and Medical Analysis of
Psychological Abuse 164

Understanding the Life Space of the Elder...................................... 165

Psychological and Developmental Factors...................................... 166

Impact and Consequences of Psychological Abuse.......................... 168

Perpetrators of Psychological Elder Abuse 169

Varieties of Psychological Abuse... 171

Challenges in Documentation: Assessment and Evaluation
Tools... 173

Abandonment: An Emerging Trend in Psychological Abuse.............. 178

Case Study 179

References... 180

Chapter 8 Multidisciplinary Collaboration **183**

Introduction 183

The Multidisciplinary Team 184

Law Enforcement 185

Medical Response 188

The Justice System 192

Bringing the Collaboration Together... 194

Case Example... 195

References 197

Chapter 9 Death Investigation **199**

Introduction 199

The Medicolegal Death Investigation.. 200

The Elder Death Investigation 203

Conclusion... 210

References 210

Chapter 10 Medication and Substance Use and Misuse in the Elderly **213**

Substance Use Disorder, Self-Neglect, and Comorbid Conditions in the Elderly 213

Alcohol Use and Polysubstance Use Disorder.................................. 216

Benzodiazepine Use Disorder 217

Opioid Use Disorder.. 218

Over-the-Counter Medications 221

Medication Diversion: The Elderly as a Drug Source 223

Chemical Restraint 224

Conclusion and Implications 225

Case Study 227

References 227

Further Reading 229

Chapter 11 The Medical Examiner Response **231**

Introduction 231

Anatomic and Physiological Factors 232

Forensic Markers of Elder Abuse 233

Injuries 234

The Autopsy Examination 237

Summary 238

References 239

Chapter 12 The Criminal Justice Response to Elder Abuse **241**

Introduction 241

Embarking on the Journey: Building a MultiDisciplinary

Approach 242

From Investigation to Prosecution 246

Types of Criminal Elder Abuse 247

Preparing the Elderly Victim for the Criminal Justice System 253

Challenges for the Future 255

References 256

Index 257

LIST OF CONTRIBUTORS

Amy Carney
School of Nursing, California State University San Marcos, San Marcos, CA, United States

Stacy A. Drake
The University of Texas Health Science Center at Houston, Houston, TX, United States

Diana K. Faugno
Eisenhower Medical Center, Rancho Mirage, CA, United States

Melanie Gibbons Hallman
Family, Community, and Health Systems, University of Alabama at Birmingham School of Nursing, Birmingham, AL, United States

Paul R. Greenwood
Former Head of Elder Abuse Prosecution Unit, San Diego District Attorney, San Diego, CA, United States

Rita A. Jablonski
School of Nursing, Department of Adult Chronic and Continuing Care, University of Alabama at Birmingham, Birmingham, AL, United States

Jennifer Lynn Johnson
Emergency Department FACT Program, AdventHealth Shawnee, Merriam, Kansas, United States; Johnson Legal Nurse Consulting, LLC, Shawnee Mission, KS, United States

Kimberly Liang
School of Nursing, California State University San Marcos, San Marcos, CA, United States

Stacey Mitchell
College of Nursing, Texas A&M University Health Science Center, Bryan, TX, United States

Russel Neuhart
Human Development Department, California State University, San Marcos, CA, United States

Patricia M. Speck
School of Nursing, Department of Family, Community, & Health Systems, University of Alabama at Birmingham, Birmingham, AL, United States

Robert Stabley
San Diego County Medical Examiners Office, San Diego, California, United States

Kathleen Thimsen
Goldfarb School of Nursing at Barnes Jewish College, St Louis, MO, United States

FOREWORD

The United Nations 2030 agenda for Sustainable Development Goals (SDGs) emphasized the importance of preparing for an aging population with a strong focus on protecting and promoting the rights of the vulnerable. This agenda includes measures directed at the elder population at risk for abuse and criminal violence. Global aging represents an underlying source of the human condition that continues to affect the biological, psychological, social, and environmental relationships between the health and justice sciences. Among the various categories of human abuse, those related to the victimization of the older adult are increasing as the rate of longevity expands. Abuse of the elder population represents an epidemic of public health concerns pervasive throughout global societies. This textbook explores the crimes against the elderly and the challenges that the healthcare and criminal justice systems face to prevent abusive caretaker behaviors that result in criminal investigations and proceedings.

The health consequences of societal violence are of paramount concern to healthcare practitioners, forensic scientists, and the criminal justice system as they endeavor to combat structural and interpersonal violence. Successful prevention and prosecutions of crimes against the elderly require an increasing recognition and reporting of abuse in a combined approach of coordination and cooperation of the forensic health sciences, legal authorities, and the public at large. Crimes against the elderly are widespread and often overlooked. Effective management of forensic cases involving the elderly patient is an area lacking in sufficient policy and legislation to ensure protection of their legal and human rights. Research related to the incidence, distribution, and control of trauma, abuse, and disease in aging populations recognizes the need for explicit policies to address critical issues related to the escalation of elder abuse.

The forensic health sciences assume a pivotal role in both hospital and community settings by assisting people who are victims of crime-related trauma, abuse, and maltreatment. Expert care for these patients requires recognition of subtle and serious injuries, which may involve forced sexual activity, among other aspects of intentional and unintentional harm. Biomedical and ethical principles form a basis for justice when managing long-term care and near-death circumstances during end-of-life care. Informed consent is a legal doctrine that requires the coordination of sensitive intervention and judgment issues that necessitate healthcare professionals to be skilled in legal and ethical care, clinical intervention, risk reduction, and prevention of crime-related trauma through antiviolence strategies. A comprehensive multidisciplinary education and training program should address relevant responsibilities within the healthcare and legal systems.

Dr. Amy Carney, an advanced practice forensic nurse clinician, academician, and Fellow of the American Academy of Forensic Sciences, has sought contributing authors from among the experts of forensic healthcare, social sciences, and criminal justice. Their accumulated knowledge and experience have provided essential insight into the complex nature of elder abuse and the effectiveness of an interdisciplinary approach to community-based interventions across global societies.

Virginia A. Lynch, RN, MSN, FCNS, DF-AAFS, FAAN

ACKNOWLEDGMENTS

Thanks to all who contributed to this work, for sharing your expertise and wealth of knowledge. The more we know, the better we are at intervening and eradicating elder abuse. Thanks also to all those who give their time and experience on a daily basis to ensure that elders who suffer mistreatment are not marginalized. Special thanks to Alayna Pettigrew and Cynthia Nguyen for their research excellence.

Dr. Amy Carney

INTRODUCTION

Elder abuse is a global phenomenon, crossing all racial and socioeconomic lines. Similar to child abuse and interpersonal violence, elder abuse is known to cause devastation, fear, and heartbreak. As with other forms of "domestic" violence, it has generally been kept away from public view and considered a private family matter. Yet, while elders suffered, professionals across a broad spectrum of service were learning, and they began to bring maltreatment of the elderly into public awareness. Medical personnel, legal professionals, law enforcement, social workers, and many others concerned with violence against older adults began to share research and information on this important demographic.

Elder Abuse: Forensic, Legal, and Medical Aspects builds on that knowledge and provides information across multiple disciplines to assist those working with the elderly, both students and professionals. The contributors come from a wide range of medical, academic, and practice professionals with one goal: to enhance knowledge of elder abuse, provide intervention, and work to eliminate mistreatment in the aging population. Beginning with the epidemiology of elder abuse, this book identifies specific types of abuse, both physical and psychological, and provides detailed examples of the consequences of trauma and neglect. The effects of dementia and medication misuse are discussed, as well as the professional response of those working with the aged. It is hoped that this information not only educates on the topic of elder abuse but also encourages both professionals and the public to become involved on behalf of this vulnerable population.

Amy Carney, NP, PhD, FAAFS

EPIDEMIOLOGY OF ELDER ABUSE AND NEGLECT

Amy Carney
School of Nursing, California State University San Marcos, San Marcos, CA, United States

CHAPTER OUTLINE
Elder Abuse: Danger for an Aging Population 1
  The Difficulty of a Definition 3
  The Multifaceted Nature of Abuse 6
  Elder Abuse and Family Law 7
  Elders Rights 9
  Aging in Place 10
Demographics: The Impact of an Aging Population 11
  Socioeconomics 12
  Incidence and Prevalence 12
Forensic, Medical, and Legal Implications 15
Case Study 15
References 16

Elder Abuse: Danger for an Aging Population

The actual study of elder abuse is relatively recent in the United States. Mentions of mistreatment in the geriatric population began back in the mid-1970s, but research and resources were years in coming. Similar to child abuse and domestic violence, harm to an older relative was considered a family matter and stayed behind closed doors. Unless an actual crime could be proven, such as homicide, charges were rarely filed against a suspected abuser. Arrest and prosecution for financial abuse or neglect was unheard of.

Elder Abuse. https://doi.org/10.1016/B978-0-12-815779-4.00001-X

Also similar to child abuse and interpersonal violence, identification and intervention in elder abuse came slowly, and much of early theory was based on patterns of family violence that had been studied in child abuse and the battered wife syndrome. The phrase "granny battering" was first used in the British Medical Journal in 1975 by Dr. G. R. Burston included in a letter to the editor, urging colleagues to give elder abuse the attention "baby battering" was receiving. During the late 1970s in the United States, Congressman Claude Pepper held well-publicized hearings on what he saw as the "hidden problem" of elder abuse and urged Congress to take action. Although this put elder abuse in the national spotlight for the first time, mistreatment was seen as an aging issue rather than a component of adult protection (Dyer, Connolly, & McFeeley, 2003).

State laws were not enacted until the late 1990s; the Elder Justice Act, the first comprehensive federal legislation to address elder abuse, was not signed into law until 2010. Unlike child abuse, an aging family member could be blamed for their own injuries due to dementia and "accidental" falls or taking too much medication. Additionally, elders had assets, which could be taken or exploited. The disappearance of cash, property, and other possessions could be blamed on the elders' forgetfulness. Caregivers, usually a family member, were often seen as stressed and overwhelmed at the prospect of the work it took to care for an aging relative, straining the relationship, and jeopardizing safety and care.

With the growing understanding of the nature and extent of elder mistreatment came the awareness of the lack of forensic and medical markers that could be useful in identifying abuse. There was no research that could assist investigators in establishing lacerations, bruising, fractures, dehydration, weight loss, or decubiti as elements of abuse or neglect. The aging patient frequently has physiological characteristics or medical conditions, which can mask or mimic markers of neglect and abuse, making it even more difficult to detect or evaluate. A fractured bone can heal without the cause of the fracture being known, but in cases of abuse, the cause is the starting point of investigation and prosecution. Improved levels of awareness of the possibility of abuse were needed to establish patterns and motives. More obvious injuries, such as from gunshot wounds, knife wounds, or rope burns, can be clear indicators of abuse. Obvious bite marks, large or multiple decubiti, and starvation also denote abuse and neglect, but most injuries were noted to fall in a gray area, difficult to identify due to underlying medical diagnoses. Actual incidents of abuse are rarely directly observed by medical personnel or legal authorities, emphasizing the need for solid forensic identifiers. With fewer support systems and physical, psychosocial, and economic burdens, the elderly died before injuries could be documented and investigated (Dyer et al., 2003).

Increasing the complexity of detection and reporting was the reluctance by the elderly to admit being abused, often due to worry about stigma, fear of their abuser, or possibly being taken out of their home. Research and data were needed to support investigation, establish assessment and measurement tools, streamline reporting practices to support prosecution, and prevent elder abuse (Table 1.1).

The Difficulty of a Definition

Definitions of what constitutes abuse have been argued by many individuals and organizations. Adding to the confusion were early debates on "neglect" versus "self-neglect." Rosalie Wolf noted in 2000 that the term "elder abuse" was all types of abuse or maltreatment toward older adults. Acts could be intentional or unintentional and could be commission (abuse) or omission (neglect). Mistreatment could be physical, psychological, emotional, financial abuse, and neglect, which leads to suffering, loss, or decreased quality of life. Whether an act was neglectful or abusive centered on duration, frequency, severity, and consequences. A single slap may not be perceived as abuse. However, the older person's perception of the action and its cultural context were significant to identification and intervention (Wolf, 2000).

Much of the difficulty stemmed from the anecdotal nature of reporting. Descriptions of maltreatment sometimes focused on the type of perpetrator, such as family or nonfamily caregiver. Alternately, discussions centered on typology of abuse or injury and the number of times the elder was a victim. Global definitions also varied. In 1995, the group Action on Elder Abuse in the United Kingdom developed a definition which stated "elder abuse is a single or repeated act, or lack of appropriate action, occurring within any relationship where there is an expectation of trust, which causes harm or distress to an older person" ("What is Elder Abuse?,"1995). This definition included physical, sexual, psychological or emotional abuse, financial and material abuse, and neglect. While elder abuse definitions have been influenced by work done in the United States, Canada, and the United Kingdom, other nations have approached defining elder mistreatment differently. In countries such as China, where there is an emphasis on harmony and respect within society, neglecting the care of an older person is abuse. Family members failing to fulfill the kinship obligations to provide food and housing are committing neglect. In Norway, researchers identified abuse with a "triangle of violence," which included a victim, a perpetrator, and others

Table 1.1 Historical Timeline of Significant Events in Elder Abuse Awareness and Legislation.

Year

1950s   The United States Congress passes legislation, as part of the Social Security Act, providing funds to the states on a three-to-one matching basis to establish protective service units.

1960s   **1969:** In the United States, Robert N. Butler, MD, Head of the District of Columbia Advisory Committee on Aging, coined the term "age-ism" (Fig. 1.1).

Figure 1.1

1970s   In the late **1970s**, the US Congress conducted hearings at the national level to move elder mistreatment to the forefront of Americans awareness (Falk, Baigis, & Kopac, 2012).
Claude Pepper and the Special Subcommittee on Aging sponsor investigations and hearings on "granny bashing (Fig. 1.2)."

Figure 1.2

1975: Dr. Alex A. Baker wrote of "Granny Battering", published in the British Medical Journal.
1975: G. R. Burston, MD, wrote of "granny bashing" in Bristol, England; In the United States, Dr. Robert Butler described the "battered old person syndrome" and went on to become the founding director of the National Institute on Aging and the National Institutes of Health.

Table 1.1 Historical Timeline of Significant Events in Elder Abuse Awareness and Legislation.—*continued*

Year

1978: Suzanne Steinmetz, Professor of Sociology at Indiana University, shared her "discovery" of battered elders. Over the succeeding years, as more cases were uncovered, initial disbelief and denial have given way to acknowledgment of the societal problems of elder neglect and abuse.

1979: The House Select Committee on Aging holds a hearing called "The Hidden Problem."

1979: "The Battered Elder Syndrome" published by Block and Sinnott increased the attention on elder abuse

1980s In the **1980s**, Surgeon General Louis Sullivan held a workshop on family violence, declaring it to be a public health and criminal justice issue that included the problems of elder abuse and neglect. Elder abuse was included under the umbrella of family violence (Fig. 1.3).

Figure 1.3

In the early **1980s**, researchers began to investigate elder mistreatment, and the House Select Committee on Aging began a series of public hearings around the country (http://medicine.jrank.org/pages/549/Elder-Abuse-Neglect.html).

In **1981**, Congress proposed legislation to establish a national center on elder abuse, but the bill never reached the floor of Congress. Finally, in 1989, Claude Pepper introduced that proposal as an amendment to the Older Americans Act.

1984: Rosalie S. Wolf published her first book on elder abuse, *Elder abuse and neglect: Final report from three model projects*. She later went on to publish many other works that contributed to elder abuse research.

1990s **1994:** The Bureau of Justice Statistics reports on elder abuse.

1999: Toshio Tatara published his book on understanding elder abuse in minority populations when much of the early research in the area of elder abuse had primarily been focused on the white elder population.

2000s Elder abuse legislation began to improve only in **2003** when Senator John Breaux introduced the Elder Justice Act in the US Senate (Falk et al., 2012).

In March of **2010,** an important victory for vulnerable older adults was won when the Elder Justice Act was passed in the sweeping health-care reform known as the Patient Protection and Affordability Act (Falk et al., 2012).

who either directly or indirectly observe those principally involved (Krug, Dahlberg, Mercy, Zwi, & Lozano, 2002, p. 127).

In the United States, the National Committee for the Prevention of Elder Abuse states that elder abuse is a term referring to any knowing, intentional, or negligent act by a caregiver, family member, or any other person that causes harm or a serious risk of harm to older people. Included in this description are abandonment, self-neglect, and spiritual neglect (Elder Abuse, n.d.). The National Center on Elder Abuse (NCEA) notes while there is no universally accepted definition of elder abuse currently, each existing definition has its own merit and value. Differences in the definitions and data elements on elder abuse make it difficult to measure elder abuse nationally and to compare the problem across states, counties, and cities, adding to the challenge of establishing trends (National Center on Elder Abuse, n.d., A).

The difficulty in defining the problem of elder abuse also helps spur research and investigation. With multiple entities examining abuse typology, injury description, and forensic markers, more focus is placed on the complex questions in elder abuse, spurring more research and establishing theory. Increased attention placed by communities, researchers, and professionals generates proposed interventions and practices.

The Multifaceted Nature of Abuse

As the population ages, there will be more elderly people to care for, and resources will be needed on multiple levels. Not only age but also fitness and state of health, both mental and physical, will determine where and how well an elder lives. Although some persons over age 65 will retire, many will stay in the workforce; almost all want to stay in their own homes and manage their own finances. The trend for aging at home has grown in recent years, with more seniors opting out of retirement facilities and nursing homes. When abuse and neglect occur in their home, it makes that living space a potential crime scene, as well as a less safe space to live. The elderly can be less likely to protect themselves and more likely to sustain injuries. Loneliness and social isolation contribute to vulnerability. With an increase in longevity, women and widows have shown to be a disproportionate segment of the population, living alone in to old age. Because of size and lack of physical strength, an elderly woman may be less able to resist a physical attack. Age-related changes in skeletal and neuromuscular systems make it more difficult to run from an attacker. A potential abuser, one who perceives they have something to gain, can take advantage of vulnerable elders who appear less capable of protecting themselves from physical and financial harm (Safarik, Jarvis, & Nussbaum, 2002).

In addition to physical vulnerability, elders may have financial assets that expose them to financial abuse. The family member might be a primary caregiver with control over the elder's finances. In many cases, the abusers consider themselves to be entitled to reciprocity for "helping out" the elder with their activities of daily living, feeding and dressing them, taking them to appointments, and generally watching over their well-being. They may assume the elder would want them to be compensated for their care or expect to be allowed to use the assets as they would like. It is in these gray areas where the elders are vulnerable to losing assets such as bank accounts, social security checks, vehicles, or their home.

While older persons can be victimized by family members, elders can also be susceptible to persons outside the family. Employing caregivers who will be paid means the caregiver is compensated but may feel they deserve more for their duties. Assets such as jewelry or other valuables may go missing, and the elder victim may not be aware of it either in the moment, or later.

All these factors contribute to the multifaceted nature of elder abuse, increasing the difficulty in identification and intervention. Loss of autonomy, the desire to stay in one's own home, and the need for control over their own circumstances may increase isolation, making the elder a more likely target of abuse.

Elder Abuse and Family Law

Laws concerning elder abuse vary widely around the world. Law as a cultural construct is shaped by a society's political, sociological, and anthropological views. How a community views its elders can influence the establishment and application of regulations to protect them. Issues of age discrimination, vulnerability, autonomy, inclusion, and justice are all matters included in elder law. Beginning with the World Assembly on Aging in Vienna in 1982, efforts were being made to address a global aging population. This effort continued with a resolution by the United Nations in 1991 and with the Second World Assembly on Aging in Madrid in 2002. Studies started to emerge, which addressed questions about liability and responsibility toward older people, and how to confront questions on elder abuse and elder's rights (Dabove, 2015).

Before enacting laws specific to elder abuse, actions such as battery or robbery, which were already established as crimes, were prosecuted without additional charges specific to the age or circumstances of the victim. In the United States, individual states take different approaches to elder law. Abuse may be covered in multiple legal areas, such as criminal codes, trust and estate codes, family law, and civil remedies. Some laws may be embedded in several code sections. One example is Adult Protective Services (APS) or elder protective services (EPS) statues. While all states have APS or EPS regulations in place, which set up systems for reporting and investigating elder abuse and service delivery, some states may have both, and some have more than one APS law.

Variation also exists in states' applications of criminal law. All 50 states in the United States have general criminal statutes on sexual assault, theft, fraud, assault, battery, and other crimes that can be applied in cases of elder abuse. Many states, such as Texas and Virginia, have specific crimes against family members. Others, including Connecticut, California, Indiana, and Florida have increased penalties for victimizing older adults. Some states identify elder abuse as one or more separate crimes: California's Penal Code 368, Florida's Chapter 825: Abuse, Neglect, and exploitation of Elderly Persons and Disabled Adults, and Nevada's Abuse, Neglect, Exploitation or Isolation of Older Persons or Vulnerable Adults. Several states have also passed laws regarding financial exploitation. In 2012, Maryland enacted a law requiring financial institutions to report suspected financial abuse of older persons to APS or law enforcement within 24 hours of suspicious activity. Missouri amended its statute on elder abuse to include undue influence as an act that, when committed against a disabled or elderly person, constitutes the crime of financial exploitation (Center for Elder and the Courts, n.d.).

Family law in the United States has historically been a matter of state law. State legislatures define what comprises a family and enacts laws regulating marriage, divorce, adoption, child welfare property rights, and other family matters. Although an increasing number of federal and international laws have been established for family legal issues and problems, state courts generally decide family law cases (Elrod, 2009). In elder abuse, state courts will examine the concept of capacity and guardianship. Black's Law Dictionary defines capacity as "the mental ability to understand the nature and effects of one's acts" (Garner, 2011, p. 95). If the state finds an elder person is unable to make personal and/or property decisions, a guardian may be appointed to assist with these decisions. This could be a family member, friend, trained volunteer, or a professional such as a lawyer. Corporation and banks may also be appointed guardians. A guardian may be appointed in cases of dementia or other cognitive impairment, intellectual disabilities, mental illness, brain injury, substance abuse, or a combination of these conditions. A court may authorize a "guardian of the person" to make personal and health-care decisions or a "guardian of property" to make financial decisions. Although guardianship is meant to protect individuals at risk for harm, it also removes some fundamental rights, including the right to control and manage assets and the right to make residential and medical decisions. This can drastically reduce the elder's self-determination and personal choice (National Center on Elder Abuse, n.d., B).

Elders Rights

In the early research on child abuse in the United States, little thought was given to the rights of the child. Considered a private family matter, parents had the obligation to care for the child but were also believed to be the authority on what was best for their children. Concerns for the safety and well-being of children lead to changes in legal approaches to investigation and prosecution of child abuse. Over time, it came to be understood that in cases of suspected child abuse or neglect, a report could be made to Child Protective Services (CPS) who would investigate and take the appropriate action to protect the child. APS has many similarities to CPS in its mandate for protection and intervention in maltreatment. Although older victims of abuse or crime are eligible for other victim services, such as domestic violence programs, sexual assault services, or victim-witness services, the elderly often do not seek these out. APS is statutorily responsible for investigating maltreatment of elderly and vulnerable adults and to take steps to protect the victims. The development of APS came about in 1975 as part of the enactment of Title XX of the Social Security Act, requiring the states to address specific goals, including remedy or prevention of abuse in children and adults who could not protect their own interests. While awareness of the prevalence of elder abuse was increasing, the need for a coordinated response was also increasing. Although funding for APS has changed through the years, its mandate has not. APS continues to investigate allegations of abuse, provide emergency medical and protective services, and initiate civil and criminal legal actions (Quinn & Benson, 2012). Questions have arisen, however, on how and when an elder can refuse services when neglect or abuse is identified. Does an elderly hoarder have the right to remain in unsafe or squalid surroundings? Does the elder victim of self-neglect have the same right to privacy as other adults?

Living in an environment which others might see as unsafe or unhygienic can be confounding for those trying to "assist" an elder into a different living situation. Keeping stacks of papers or other belongings heaped around the home or having multiple pets might be seen as a poor choice to an outsider, but it brings comfort and familiarity to the elderly. If the older adult has cognitive capacity, they can choose not to participate in programs or activities as advised by APS. Elder victims of mistreatment have the right to determine their own fate and may choose a course of action they deem fit for themselves. The same holds true for self-determination in health care: If patients are able to act on their own behalf, then they have the right to have their preferences and determine their choices in medical treatment, based on their own values, experiences, and goals (Burnes, 2017; Stilwell, 2015).

Elders also have the right to privacy. With the widespread use of social media and mobile devices, there is concern for patient images or protected information to be posted without consent. Sharing of photos, videos, or audio recordings without consent of the patient violates the right to self-determine what information is revealed in public. Malicious and intentional posting of embarrassing photos has been reported, but some unintentional social media posts have revealed images and comments with personal details (PPS Alert for Long Term Care, Feb. 2016). As with health-care decisions, the elderly have the right to determine how much personal information is revealed about them and with which persons or media sites.

In a statement by the United Nations in 2011, it was noted that the International Covenant on Economic, Social and Cultural Rights provides for several specific rights relevant to the challenges faced by older persons, including the right to the enjoyment of the highest attainable standard of physical and mental health, the right to an adequate standard of living, including food, clothing, and housing, the right to work, and the right to education (United Nations, 2011). Each country has the obligation to support the rights of its citizens, regardless of age. Safety, health-care decision making, and privacy are fundamental in the security of any nation's elderly.

Aging in Place

Past research has shown that older adults want to live in their own homes as long as possible, as this environment provides independence and security. "Aging in place" refers to individuals who want to stay in their home as they grow older. "Home" can refer to a variety of lifestyles and circumstances, but in general, it is where the elder wants to reside for as long as possible. Many elements come in to play from the time the individual decides what their living environment will be and what this lifestyle will look like. If the elder individual needs in-home care only part of the time, a caregiver can come as needed. However, if the individual's health deteriorates, round-the-clock care may be needed, changing the environment and self-perception about the ability to care for one's self. Loss or absence of social support, such as the loss of a spouse, can also change the living arrangement (Park, Han, Kim, & Dunkle, 2017). Over time, preferences may change, or other circumstances such as changes in mental health may require a change in living space. As frailty increases, arrangements in physical space may need to occur. Architecturally friendly homes, such as one-storey dwellings without stairs and with doorways that can accommodate a wheelchair or walker, encourage safety and security.

One of the biggest challenges in aging in place is financial feasibility. Although there continues to be growth in home and community-based services for elders, these can be costly and not always covered by insurance or Medicare. Meals on wheels, local companion services, and adult day-care centers make it possible for the elderly to enjoy services while remaining in their home but may come at a price out of reach for seniors on fixed incomes. Improved old age life expectancy means income or savings needs to cover more years. Making a home "architecturally friendly," as mentioned previously, may require the addition of improved lighting around the home, addition of grab bars in the bathroom and handrails to stairs, or building a ramp to replace outside steps (Cutler, 2011). Without adequate financial planning, these home modifications may not be possible. The individual may need to choose another living environment, such as a board and care facility, or assisted living.

Demographics: The Impact of an Aging Population

With increased longevity and a decline in birth rates in many countries, the population of the aging continues to grow. By 2050, the number of persons over age 65 is expected to exceed 20% in the United States. An increase in the lifespan that results from better health care, increased access to health care, and changes in lifestyle pose real challenges when faced with the numbers of elderly individuals who will require services and resources. Availability of economic and social support systems will impact communities' ability to care for the elderly.

As the numbers grow, so does the need for prepared professionals familiar with this demographic. Cognitive decline and prevalence of dementia will require mental health professionals to anticipate an increase in patient numbers. In addition to clinical competence, multicultural competence will be required in an increasingly diverse older population (Barnett & Quenzel, 2017). As more elders remain at home, the number who will also die in their homes increases. Differentiating accidental death and suicide will be of increased concern in the isolated elderly. Legal and financial concerns will necessitate the intervention of attorneys and other advocates who are familiar with elders' interests. Increases in participation of services for the elderly will also require active death investigation teams, gerontology specialists, and qualified forensic experts in this demographic.

Socioeconomics

In addition to the mental and physical impact of aging, the influence of financial changes also shape communities. While some people will continue to work into their 70s and beyond, many will retire and their earned income will decline. The increased need for services coupled with a fixed income will impact quality of life. As people age, they tend to spend less, contributing a smaller amount to the economy. "Downsizing" may include smaller homes, giving up a car, or sharing homes and resources.

In America, each state decides how it will tax retirement income and pensions. More retired persons and less taxation in retirement means less state revenue, and every state is seeing the impact. States that have relied on taxes from gambling, or sales of cigarettes and alcohol, have seen a decline in those sources as older people tend to drink, smoke, and gamble less than younger people. Increasing taxes on retirement income is not a popular option, as older people do still tend to vote in elections (Barrett & Greene, 2017). The states are then left with the rising elderly population, decreased revenue, and increased need for services.

Incidence and Prevalence

One of the major problems that investigators and prosecutors have faced is the lack of reporting in elder abuse. While some studies have attempted to establish prevalence in certain locations, such as emergency departments or senior homes, it is widely held these numbers are under reported. Intervention can only take place if incidence is known. Fear of reporting by the victim, lack of awareness by medical personnel, and incomplete knowledge of forensic indicators of abuse complicate establishing prevalence.

The NCEA has reported through a variety of reviews that while exact numbers are not known, studies have attempted to quantify abuse of many types. Prevalence of approximately 10% was found for physical, psychological, and verbal abuse, as well as neglect and financial exploitation. A study in New York State found that 1 in 13 older adults had been victims of at least one type of abuse in the preceding year. Abuse by family members, collected on abuse by type, showed verbal mistreatment was most frequent, followed by financial and physical abuse. The NCEA also noted that APS data showed an increasing trend in abuse reporting (National Center on Elder Abuse, n.d., A).

An analysis of the data collected for the National Intimate Partner and Sexual Violence Survey found that 1 in 10 elders over the age of 70 had experienced abuse in the past year. Psychological abuse was more prevalent than physical abuse, but many reported coercive control and expressive aggression; some reported experiencing both. Most of the abuse was perpetrated by nonintimate partners, someone the victim was not romantically involved with. Risk factors for abuse included low social support, prior trauma, poor health, functional impairment, and difficulties with activities of daily living. Low income was also identified as a risk factor, with many respondents reporting both financial and food insecurity (Rosay & Mulford, 2017). Financial crimes also continue to grow, with property crime and identity theft more prevalent in the older population (Morgan & Mason, 2014, pp. 1–24).

Many of the trends in the United States mirror what is happening globally. Abuse of the elderly was originally identified in developed countries, where most of the research had been conducted. However, anecdotal reports and other evidence from developing countries have shown elder maltreatment to be universal. Concerns about human rights, gender equality, domestic violence, and population aging are worldwide. One of the difficulties in comparing reports from diverse countries is what is defined as "elder." In Western societies, this coincides with the age of retirement, at 60–65 years. In developing countries, the number in years has less impact than the roles the individual held in their lifetime, and old age is identified with physical decline, when that role can no longer be maintained. Changing family structure has also impacted elder care. Patterns of interdependence between generations have changed in some societies with an increase in mobility and industrialization, weakening the support to older persons. Social and economic change can bring material and emotional hardship; most of the world's elderly are not covered by pensions and lack retirement income, leading to an increase in poverty and vulnerability (Krug et al., 2002).

Obtaining data on prevalence is affected by community and cultural norms. In the United States, Canada, and Mexico, statistics on crimes against the elderly by type are collected and published by various entities, often collected from reporting parties such as law enforcement and adult protection and welfare agencies, similar to in Europe and elsewhere. As with other countries, much of what is prosecuted is dependent on what elders themselves are willing to report. In Asia, the concept of filial piety, from Confucian teachings, emphasizes benevolence and propriety. This principle establishes that adult children should obey their elders and provide them care, respect, and financial support. As cultural norms change, however, filial duty is interpreted differently by adult children and older generations. The elderly may hold high personal expectations of filial piety going in to old age, whereas the younger generation may interpret the concept as paying for institutional care, depending on their future circumstances. Disrespect is seen as a form of elder abuse and is a type of mistreatment not necessarily seen as abusive in western culture. Being rude to an elder, or ignoring them and their wishes, goes against the teaching of filial piety. For many elders, admitting this behavior occurs means telling others their adult children are not fulfilling their obligations of respect and obedience and is a source of embarrassment and loss of face (Yan, Chan, & Tiwari, 2015).

In Nepal, it was found that being a member of the Dalit community, a member of the untouchable class in the Hindu Caste system, as well as smoking, both contributed to being at risk for mistreatment. About 49% of the respondents reported abuse in the last 3 months. As with other countries, changing generational norms were found to have an effect on incidence of elder abuse. In Brazil, it has been noted that abuse of elderly men was poorly recognized and underreported due to traditional, sexist social, and cultural norms, preventing older men from divulging maltreatment (Rodrigues et al., 2017; Yadav & Paudel, 2016). In a community in Nigeria, a high rate of emotional abuse was reported. In traditional African society, elders are treated with respect, and culturally, there are accepted ways of addressing the elderly, and deviations are highly noticeable (Cadmus & Owoaje, 2012).

Many similar studies exist in countries that are just starting to collect and assess data on elder abuse. Cultural norms and responses vary, but the need remains the same: as a population ages, it requires services, support, and interventions in elder abuse.

Forensic, Medical, and Legal Implications

As communities take more of an active approach in elder mistreatment, more research will be generated. One of the goals of research in abuse will be to find common themes and more understanding of definitions across societies. Increases in reporting and investigation will contribute to data on forensic markers and establishing evidence in abuse of elders. State, national, and international law influence the directions the courts will take, contributing to the enactment of laws for increased safety and security of elders. Lastly, identification of trends in prevalence will help focus on specific needs and interventions, assisting with allocation of resources and identifying gaps in provision of services.

Case Study

A 48-year-old woman called paramedics to attend to her mother, who she described in deteriorating condition. On arrival, the paramedics found an 83-year-old patient under four blankets in a steaming hot room. She was in serious condition with multiple bedsores. She had not been seen by her neighbors in some time but the daughter and her boyfriend were seen at the home. She was taken to the hospital, where she died a week later. The daughter was arrested for elder abuse causing great bodily injury and theft by a caretaker of more than $150,000. The boyfriend was also arrested, but the charges were later dropped.

At a preliminary hearing, a paramedic testified to the woman's condition and the smell he described as a stench of urine, feces, and rotting flesh. The daughter's attorney told the court that the defendant was doing the best she could, given her mother's failing health. Facing a sentence of up to 12 years and 8 months, the daughter plead guilty to willful cruelty of an elder as part of a deal and was sentenced to a 2-year prison term.

This case illustrates the vulnerable position a dependent elderly woman can find herself in. Although living in her own home, she needed to be cared for by others, who then neglected her physically and stole from her. The neighbors had only seen the daughter and boyfriend, and no one thought to check her welfare as they assumed her family was there for her. This case typifies multiple incidences of physical and financial abuse, as well as neglect, as comorbidities.

References

Barnett, J., & Quenzel, A. (2017). Innovating to meet the needs of our aging population. *Practice Innovations, 2*(3), 136–149.

Barrett, K., & Greene, R. (2017). States revenues and the aging population. *PA Times, 3*(1), 2–26.

Burnes, D. (2017). Community elder mistreatment intervention with capable older adults: Toward a conceptual practice model. *The Gerontologist, 57*(3), 409–416.

Cadmus, E., & Owoaje, E. (2012). Prevalence and correlates of elder abuse among older women in rural and urban communities in south western Nigeria. *Health Care for Women International, 33*, 973–984.

Center for elders and the courts. (n.d.). Retrieved from http://www.eldersandcourts.org/Elder- Abuse/Elder-Abuse-Material-For-Right-Rail-Menu-for-Elder-Abuse/Basics/Elder-Abuse-Laws.aspx.

Cutler, N. (2011). The fear and the preference: Financial planning for aging in place. *Journal of Financial Service Professionals*, 23–26. November.

Dabove, M. (2015). Elder law: A need that emerges in the course of life. *Aging International, 40*, 138–148.

Dyer, C. B., Connolly, M. T., & McFeeley, P. (2003). National research council (US) panel to review risk and prevalence of elder abuse and neglect. In R. Bonnie, & R. Wallace (Eds.), *Elder mistreatment: Abuse, neglect, and exploitation in an aging America* (p. 12). Washington (DC): National Academies Press (US). Available from: https://www.ncbi.nlm.nih.gov/books/NBK98806/.

Elder Abuse. (n.d.). *National committee for the prevention of elder abuse.* Retrieved from https://www.ifa-fiv.org/wp-content/uploads/2012/11/community-tool-kit-powerpoint-english.pdf.

Elrod, L. (2009). The federalization of family law. *Human Rights, 36*, 1–9. Retrieved from https://www.americanbar.org/publications/human_rights_magazine_home/human_rights_vol36_2009/summer2009/the_federalization_of_family_law.html.

Falk, N., Baigis, J., & Kopac, C. (2012). Elder mistreatment and the elder justice act. *OJIN The Online Journal of Issues in Nursing, 17*(3). Retrieved from http://www.nursingworld.org/MainMenuCategories/ANAMarketplace/ANAPeriodicals/OJIN/TableofContents/Vol-17-2012/No3-Sept-2012/Articles-Previous-Topics/Elder-Mistreatment-and-Elder-Justice-Act.html.

Garner, B. (Ed.). (2011). *Black's Law Dictionary*. St Paul Minnesota: West Publishing Company.

Krug, E., Dahlberg, L., Mercy, J., Zwi, A., & Lozano, R. (2002). *World report on violence and health*. Geneva: World Health Organization.

Morgan, R., & Mason, B. (2014). *Crimes against the elderly, 2003-2013*. U.S. Department Of Justice, Office of Justice Programs, Bureau of Justice Statistics.

National center on elder abuse. (n.d., A). Retrieved from https://ncea.acl.gov/whatwedo/research/statistics.html.

National Center on Elder Abuse. (n.d., B). *Fact sheet: role of guardian standards in addressingelder abuse.* Retrieved from http://eldermistreatment.usc.edu/wp-content/uploads/2017/02/NCEA_GuardianStandardsFS2017_508web.pdf.

Park, S., Han, Y., Kim, B., & Dunkle, R. (2017). Aging in place of vulnerable older adults: Person-environment fit perspective. *Journal of Applied Gerontology, 36*(11), 1327−1350.

PPS Alert for Long Term Care. (February 2016). Elder abuse incidents underscore new social media, privacy concerns. *Hcpro.com, 19*(2), 6−8.

Quinn, K., & Benson, W. (2012). The states elder abuse victim services: A system still in search of support. *Generations Journal of the American Society on Aging, 36*(3), 66−72.

Rodrigues, R., Monteiro, E., dos Santos, A., Pontes, M., Fhon, J., Bolina, A., … Silva, L. (2017). Older adults abuse in three Brazilian cities. *Revista Brasileira de Enfermagem, 70*(4), 783−791.

Rosay, A., & Mulford, C. (2017). Prevalence estimates and correlates of elder abuse in the United States: The national intimate partner and sexual violence survey. *Journal of Elder Abuse and Neglect, 29*(1), 1−14.

Safarik, M., Jarvis, J., & Nussbaum, K. (2002). Sexual homicide of elderly females. *Journal of Interpersonal Violence, 17*(5), 500−525.

Stilwell, D. (2015). Health literacy and numeracy: The overlooked challenge for elders who want to guide their own healthcare. *Generations Journal of the American Society on Aging, 39*(1), 88−91.

United Nations. (2011). *Follow-up to the second world assembly on ageing.* Retrieved from http://www.un.org/en/ga/search/view_doc.asp?symbol=A/66/173.

What is Elder Abuse?. (1995). *Action on elder abuse bulletin, 11, (May-June).* Retrieved from https://www.elderabuse.org.uk/Pages/Category/what-is-it.

Wolf, R. (2000). The nature and scope of elder abuse. *Generations, 24*(2), 6−11.

Yadav, U., & Paudel, G. (2016). Prevalence and associated factors of elder mistreatment: A cross sectional study from urban Nepal. *Age and Aging, 45,* 609−614.

Yan, E., Chan, K., & Tiwari, A. (2015). A systematic review of prevalence and risk factors for elder abuse in Asia. *Trauma, Violence, and Abuse, 16*(2), 199−219.

2

IDENTIFICATION OF ELDER ABUSE

Amy Carney
School of Nursing, California State University San Marcos, San Marcos, CA, United States

CHAPTER OUTLINE

Risk and Vulnerability   19
    Aging and Victimization   21
    Institutional Abuse   22
    Diseases and Disorders that Mimic Abuse   24
    Neglect and Self-Neglect   29
Observable Injury versus Suspected Abuse   30
    Accidental Injury and Inflicted Injury   31
    Challenges in Identification   32
    Fear of Disclosure   33
Documenting Elder Abuse   34
    Tools and Measures   35
    Documenting and Reporting   37
Cultural Awareness   38
    Identification and Awareness in Diverse Populations   39
    Emerging Research   42
Intervention and Advocacy   44
    Identifying Sources of Assistance   46
Identification of Elder Abuse   49
Case Study   50
References   51
Further Reading   54

Risk and Vulnerability

"Elder abuse" is a term that typically includes specific harms against older adults: physical abuse, psychological abuse, caregiver

Elder Abuse. https://doi.org/10.1016/B978-0-12-815779-4.00002-1

neglect, financial exploitation, sexual abuse, and abandonment (Jackson, 2017). The World Health Organization published a fact sheet in June of 2017, outlining best evidence from 52 studies in 28 countries, on the scope of elder abuse. Psychological abuse was found to be most prevalent, followed by financial abuse, neglect, physical abuse, and sexual abuse. Risk factors for abuse were categorized as individual, relationship, community, and sociocultural. Poor mental and physical health were also noted to put individuals in jeopardy, while certain living situations posed a relationship danger. However, it is not clear if a spouse or a child was more likely to be a perpetrator of abuse. Isolation and lack of social support constituted a community risk factor, particularly in cases of poor family relationships, which increased the stress of caregiving. Sociocultural norms were also implicated, including the erosions of the bonds between generations and the migration of young couples away from aging parents (World Health Organization, 2017). Less clear are the circumstances that make the elderly a more vulnerable population. Age, if accompanied by few resources or lack of physical strength, can contribute to vulnerability, but not all aging persons are weak or ill. In communities around the world, individuals in aging populations known as "blue zones" are living much longer than average. In five specific areas from Okinawa, Japan to Icaria, Greece, the elderly are living healthy lives into their 90's. While these groups share some common characteristics (moderate calorie intake, low alcohol intake, plant-based diet), they also focused on putting family first and staying socially integrated in their communities. What is not known is if these lifestyle and social choices decreased their vulnerability to harm, allowing them to live to old age, or if staying visible and active in their families and social circles makes it more difficult to encounter harm. Similarly, merely identifying risk factors does not keep elders safe. While a senior lending money to an adult child in need is not of itself inherently dangerous, when the adult child lives with the elder parent and has a substance abuse problem, the possibility for maltreatment increases. Research has documented this set of facts, and yet elders continue to be victims of abuse in these circumstances. Early identification of risk, coupled with thorough physical assessment by professionals, such as a comprehensive geriatric assessment, has also shown to increase the opportunity for early intervention and identification; yet few family practice and nongeriatric specialists are likely to utilize them (Burnett, Achenbaum, & Murphy, 2014). If effective research in interventions and assessment has been documented, how do we as a society keep the elderly from falling victims to abuse?

Aging and Victimization

Aging well has been described as a combination of actions and attitudes that promote physical and mental health and increase well-being regardless of age. A positive lifestyle, which includes staying physically fit, paying attention to diet, and keeping mentally active with hobbies and interests, has shown a beneficial impact on both longevity and happiness. A proactive approach to aging also includes reduction of negative stereotypes, especially when applied by the elder themselves: assuming that dementia is inevitable increases fear and worry and can lead to depression. Some signs of aging are benign, such as wrinkled skin or gray hair and others, such as a decrease in taste or hearing, can affect quality of life, despite a senior's best effort to eat well or stay active. Certain circumstances in life can change the expectation of how the elderly move into old age: the death of a spouse, necessitating a change in living arrangements; sudden financial loss; and a sudden or severe health complication. Changes such as these can increase the older person's sense of vulnerability and the feeling of no longer being in control of their own preferences and decision-making.

The idea of "vulnerability" has been described in a combination of concepts as it applies to old age and includes the capacity of the victim to defend against abuse or neglect. Health status and the physical ability to endure harm, the possibility of suffering long-term effects of abuse, and the mental capability to cope with maltreatment all affect the potential outcome of neglect and mistreatment. Aging by itself does not create vulnerability, but it can expose the elderly to situations and conditions where abuse can occur. Physical and cognitive decline can increase frailty and exposure to harm (Goergen & Beaulieu, 2013). Circumstances surrounding issues in aging can also increase vulnerability. An elder may have no choice but to move in with an adult child, who may or may not have the ability to care for an aging relative. Declining mental function or the presence of mental illness in the older adult can increase stress on the caregiver and put strain on the living situation. The expense of caring for an elder is also a factor in quality of care; medications, hospital bills, the need for durable medical equipment or specific diet can increase the burden of elder care by putting pressure on the caretaker, and adding to the sense of vulnerability on the part of the parent. Diminished capacity can also mean the adult child must take a greater role in decision-making, such as end of life care, increasing the pressure on the relationship.

Other circumstances in the elder's life, such as violence or dependence on others to handle activities such as finances, can also lead to an increase in feeling vulnerable. As in child abuse research when interpersonal violence is witnessed in the home, a dependent elder observing violence or watching a loved one be harmed can increase their sense of fear or danger. Having a pet has been shown to increase a feeling of love and security in the elderly, but seeing that pet threatened or harmed can greatly increase distress. Just as aging by itself does not create vulnerability, the presence of assets on the part of the elder does not automatically increase the likelihood of financial abuse. However, not being able to care for their finances themselves and being dependent on someone else to handle them safely leaves the elder open to the possibility of abuse.

Institutional Abuse

Around the world, a variety of out-of-home options exist for seniors who can no longer live on their own or who choose to age with people of similar interests and functional capacity. Although aging in place is one option, many elderly have no desire to continue to manage their own home or to plan meals and manage housekeeping. In the United States, these options include "active senior communities" with a mix of housing (apartments, single family homes) and various amenities, such as golf course or clubhouses. These are often restricted to individuals of age 55 and older and are built with seniors in mind, with accessible features and a variety of resources. In some, the residents actively participate in the design and operation of the community. Other facilities may offer more health-care options, such as skilled nursing and assisted living. These facilities may aid the elderly in remaining as independent as possible while offering health care and management of medications. Some offer round-the-clock care to meet the elders' needs (AARP, n.d.). Some board and care facilities may be independently owned and operated, while other types of facilities may be run by corporations or partnerships, both for profit and non profit.

One of the barriers to such care is cost. Although some seniors can afford a range of living and retirement opportunities, others find them out of reach. Skilled nursing care can be very expensive, and competition for affordable living situations increases with the number in the aging population. The level of care required may also influence cost and payment. For example, in the United States, a recipient of Medicare Part A may qualify for a stay in a Medicare-certified skilled nursing facility if they have met certain requirements: a minimum inpatient stay in a hospital, requiring further skilled nursing and which goes beyond simple needs such as bathing and dressing. Although some insurance policies, such as long-term care policies, provide for a range of benefits over time, they do not guarantee the quality of care in any particular instance or institution. Laws and regulations regarding assisted living facilities, board and care homes, and "foster care homes" differ state to state. Most nursing homes receive federal Medicare and state Medicaid funding and must follow established safety and welfare guidelines or risk losing licensing and payment. Medicaid accounts for over a third of total spending on long-term care services in the United States (Howard, 2014). However, depending on the size and type of facility and level of care offered, a background check for employees may not be required or may only include cursory information.

Lack of a vigorous background check may lead to a variation in the quality and type of care an elder receives. Another contributor to differences in care is the use of unlicensed assistive personnel. The first assisted living facilities were designed as an alternative to more expensive nursing care homes, where the elderly required some care, but not the level of care provided by a licensed professional nurse. These elders were presumed to have stable health conditions and were capable of a certain amount of self-care. As they aged, however, their health became more unstable, and transferring care to a nursing home increased the cost level. Often, the unlicensed personnel did not have the assessment skills to recognize when a change in the level of care was needed, leading to the neglect and subsequent decline of the elder (Phillips & Ziminski, 2012).

Abuse that takes place in an institution includes many of the same risk factors and consequences seen in abuse in private homes or other settings. In an institutional setting, physical abuse may take the form of hygiene neglect, with subsequent skin breakdown. Decubiti are a common finding in institutional neglect and abuse. Medication withholding and medical neglect have also been reported. Psychological abuse is seen in the use of threats of death or harm. Patients with disabilities are often at a higher risk, unable to protect themselves, or remove themselves from the abuse. Denial of food, unnecessary use of restraints, and lack of timely care for injuries contributes to decreased health. The pattern of underreporting follows some of the explanations present in home living situations: Shame, fear of retaliation, and fear of being moved to a worse living situation may keep an elder from reporting abuse. In institutional facilities, employees may be reluctant to report a coworker, anxious that they may lose their job. Lack of understanding of risk factors and symptoms of abuse also lead to a decrease in reporting. Even lack of policies on when and how to report known or suspected abuse increase the danger in these settings (Frazao, Correia, Norton, & Magalhaes, 2015). This in turn leads to an increase in health-care costs, as well as mortality.

Two of the key areas of identification in institutional abuse are emergency prehospital providers and emergency departments (EDs). Prehospital providers not only transport the elderly from their living situation but also are in a unique position to see what that situation is like. Areas the first responder can assess while on scene and report to the hospital include the following: if the facility is clean, with hallways wide and clear enough for wheelchairs and ambulation; if the patient's room has sufficient ventilation and privacy; and if the personnel are knowledgeable about the patient's health and circumstances. Historically, ED personnel have often been the first to identify indicators of intimate partner violence (IPV) and child abuse, providing interventions and decreasing morbidity. An increase in mandated reporting across the United States has also lead to improvements in medical care and safety. Yet much like IPV and child abuse, ED providers must be able to identify signs of abuse and maintain a high index of suspicion for certain findings and conditions. Education on physical and psychological abuse, as well as when and where to report, should be included in basic ED training (Evans, Hunold, Rosen, & Platts-Mills, 2017). Similarly, emergency medical service (EMS) protocols need to identify elder abuse and how to manage cases of abuse. Namboodri et al. (2018) reviewed 35 statewide EMS protocols and found only 14 mentioned elder abuse. Of those that did include elder abuse, only some mentioned definitions, indicators, and management. It was noted that nearly twice as many states covered all of these areas in instances of child abuse. Educating these key providers on what to look for and when to report will lead to an increase in medical care and safety in persons who receive institutional care.

Diseases and Disorders that Mimic Abuse

Not every bruise is abuse, and not every fall is suspicious. Although there is an emphasis on identification and reporting of abuse, it is also important to be able to identify disease processes and accidental injury that mimic maltreatment. Certain common conditions in the elderly require medications, which may lead to dizziness, such as blood pressure medication,

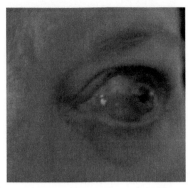

Figure 2.1 Subconjunctival hemorrhage in a 62-year-old female.

or to spontaneous "bruising," which can be seen with blood thinners. Some common mimics include the following:

Subconjunctival hemorrhage: Blunt force trauma to the eye area can cause bruising of the soft tissues, fractures of the bony orbit, and damage to the globe itself. Asphyxia from smothering or strangulation can result in petechial hemorrhage. But even minor trauma, such as rubbing of the eye, can result in bleeding of a small capillary under the conjunctiva. The capillary can also rupture spontaneously. The resulting hemorrhage can appear as dramatic bleeding in the eye but is often painless (Fig. 2.1).

Soft tissue injury to the face: Trauma to the face can result in bruising over both soft and bony areas. Depending on the patient's age, and the underlying condition of the skin, the resulting bruise may look suspicious as opposed to accidental. These same conditions may result in slow healing and lingering discoloration. The mechanism of injury may be something as innocent as the elderly person getting up to use the bathroom at night and failing to turn on a light, resulting in a fall and trauma (Fig. 2.2).

Injury to the skin: A "patterned injury" of the soft tissue shows a mark or impression, often resulting in a bruise or wound, which shows repetitive striking with an instrument, such as a ruler or belt. Some injuries can exhibit this appearance from falling on to a surface or object, with a "pattern-like" result (Fig. 2.3).

Open wounds: Obvious wounds can be the result of weapons, falls from being pushed, altercations, and intentional blunt force trauma. Some accidents in the elderly can also result in open wounds. Falling against the corner of a stationary object, such as a table, or being struck by a moving object, such as a door, can cause both superficial and deep wounds. Evaluation of the injury must include the possibility of an underlying fracture or undetected internal bleeding (Figs. 2.4 and 2.5).

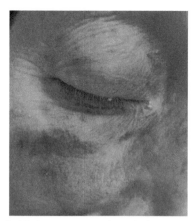

Figure 2.2 Periorbital eye trauma after tripping over the family pet.

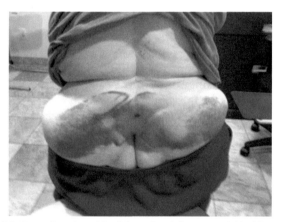

Figure 2.3 Posterior gluteal bruising after fall on to a folded lawn chair.

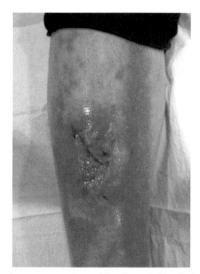

Figure 2.4 Jagged open wound resulting from falling industrail cookware.

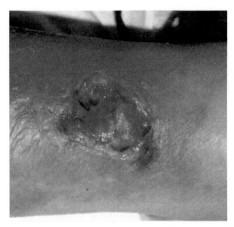

Figure 2.5 Round open red wound from accidental trauma with delayed care.

Bruising: As will be discussed in coming sections, bruising can be an indication of both accident and inflicted trauma and can be difficult to assess accurately. A history of the mechanism of the bruise is important, but the elder may not be able to give a complete history due to dementia, aphasia, or short-term memory impairment. Bruises to the extremities may be easily seen and can be explained secondary to an accident; bruises to the torso or in other unusual places, or hidden under clothing, may be less easy to explain (Fig. 2.6).

Abrasion: The appearance of abrasions can vary on skip type, color, and mechanism. Delayed healing, such as is common in elders with diabetes, may further complicate the appearance of scrapes or scratches, particularly if accompanied by cuts or erythema (Fig. 2.7).

In addition to wounds and bruising, a number of medications and medical conditions can mimic trauma. Senile purpura, also

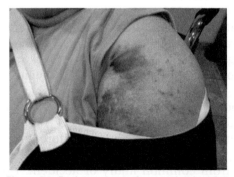

Figure 2.6 Bruise on arm after mechanical fall.

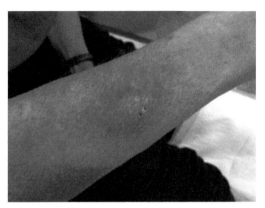

Figure 2.7 Healing abrasion in a diabetic patient.

called solar purpura, appear as discolorations on sun-exposed areas, such as arms and hands. Thinner, more delicate skin tends to show these more easily. Steroid medications, both topically and systemically, can cause skin to be more fragile and tear and discolor easily. The use of anticoagulants can lead to easy bruising as well as slow resolution of bruises. Some traditional methods of healing, such as coin rubbing or cupping, may leave marks that mimic abuse.

Other disorders, which could raise suspicion for abuse, may mimic sexual assault. Lichen sclerosus, which presents as thin white patches, can appear anywhere on the body but often manifests on the genitalia and is seen in both men and women. Decreased estrogen in the postmenopausal elderly woman can lead to excoriation and bleeding of the genitals with only minimal or moderate contact. Anal excoriation secondary to inflammatory bowel disease or constipation can be mistaken for trauma. Irritation from incontinence, or bruising and bleeding from difficult catheterization, can also be confused for mistreatment (Palmer, Brodell, & Mostow, 2013).

Inflammation or bleeding of the oral mucosa can be indicative of inflicted trauma, such as forced feeding, but may also be due to poorly fitting dentures. Weight loss from lack of dentition and poor nutrition can present as neglect. Cheilitis, cracked and swollen skin at the angles of the mouth, which can be due to decreased perception of thirst and poor fluid or nutritional intake, can also be mistaken for neglect.

As with any indicator for abuse, a thorough physical exam and eliciting as much history as possible can separate abuse and neglect from common injury or accident. Documentation of findings with illustrations, drawings, and photographs can support a case that goes to court, as well as provide a record of the course of healing.

Neglect and Self-Neglect

Neglect can occur as the result of someone in the role of caregiver failing to provide for the needs of an elder or by the failure of elders to care for themselves. The United Nations Economic Commission for Europe published a policy brief in 2014 on the abuse of older persons, with input from 11 countries and the European Commission. They defined neglect as "an intentional or unintentional refusal or failure to fulfill a caretaking obligation, for example insufficiency of nutrition, personal hygiene, health care or company," and self-neglect as "refusal or being unable to care about own health or safety" (p. 3). The Elder Justice Act, passed in to law in the United States in 2010, defined neglect as the inability to perform self-care tasks. This can be due to diminished capacity or physical or mental impairment. Some of these tasks included being unable to manage finances, obtaining food, medical care, clothing, or shelter, or maintaining personal safety. Much of the discussion on self-neglect centers on autonomy versus dependence in the elderly. If an older adult has the capacity to manage their own affairs, they are seen as having the ability to make their own decisions, even if family or friends do not agree with those decisions. Questions may arise on both legal and moral issues when assistance is offered or imposed on an elder or when self-neglect appears to be harming an elderly person. Caregiver neglect, however, is the actual failure to provide for an elder who requires it. A caregiver can be paid or unpaid, family member or nonrelative, or who fails to act on behalf of an elder or does something that causes harm. In establishing neglect by a caregiver, legal questions arise regarding the relationship and the duty of care. For example, was the behavior of the caretaker something a reasonable person would do in comparable circumstances? Although laws differ across states in the United States, there are commonalities in issues of caregiver neglect. Courts examine if there was a duty on behalf of the caretaker to provide for an elder, to what extent physically or financially that care exists, if the caretaker has the capacity to care for a dependent elder, and how much input the elder has in the relationship (Heisler, 2017).

What might be viewed as neglect or self-neglect requiring intervention in one country may not be viewed as abuse at all in another. In a 2014 publication by the Elder Abuse Prevention Unit (EAPU) of Queensland, Australia, the topic of elder neglect is covered in detail with specific examples, while also stating that self-neglect is not considered abuse by the EAPU. Specifically, "the respect of a person's rights to make their own decisions on matters affecting their lives is of paramount importance to the EAPU" (para. 5). It goes on to discuss when intervention may be warranted, for instance, if self-neglect is unintentional due to mental illness or through lack of access to services. In some countries, neglect does not have to be physical to be seen as abuse. Psychological abuse, including verbal and emotional abuse and psychological neglect, has been identified as the most prevalent form of abuse in some Japanese and Korean elders (Lee & Lightfoot, 2014). A study done in the Netherlands described seniors who felt neglected by society, leaving them lonely and vulnerable (Mysyuk, Westendor, & Lindenberg, 2016).

As more becomes known about neglect and self-neglect, identification by medical providers, law enforcement, and forensic experts will improve. As with elder abuse in general, common definitions need to be established and applied across research to help follow trends and track prevalence rates.

Observable Injury versus Suspected Abuse

One of the biggest challenges for those working in the field of elder abuse is being able to identify if and when abuse occurs, particularly if the elder victim is unable or afraid of communicating. Most incidents of abuse occur inside homes or facilities and usually are not witnessed events. Without a witness or specific forensic markers for abuse, mechanism of injury can be disputed, and cases of abuse can be missed.

With a lack of testimony or physical evidence, prosecution may be impossible. Even when injuries can be identified, those who see them may be reluctant to report. Fear of being wrong and reporting something as abuse when it might not be can keep observers from coming forward. Privacy concerns, personal feelings, and fear of retaliation can also prevent reporting. Verbal abuse, while harming an elder, leaves no obvious physical mark. Clues such as physical decline or withdrawal may indicate that abuse is occurring, but they are not themselves solid indicators of abusive behavior. While a high index of suspicion is useful in identifying abuse, other events and circumstances can also help identify episodes of mistreatment.

Accidental Injury and Inflicted Injury

The cause of injury in the elder should be investigated to differentiate accidental injury and inflicted injury. An active senior lifestyle has been promoted as keeping older people healthy and involved. Depending on the activity, there may be risks of injury, where the mechanism or outcome is easily understood. Twisting an ankle while walking, or falling during a round of golf, may not raise any question of abuse. However, unexplained falls in someone who is usually steady on their feet requires further investigation. In some cases, physical signs are more subtle and can be harder to establish as maltreatment.

While brain atrophy secondary to aging can contribute to falling and osteoporosis can result in a fracture following a simple fall, these injuries may be obvious and explainable. Injuries in specific locations on the body may be clues of abuse, as opposed to accidental injury. Common sites where marks of abuse can be seen are the upper extremities, head, neck, face, and skull. Bruises from being grabbed on the upper arms can leave characteristic "fingertip" bruising. Injuries to the eyelid and periocular area are also suspicious for abuse (Murphy, Waa, Jaffer, Sauter, & Chan, 2013). Patches of alopecia with erythema of the scalp may indicate traumatic hair removal. Blunt force trauma can result in skin tears and open wounds.

Often, marks of abuse are hidden in areas covered by clothing. The torso and legs are two locations where abuse is inflicted and often missed due to clothing not being removed for injury evaluation. Wounds to the scalp can be missed due to hair or head coverings. Lacerations and other wounds that could not be self-inflicted due to their location should be questioned. A detailed exam should include the posterior upper legs, feet, and the area behind the ears of any elder suspected of having been abused.

Injuries may not be severe enough at any one time to warrant a visit to the ED; the elder may be unwilling or unable to seek care. Although the injuries may be considered mild, they contribute to an identifiable pattern of abuse and could be identified at an office visit with a primary care provider or other medical professional. More serious injuries may only be found with imaging; skull or other bony fractures may present as a single occurrence or in various stages of healing, indicating an ongoing pattern of maltreatment.

An alteration in an elder's personality can indicate mental decline in the normal course of aging or suggest that something has changed in their personal lives. Decreased mental acuity or withdrawal from socializing may signify fear, increasing an elder's sense of isolation. Excuses on the part of caregivers for incidents of trauma, or not letting older persons speak for themselves during an exam, may also suggest mistreatment.

A recent area of research in elder abuse is animal cruelty. Although much has been written about children and animals, only in the last several years has animal mistreatment been evaluated as a possible indicator of interpersonal violence and elder abuse. As with varying definitions of elder abuse, "animal abuse" has been used as a broad term to describe crimes toward animals, such as neglect or failing to protect. "Animal cruelty" refers to intentional criminal conduct. The National Link Coalition has stated that animal mistreatment should not be seen as an isolated incident but as an indicator or predictor of crime and as a warning sign that other family members may not be safe (Ansello, 2016). Asking an elder patient about harm to pets in the home may be clues to human abuse as well. With an increase in the elder population as well as the number of pets and service animals, it is estimated that 16 million pets could reside in older people's home by the year 2020. Having a companion animal may influence physical and mental health positively but can also have negative effects, as in animal hoarding. It has been suggested that animal welfare issues should be evaluated during screening by Adult Protective Services (APS) professionals, which could lead to more useful information on abuse and neglect in the elder's home (Peak, Ascione, & Doney, 2012).

Challenges in Identification

Physical injuries need to be carefully evaluated as Indicators of Abuse (IOA). Bruises and their location can be indicators of both abuse and accident and are common in the elderly. As stated previously, aging skin may show changes differently than younger skin. Changes in the epidermis include fewer fat cells, leading to drier skin. Epidermal cell turnover slows, leading to decreased healing rates. Solar damage can increase dilation of small blood vessels and alter the strength of connective tissue, resulting in uneven pigmentation. Bruising is the result of disrupted blood vessels due to trauma. Depending on the mechanism of injury, bruising can occur not just in the skin but also in the bone, muscle, and soft tissue. Hematoma, a raised bruise, can also occur with blunt force trauma (Gibbs, 2014).

Color is one of the primary parameters used to evaluate bruises, but it is not predictable over the life of a bruise. Redness can remain throughout the time it takes for bruising to resolve; the presence of yellow in the bruise can be early or late and may eventually become purple. Skin tone can change the appearance of color in a bruise (Mosqueda, Burnight, & Liao, 2005). It should also be noted that at the time an elder is examined for potential abuse, it may be too soon for a bruise to have appeared (Wiglesworth et al., 2009). Although location of bruising and mechanism of injury provide important forensic markers of abuse, the patient and their circumstances should always be evaluated in full. For example, mobility status of a patient may contribute valuable history in cases of abuse; bruises consistent with gait instability or falls would not be present in an immobilized older person (Carney, 2015a).

Another challenge in abuse identification is the setting in which the mistreatment is suspected to have taken place. As noted previously in the section on institutional abuse, there may be a lack of understanding on how and when to report. However, gaining access to assess for abuse may also be a challenge. Questions of privacy for the patients in nursing homes or board and care facilities may prevent professionals, even with a high index of suspicion, from speaking to the elderly. This confusion may stem from which agency should receive a report of suspected or known maltreatment. In the US APS, long-term care ombudsman and law enforcement all have a role to play in elder safety. As laws and rules of enforcement vary across states, it may be unclear who should receive the initial report. Mandated reporters, those who are required by law to report mistreatment, were established by 2013 in all states in the United States and District of Columbia for cases of child abuse. Although all states now have mandated reporting rules for elder abuse, they differ in what is required to report. What persons are the actual mandated reporters, what activities they are required to report, where the victim resides (home, nursing home, care facility), and whether or not the victim lacks capacity may change from state to state (Stetson Law, 2016).

Fear of Disclosure

It has been noted that elders, caregivers, and professionals have disclosed reluctance to divulge abuse, for a variety of reasons. Noncompliance with mandated reporting laws has been documented, even in states where noncompliance is a misdemeanor, punishable by penalties ranging from fines to time in jail. Although these penalties are known by those mandated to report, there is inconsistent compliance. In some cases where maltreatment was detected, only half were reported. When asked why incidents were not reported physicians felt that to do so would negatively affect the relationship with their patients and did not think reporting would improve their quality of life. They also cited absence of physical signs of maltreatment at the time of the exam and victim denial as reasons not to report. Additionally, it was felt that limited funding at both the state and federal levels had hampered APS efforts to provide services after referrals were made (DeLiema, Navarro, Enguidanos, & Wilber, 2015).

Fear of being wrong that abuse is actually taking place also occurs. Some states have laws and penalties for making a false report. Fear of losing patients in a specific practice setting, and thus business, also keeps some licensed professionals from reporting, worried that word will get out that they filed a report. Loss of staff is also possible, if issues arise in which some providers believe in reporting and others do not.

When elders who may have been abused by caregivers fear reporting, it is important to interview the elder and the caregiver separately. While hovering over a patient, finishing their sentences for them or answering questions instead of letting them speak may appear to be intimidating that they are not specific IOA. Diversion of medication by the caregiver can have serious consequences, and the elder patient may not feel comfortable discussing this with anyone but the interviewer (Hoover & Polson, 2014).

Frightened that the abuse might escalate may prevent disclosure, with the elder fearing that reporting mistreatment would only make it worse. A private, thorough, and careful interview, in a safe place, may assist the older person with their willingness to reveal maltreatment.

Documenting Elder Abuse

Tools for assessment and documentation of elder abuse have evolved since the 1960's, due much in part to the early work in child abuse and IPV. Many of the same challenges are faced in uncovering cases of elder abuse as were encountered in IPV: fear of retaliation, loss of home and living situation, and loss of family and other support inhibit reporting. When interpersonal violence was first being assessed, simple questions about actual or potential abuse were included in the health history, often by clinicians and other health providers simply asking if the person was in an abusive relationship. Short questionnaires and scales were developed, and some were designed to be self-administered. Although these were easy to use and required no special training, it was found that not every victim of IPV self-reported the full nature or extent of abuse (Carney, 2015b). Batterers were likely to answer in ways that minimized abuse or omit information completely.

Additionally, those collecting the information were left to decide on how to evaluate it and how to use it to help the victim of IPV.

In the decades since written tools were established, other methods of documentation have also been applied. Video and still photography, digital imaging, and audio recording have all been shown as effective in detailing abuse and providing evidence in a court of law. Wide spread education in their use now includes APS workers, case managers, law enforcement, and other elder care workers who encounter abuse.

Tools and Measures

Many tools now exist for the assessment of elder abuse and neglect. In the early years of maltreatment intervention, assessment instruments were adopted from IPV, for lack of an alternative. The Conflict Tactics Scales, developed in the late 1970s, was used to measure tactics used by family members in a position of conflict, specifically in abuse of spouses and children. It was designed to measure the extent family members used reasoning, verbal aggression, and physical aggression or in intrafamily violence (Straus, 1987, pp. 1–53). Modified in several versions over the last 40 years, it is still one of the most widely used tools in elder abuse research in multiple cultures and countries. From the 1980s and into the 1990s, tools were being developed specifically for evaluating elder abuse. Hwalek and Sengstock devised a 15-item paper-and-pencil test to evaluate elder abuse and neglect, with simple "yes" or "no" answers from elders themselves. Although the Hwalek-Sengstock Elder Abuse Screening Test was brief and easy to administer, it was intended to be followed up with an in-depth interview if the score indicated a potential for abuse. The Elder Assessment Instrument (EAI), without using a scoring system, was designed for clinical use. This 35-item screen uses both subjective and objective items to evaluate persons at high risk of mistreatment to refer them for further assessment. Some screens were developed for use by the caretaker, or both the caretaker and care recipient. The Caregiver Abuse Screen, with only eight items, was completed not by interviewers but by caregivers themselves. It was specifically worded to be nonblaming and avoided questions regarding mistreatment behaviors. Conversely, the IOA Screen were designed to be used by professionals, to evaluate both the caretaker and the care receiver, after a comprehensive in-home assessment. Although training was required before it being used, it was written to assess multiple forms of abuse (Acierno, 2003).

Many tools continued to evolve as research in to elder mistreatment expanded and were developed and used internationally. The Caregiver Abuse Screen for the Elderly (CASE) and the Brief Abuse Screen for the Elderly (BASE) were both part of the Canadian National "Project Care," which was established to combat neglect and abuse by caregivers. CASE, with only eight "yes" or "no" items, evaluated the possibility that a caretaker could be a potential abuser. BASE, with only five questions, was designed to be administered in 1 minute. The five questions concentrate on type of abuse, level of suspicion, and immediacy of response. It was meant to be used by health professionals, with specific training. Similar to BASE, the Elderly Indicators of Abuse (E-IOA) scale was meant to be administered by professionals. Based on the original IOA scale, it was tested on a large cohort in two Jerusalem hospitals. While it included an analysis of the nutritional and functional status of the elder, it was weak in identifying financial abuse and took 2 hours to administer. It was noted that the use of IOA or E-IOA administered in combination with CASE enhanced the effectiveness of the CASE evaluation (Gallione et al., 2017).

Some tools are designed to be used with specific population in certain locations. Designed to be used in EDs, the EAI evaluates negligence along with physical and financial abuse. "Negligence" included signs of dehydration, presence of pressure ulcers, poor hygiene, under- or overdosing of medication, and hypothermia. Taking about 15 minutes to complete, the nursing staff utilized a one-on-one interview format combined with a physical assessment to complete the EAI. The Vulnerability Abuse Screening Scale (VASS) was created in a longitudinal study, the Australian Longitudinal Study on Women's Health, which lasted 20 years. It evaluated four areas in elder maltreatment: dependence, dejection, vulnerability, and coercion. It was found that the VASS could predict a decline in both mental and physical health over a 3-year period. The Canadian Elder Abuse Suspicion Index was used to test elderly persons who could understand and speak either French or English. It was found to be culturally transferable, with short administration times, and could be used to exclude abuse. However, its generalizability was limited as it was only evaluated on those elders who were cognitively intact, with a Mini Mental Status Exam (MMSE) score equal to or greater than 24 (Gallione et al., 2017).

Ultimately, each agency and institution need to decide which tool best fits its elder population, taking into consideration the persons who will be required to apply it. The need for training in a tool's use, length of time for administration, and whether it can be used alone or must be used in conjunction with other tests, such as the MMSE, all need to be reviewed before a measure is chosen. Additionally, a decision must be in place on how the information will be used once it is collected and whether it is required to be reported.

Documenting and Reporting

The goal in identification of abuse should be to intervene on behalf the abused elder. With documentation comes the need to decide on what needs to be done with this information, who is bound to provide it, and where and when it needs to be disclosed. In the United States, this varies from state to state. The discussion on confidentiality, privacy and mandated reporting has taken place across agencies and organizations since before child abuse was first required to be reported. Like child abuse reporting, standardized measures needed to be established for elder abuse to assure the safety of the elder and the positive outcome of legal proceedings. As discussed in Chapter 1, difficulties in establishing definitions of abuse had to be overcome. Each state then had to establish who was mandated to report and how that report would take place. Over time, statues were put in place defining what constitutes abuse, what information had to be reported, and about whom. Individual states also had to decide what exceptions, if any, would apply to mandated elder abuse reporting.

It's been estimated that close to four million Americans live in long-term care facilities. The majority of these are over age 65. Depending on the state, there may be an extensive list on who in these facilities must report, while some states limit mandated reporting to certain professionals, and allow that other persons "may" report. Some states impose criminal liability for failure to report, other impose civil liability. Criminal liability may be either a felony or a misdemeanor, depending on the state and its statues. While civil penalties may be imposed on an individual for failure to report, some states have laws that hold the institution responsible if the designated mandated reporter fails to disclose incidents of abuse. Even if state law directs who in a facility is a mandated reporter, reports often do not come from the facility itself but from concerned family members or other outside parties. Arguments against mandated reporting have included that such reporting is "ageist," undermining the autonomy of the elder and not taking into account that a cognitively intact older person could make the decision on whether they want a report made. The problem for the mandated reporter then becomes balancing the interest in protecting an elder from further abuse and protecting their sense of self-worth and self-direction. Arguments in support of mandated reporting hold that even more abuse would go unreported if such laws did not exist, putting more elders in harm's way (Bernal, 2017).

The same problems exist for those who encounter elder maltreatment in clinic or hospital settings, at home visits, or in other encounters with adults, when abuse may be suspected. Submitting a report on paper, such as with an official county or state form, or documentation with photographs or other imaging may lead to increased intervention and safety for the elder. It may also increase successful prosecution in a court of law. Other consequences may come as a surprise to the elderly victim, such as a change in where they live, who will care for them, and who is involved in their decision-making. The victim of elder abuse should be kept informed of what steps are taken to protect them, what information is being disclosed, and how that will affect them. That includes the need for mandated reporting and what follows such a report.

Cultural Awareness

From early research in elder mistreatment, it has been recognized that abuse is not confined to one population or ethnic group. Around the world, many countries are facing the same elder population explosion, and confronting abuse and mistreatment in their aging citizens. In the United States, it was noted that data were often focused on the Caucasian elderly, usually Caucasian females, possibly due to their use of social service agencies. In 1999, "*Understanding Elder Abuse in Minority Populations*" was published, edited by Toshio Tatara. The authors included evaluations of demographic changes in minority populations and examined mistreatment in multiple minority groups including Native American, African American, Hispanic, Japanese, Puerto Rican, and Korean elders. The authors cited the need for careful and culturally appropriate outreach, as discussions of elder abuse were still taboo outside the family. In a study a decade earlier, Tatara noted that maltreatment was grossly underreported across the United States despite mandated reporting in many states. Even when intervention was possible, it was recognized that researchers were only seeing the tip of the iceberg across minority communities (Tatara, 1989).

Since that time, many more researchers have explored elder abuse in diverse communities. Studies have begun to emerge not only in specific ethnic populations but across prison populations, tribal communities, and in lesbian, gay, bisexual, and transgender elders as well.

Identification and Awareness in Diverse Populations

Multiple factors have been identified that contribute to elders becoming vulnerable. Isolation, economic status, lack of a support system, unemployment, and housing insecurity can have an impact on an elder's well-being. Immigrants with green cards who are dependent on their sponsor children may be reluctant to report them as abusers. Additionally, being a member of a specific cultural group may prevent an elder from reporting abuse or receiving care.

Being an immigrant into a new culture can be confusing and isolating, particularly if there is a language barrier. The inability to communicate can increase the abused elder's sense of vulnerability. A lack of understanding of local laws and statutes, as well as available sources of support, can make attempting to seek help virtually impossible. This is particularly true in rural communities, where obtaining health care in general may be a challenge. Lack of ability to drive or use public transportation, when it exists, further complicates seeking help.

In the United States, research studies with some cultural groups have benefited not only the elders but also the people who work with them. It has been noted that research with Asian American elders has been lacking until the last several years. This population, which includes Asian, Hawaiian, and Pacific Islanders, is expected to grow to 7.6 million by the year 2050. The idea of culturally mandated care for the elderly by their children has deep roots in much of this culture and often it was assumed that this duty was being fulfilled. However, filial piety is less followed in modern American society. Those service providers working with this population found that a better understanding of cultural beliefs, gender roles, family shame, and parent–child relationships in general assisted in being able to intervene in elder abuse. Finding providers who spoke the native language of the elder was also an identified need (Bennett, 2014). Law Enforcement and Adult Protective Service workers learned they need to establish a level of trust and to utilize existing community resources within these groups, such as spiritual leaders, to assess safety.

Physical abuse is often not the most reported type of maltreatment in immigrant populations. Among Chinese and Korean older persons, disrespect is often the most common form of emotional abuse. This can take the form of treating the elder like an infant, or ignoring the elder, and using the "silent treatment" to shut them out of the family dynamic. Although nonphysical, this silent form of nonverbal aggression is seen as punishing and humiliating. Another form of nonphysical abuse is separating grandparents from grandchildren. Grandparents often care for grandchildren in multigenerational households and are often brought to the United States for that specific purpose; to be deliberately separated from them disrupts the harmony of the family and further isolates the elder. Another difference in this population is in help seeking behavior: the abused elder often avoids utilizing professional involvement, such as APS and law enforcement, and instead relies on informal sources, such as relatives and family members. By not involving outsiders, this also serves to help the family "save face" by avoiding shame (Chang, 2016; Lee, Kaplan, & Perez-Stable, 2014).

Similar to elders in Asian households, Latino elders may be dependent on their families for shelter and long-term care. Other risk factors for abuse include low income, low education levels, and isolation. Preserving the family to avoid shame has been noted to promote tolerance of abuse and prevent reporting. Latino elders also avoid seeking formal help. This can be attributed not only to retaliation by the family member or caregiver but also fear of government interference and deportation (DeLiema, Gassoumis, Homeier, & Wilber, 2012).

In 1999, Griffin noted that research in elder abuse centered on the majority's definition and description of what constituted abuse and who the perpetrators were, assuming the same was true in minority populations, or that in these groups maltreatment did not occur at all. This was particularly problematic with African American victims of abuse, who were often only included in smaller numbers than other groups of elders. Although similarities existed, such as older people living with their children, in African American communities, it was often the adult children who moved into their parent's home. This was usually a daughter who was divorced, widowed, or separated, bringing her children to live in the elder's house as well. Issues of culture and context were not evaluated; clarity on what maltreatment was and how it presented in the African American community was lacking.

Since that time, more attention has been paid to the differences and similarities in the African American experience of elder abuse. Risks and protective factors have both been evaluated, in cultural context. While African American women may be less likely to be socially isolated compared with Caucasian women, poor health and financial status may make them dependent on family as caregivers. Similar to other minority groups, lower socioeconomic status and lack of ready access to health care may contribute to vulnerability. Psychological mistreatment is often more commonly found than physical abuse. Financial abuse was also common, with some African American elders feeling that having more money and assets than other family members made them more susceptible to financial crimes. Older persons in this group were also found to be in danger for self-neglect, with research showing increased mortality risk (Beach, Schulz, Castle, & Rosen, 2010; Dong, 2014; Dong et al., 2011; Paranjape, Corbie-Smith, Thompson, & Kaslow, 2009). Professionals working with elders in this group can use this information with available screening tools to evaluate subtle signs of psychological maltreatment, as well of signs of neglect and self-neglect, that may lead to deterioration of health.

Recent reporting in studies with American Indian/Alaska Native (AI/AN) elders revealed that for many years, it was believed that the elderly in these populations were never abused, protected by the belief that elders were revered and supported in old age. Common themes of fear, shame, pride, and the need to protect the family were found to prevent reports of elder maltreatment. The AI/AN nations, however, have a unique relationship with the United States federal government, unlike other populations. Treaties negotiated between sovereign Indian nations and the US federal government included the federal obligation to provide health care to Indian people in the United States. This requires the federal government to work with tribal communities to address elder abuse issues and to protect elders from incidents of abuse. The Department of Health and Human Services, Centers for Medicare and Medicaid Services (2015) has noted that a loss in traditional cultural values can lead to a lack of appreciation for elders, making them more susceptible to elder abuse. Lack of long-term care and support can mean families caring for elderly members may not have access to respite care or home health services. Neglect and financial exploitation may go undetected for long periods of time. It was recommended that better coordination of services, more direct tribal involvement in elder abuse prevention, and increased financial support for tribal initiatives could help protect AI/AN elders.

Some immigrant populations are also seeing increasingly visible signs of elder abuse. Migration from South American countries and the Middle East into the United States has brought cultural change for these immigrants, but also stress, fear, and financial insecurity. However, research is lacking in elder abuse in these groups. In Europe, the large influx of migrants has brought families with senior members who are ill and unable to work and may be seen as a burden on the family. Other cultures have seen similar trends, with aging populations and increased caregiver demand, highlighting elder mistreatment as a global problem.

Emerging Research

As elder abuse is more globally identified, more persons of diverse cultures and beliefs will be recognized as needing assistance in staying safe. In America, among these groups are the lesbian, gay, bisexual, transgender, queer/questioning (LGBTQ) population and those serving time in prison.

In the United States, the LGBTQ community has seen positive changes in obtaining legal protections and improving equality in civil rights. Until recently, little focus was placed on elder LGBTQ issues, including elder abuse. Many had suffered prejudice, fear, and discrimination in their lives and knew it could be dangerous to reveal their sexual orientation. Some had been rejected by families and kept from seeing grandchildren. Younger professionals who work with these victims of elder abuse may not understand the history or the bigotry suffered by many. As with other older persons, LGBTQ elders suffer the same type of abuse and have many of the same fears of reporting maltreatment, such as losing their housing, independence, or financial security. However, there are unique types of abuse that effect these elders. It may be easier for the abuser to keep them isolated, encouraging the elder to fear how they will be treated in the larger community. Elders may feel safer keeping their gender identity or sexual orientation private and then face the threat of being "outed" by an abuser. Reporting an abuse perpetrator, who leaves or is removed from the home situation, may result in the older person living alone, further isolated from society. Many fear-seeking services in locations such as senior centers, afraid of discrimination, may not be aware of available resources (Cook-Daniels, 2013a).

Many LGBTQ elders, particularly gay men, reach old age without a partner or children, or what many consider a "traditional" family. This leaves these elderly without support to provide care when needed. Some report poorer health overall and greater psychological distress. With fewer provisions for care in later life, they may fear dying alone, or in a place where they face discrimination, where their rights are not protected. Although friends may be available to care for each other, they may also be of similar age, with comparable health issues, limiting the assistance they can offer (de Vries & Gutman, 2016). Because of these circumstances, many will need care in nursing homes or other residential facilities. This may leave them vulnerable to further threats to their health such as discrimination, isolation, and abuse from staff or other residents. Physical or verbal harassment can also be common. Many elders remember when homosexuality was considered a mental illness and fear being open with staff. Other older residents may remember when homophobia was commonplace and even accepted and may exhibit these feelings as harassment. Staff may refuse to touch LGBTQ patients and withhold care that is given to other residents, such as feeding, bathing, toileting, and dressing. Some of these concerns are being addressed in the United States with state and federal laws and social reforms. The Federal Nursing Home Reform Act mandates a minimum standard of care and states that these elderly have the right to free of mental or physical abuse and involuntary seclusion. The Fair Housing Act prohibits discrimination on the basis of sex. Although elders in nursing homes are protected by these federal statutes, standards for assisted living facilities are regulated state by state. In 2009, California passed a law requiring nurses, certified nursing assistants, and physicians to undergo cultural competency training with respect to issues of gender and sex to prevent or eliminate discrimination against LGBTQ residents. Organizations such as Advocacy and Services for Gay, Lesbian, Bisexual, and Transgender Elders have urged facilities to develop nondiscrimination policies and to institute cultural awareness and sensitivity training (Wolfenson, 2017).

Some directions have been suggested to focus more attention in this area and assist those working with LGBTQ elder clients. Research needs to be undertaken specific to this population. APS workers often fail to ask questions regarding gender or sexual orientation, so few statistics exist. As with other areas of elder abuse, definitions need to be refined, and terminology more established, to increase common understanding. Knowledge of the available resources is important, as it is allowing the client to divulge as much or little information about themselves as they choose. They may or may not want to discuss issues of gender or family, and respecting their privacy is vital. Awareness of applicable laws and reporting requirements is helpful in preparing the elderly client for what information has to be communicated and with whom; there may not be a need to divulge that they are LGBTQ, and permission should be requested from them before sharing this (Cook- Daniels, 2017).

The elderly in prison is also an area of emerging research, with less of an understanding of the experience of elder abuse in this population. In 2017, it was estimated that about 1,330,000 inmates were incarcerated in state prisons in the United States, with the highest number in Florida, California, and Texas. Beginning in the 19th century, individual States have regulated the provision of health care to prisoners and like other entities, have seen costs rise rapidly. This is due in part to an aging inmate population (Sonntag, 2017). The number of incarcerated elders is expected to triple by 2019. Prisoners age 50 and over could make up almost 28% of the Bureau of Prison population by 2019, up 10% from 2011. Compared with elders out in the community, prisoners tend to have greater incidence of disease, including hepatitis C, mental health disorders, hypertension, and substance abuse, leading this group to have a physiological age similar to nonincarcerated individuals who are 10–15 years younger. Elderly prisoners are also more vulnerable to victimization. Older inmates often require care that younger inmates do not, such as more time to complete chores, extra blankets in winter to stay warm, and increased surveillance and protection not to be victimized (Kim & Peterson, 2014, pp. ii–29). One piece of legislation, the Prison Rape Elimination Act (PREA), sought to focus attention on sexual abuse of prisoners. It mandated requirements for each agency or facility, such as the provision for private reporting by inmates of sexual assault, access to contacting advocates and community resources outside of prison, training for employees in areas such as the rights of inmates to be free from sexual harassment and abuse, and how to detect and respond to threatened and actual incidents of sexual abuse. Guidelines for the PREA require screening of incoming inmates for a number of criteria to assess for sexual victimization risk, including whether the victim has a physical, mental, or developmental disability; whether they have experienced sexual victimization in the past; the inmate's own perception of vulnerability; and the age of the inmate (Cook-Daniels, 2013b). Research in other areas of abuse needs to be undertaken with the incarcerated elderly to assess incidence and prevalence and to establish guidelines such as those used with PREA.

Intervention and Advocacy

Around the world, countries are making strides in detection and intervention of elder mistreatment. An increasing number of sources of assistance have emerged as elder abuse has become more studied. Forensic documentation has also evolved, as has medical awareness and treatment. In the United States, response has grown at the local, state, and national levels. One of the earliest programs, APS, provides social services to neglected, abused, or exploited older adults and adults with significant disabilities. Eligibility and service requirements vary from state to state. In 1950, the Department of Health, Education, and Welfare provided federal funds for demonstration projects for protective services units. These funds incentivized the development of state protective services for vulnerable, impoverished, and frail older Americans. Many years passed until 1974 when APS was authorized under title XX of the Social Security Act. This provided funding for individual states to create their own protective programs. To receive federal funds, states were mandated to develop APS units to remedy or prevent exploitation of adults unable to protect their own interests. Congress began holding hearings on elder abuse, with the first one held in the House of Representatives in 1978, and the first joint hearing in 1980. Anticipating federal funding, states began developing programs for older individuals. In 1987, nursing home reform was enacted through the Omnibus Budget and Reconciliation Act, and in 1990, the National Center on Elder Abuse was created. In 2002, the Elder Justice Act was introduced but as noted previously was not enacted until 2010. Although this authorized the first dedicated federal funding for APS, no money was appropriated in fiscal years 2011−14. It was not until 2015 that appropriation for APS appeared in a Presidential budget. With lack of federal financial support, states had to institute programs on their own. As a result of states defining elder abuse differently, each has its own screening procedures and response to elder maltreatment. What has resulted is a mixture of services that can vary across states and sometimes across counties. For example, most, but not all, states triage reports at the intake of the case, maintain regular contact with the client, and are required to make a report to law enforcement, in at least some of the cases (Jackson, 2017; Snyder & Benson, 2017).

Similar to APS, the Aging Network started forming in the 1960's. President Lyndon Johnson signed the Older Americans Act (OAA) into law in 1965, beginning the development of a structure of state and local services for older adults. Under the Administration on Aging (AoA), an agency in the US Administration for Community Living, Area Agencies on Aging were established in designated service areas. Because of the structure of the Aging Network, entities at the local, state, and federal level communicate with each other, and with other agencies at their level, to provide care for services such as meals and nutrition programs, senior centers, and legal services. This allows for monies to be allocated down to the local level, with input based on the needs of the community. It also specifically addresses the needs of indigenous populations, providing funding for services for Native Hawaiian, ANs, and AI elders. Within this structure, more focus has been placed on elder abuse. Title VII of the OAA authorized the establishment of the National Center on Elder Abuse, which provides technical assistance, training, and support to both elder abuse professionals and the general public. It also provided funds for the Prevention of Elder Abuse, Neglect, and Exploitation Program and the Long-Term Care Ombudsman Program (Yonashiro-Cho, Meyer, & Wilber, 2017). These programs, along with community, faith-based, and private-public entities, have increased the opportunities to identify elder abuse (Table 2.1).

Identifying Sources of Assistance

Within communities sources of assistance for victims of elder, abuse may be well known to professionals, but not at all to the elders themselves. Finding these resources can be the first hurdle in seeking help. Increased public awareness, such as public services announcements in the media or outreach programs from banking institutions, is starting to be more common.

Elder Mistreatment Response Programs are community organizations working directly with victims to intervene in elder maltreatment and prevent revictimization. Often this is a state or local APS agency but may also include faith-based programs or community resource centers for the elderly. Although practices among service providers may differ, all have the common goal of reducing or eliminating risk of abuse. Use of these services is voluntary on the part of the elder; if they are cognitively able to make their own decisions, the elderly can choose which services to accept or refuse. This is true even if the elder's selected course of action may seem arbitrary or unsafe. Refusal of services on the part of an at-risk person is often seen as a major problem, and the challenge becomes providing safety versus the elders' right to make their own choices (Burnes, 2017).

Family members are commonly the caregivers to the elderly, whether or not they have had training or education in caregiving. Additionally, the family member may have little ability or interest in giving care. Attention to prevention programs aimed at family caregivers is becoming more common, with the knowledge that

Table 2.1 The Aging Network in the United States; Services for Disabled Persons and the Elderly.

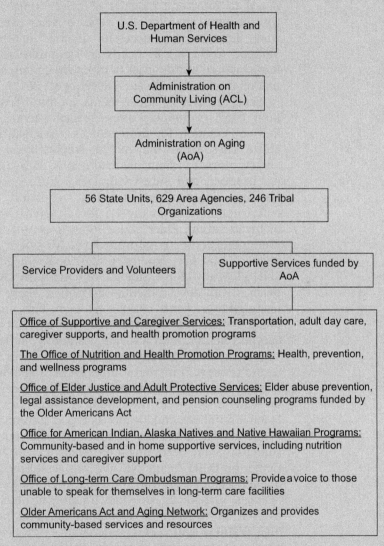

U.S. Department of Health and Human Services

Administration on Community Living (ACL)

Administration on Aging (AoA)

56 State Units, 629 Area Agencies, 246 Tribal Organizations

Service Providers and Volunteers

Supportive Services funded by AoA

Office of Supportive and Caregiver Services: Transportation, adult day care, caregiver supports, and health promotion programs

The Office of Nutrition and Health Promotion Programs: Health, prevention, and wellness programs

Office of Elder Justice and Adult Protective Services: Elder abuse prevention, legal assistance development, and pension counseling programs funded by the Older Americans Act

Office for American Indian, Alaska Natives and Native Hawaiian Programs: Community-based and in home supportive services, including nutrition services and caregiver support

Office of Long-term Care Ombudsman Programs: Provide a voice to those unable to speak for themselves in long-term care facilities

Older Americans Act and Aging Network: Organizes and provides community-based services and resources

Hornyak, B. (n.d). AoA and the Aging Network; Administration for Community Living. (2017). About the Administration on Aging (AoA).

family members are often the perpetrator of abuse. Providing information on caregiver stress, the needs of the elderly, and coping may assist a care provider who is feeling overwhelmed. Home visiting programs, such as those used in child abuse programs dating back to the 1970's in the United States, have been proposed to intervene in elder caregiver abuse. Visits combined with in-home training, as a series of visits over several months, were shown to be successful in child maltreatment models. Tailored to the family needs and culture, this model could be implemented at the onset of caregiving, intervening before elder maltreatment might occur (Meyer et al., 2017).

Specialized elder abuse teams are also becoming more common. FAST, or financial abuse specialist teams, provide support and consultation for professionals investigating financial elder abuse. These teams may include stockbrokers, insurance agents, and employees of financial institutions, with knowledge of financial products and industry practices and regulations. They may also include members of federal regulatory agencies or law enforcement, such as the US Postal Service or Federal Bureau of Investigation. Elder abuse forensic center teams also utilize multiple experts across professions. Members may include civil and criminal law experts, professionals in geriatric medicine, and advocates for residents of long-term care facilities and persons with developmental disabilities. These cross-disciplinary teams address clients' social, emotional, legal, and financial needs. Members provide consultation, conduct home assessments, accept referrals, and provide testimony in legal proceedings. Teams can also identify areas of unmet needs, such as medical record reviews, or more resources for neuropsychiatric evaluations (Nerenberg, Davies, & Navarro, 2012). Resources for self-help can be made available to the elderly at home visits, such as 1–800 Hotline numbers, and locations of food assistance.

Elder LGBTQ victims of abuse may not be aware of the resources that are becoming more available. The National Resource Center on LGBT Aging (NRCLA) was established in 2010 through a federal grant from the US Department of Health and Human Services. The NRCLA provides training and technical assistance, as well as educational resources to aging providers, LGBTQ organizations, and LGBTQ older adults. Their website lists multiple resources for victims of elder abuse addressing diverse topics such as elder sweetheart scams, fraud prevention, and where to seek assistance should an elder become a victim, some of which are in Spanish. It also provides links to training resources for professionals and LGBTQ long-term care (The National Resource Center on LGBT Aging, n.d.)

In addition to identifying sources of support for elders themselves, medical and forensic professionals are being provided more sources of education and training. Around the world meetings are held annually for the public and experts alike, such as the fifth Annual National Elder Abuse Conference of 2018 in Sydney, Australia; the International Conference on Geriatrics, Gerontology, and Palliative Nursing in Barcelona, Spain; and the University of Southern California Tamkin International Symposium on Elder Abuse. In 2006, the International Network for Prevention of Elder Abuse, founded by Rosalie Wolf, designated June 15 as World Elder Abuse Awareness Day, and numerous events are held across the globe to raise awareness of elder abuse and its prevention and intervention. Education ranges from wound identification and documentation, evidence collection, and service provision, to forensic interviewing of the elderly, laws and statutes, working with law enforcement, and best practices when working with elder victims.

Identification of Elder Abuse

As awareness and technology improve, so will identification of all forms of elder maltreatment. Those working with the elderly should maintain a high index of suspicion when they encounter something that does not look or feel right with an older person, but also avoid stereotypes. Assumptions based on preconceived ideas of how a specific elder, group, or community "should" act could mean missing indications of mistreatment. Medical personnel can act to assist law enforcement and forensic specialists by being prepared to identify and document abuse. It's been noted that the application of the "forensic lens," which uses medical expertise to answer questions relating to law and criminal justice, can assist investigators in evaluating cases of suspected abuse. In the United States, the use of the correct ICD-10 diagnosis code "adult maltreatment (unspecified) *suspected* T76.91" or "*confirmed* T74.91" can help specify abuse for investigators when records are subpoenaed. Objective documentation of signs of mistreatment and neglect are important in health records that become part of criminal prosecution (DeLiema, Homeier, Anglin, Li, & Wilber, 2016). The use of the observed and collected information can support social work, APS, law enforcement, and forensic specialists in elder abuse with assisting elders to safety and reducing risk of repeated harm.

Case Study

In 2010, an 88-year-old man needed help in caring for his 91-year-old wife, who was in the end stages of lung cancer. He was a retired mapmaker who his family described as "frugal" but having enough money to care for himself and his wife at that time of their lives. He had planned for his money to go to his daughter after his death. Through a service, he hired a 44-year-old caregiver to come in to his home and care for his wife. He soon began to trust her and allowed her access to his money when she convinced him she could help with his finances. After the wife died, the caregiver was able to gain control over the husband's assets, sell his home, and funnel his money into her own accounts. She forged his name on numerous documents and ended up with $594,000, which she used to buy rental properties and a home.

In October 2010, the retired mapmaker disappeared. The caregiver told his family he had gotten remarried in Las Vegas, and she persuaded a woman to pretend to be the new wife and leave a message for his daughter, telling the family they wanted time for themselves. The family became suspicious, and after opening an investigation, the caregiver was arrested in July 2011 while boarding a plane for Europe. At trial, she was charged with first degree murder and murder for financial gain. Her attorney argued that she had taken money but did not kill her elderly employer. She was convicted of first degree murder and a special circumstance allegation of murder for financial gain. She was also found guilty of several other charges, including fraudulent appropriation of a trustee, caretaker theft from an elder, and grand theft of personal property and forgery. She was acquitted of a charge related to theft of another elderly man in 2009 and 2010. She was sentenced to life in prison without the possibility of parole and is serving her sentence at the Central California Women's Facility in Chowchilla, California. The elderly mapmaker's body was never found (Littlefield, 2014; "Caregiver Gets Life", 2015).

This case illustrates the vulnerability of an elder, with considerable assets, needing help for his elderly wife. He had the financial means to care for himself and for her but needed someone to physically help with care in the home. Suspicion on the part of the family, as well as proper documentation and investigation, helped to identify the multiple types of abuse. With the sentence of life without parole, this perpetrator will not be able to harm another elder in the community.

References

AARP. (n.d.). https://www.aarp.org/home-garden/housing/info-08-2009/ginzler_housing_choices.html.

Acierno, R. (2003). Elder mistreatment: Epidemiological assessment methodology. In Bonnie, & Wallace (Eds.), *Elder mistreatment* (pp. 261–302). Washington DC: The National Academies Press.

Administration for Community Living. (2017). *About the Administration on Aging (AoA)*. Retrieved from https://www.acl.gov/node/915.

Ansello, E. (2016). Animal cruelty and elder abuse. *Agents and Actions, 31*, 1–3.

Beach, S., Schulz, R., Castle, N., & Rosen, J. (2010). Financial exploitation and psychological mistreatment among older adults: Differences between African Americans and non-African Americans in a population-based survey. *The Gerontologist, 50*(6), 744–757.

Bennett, A. (2014). Cultural standards for Asian Americans weigh heavily on both young and old. *Victimization of the elderly and Disabled*. September/October, 37–38, 47.

Bernal, R. (2017). Do I really have to?: An examination of mandatory reporting statutes and the civil and criminal penalties imposed for failure to report elder abuse. *The Elder Law Journal, 25*(1), 133–160.

Burnes, D. (2017). Community elder mistreatment intervention wit capable older adults: Toward a conceptual practice model. *The Gerontologist, 57*(3), 409–416.

Burnett, J., Achenbaum, W., & Murphy, K. (2014). Prevention and early identification of elder abuse. *Clinics in Geriatric Medicine, 30*(4), 743–759.

Caregiver gets life for murder of elderly man.(2015). Retrieved from https://fox5sandiego.com/2015/01/30/caregiver-gets-life-in-prison-for-murder-of-elderly-man/.

Carney, A. (2015a). Indicators of abuse in the elderly ICU patient. *Critical Care Nursing Quarterly, 38*, 293–297.

Carney, A. (2015b). Assessing for intimate partner violence. In P. T. Clements, et al. (Eds.), *Violence against women* (pp. 17–31). St Louis Missouri: STM Learning, Inc.

Chang, M. (2016). Experience of elder abuse among older Korean immigrants. *Journal of Elder Abuse and Neglect, 28*(2), 76–94.

Cook-Daniels, L. (2013a). Identifying and assisting abuse among LGBT elder clients. *Victimization of the Elderly and Disabled, 15*(6), 81–96.

Cook-Daniels, L. (2013b). Prison rape elimination act looks at elder and disabled sexual abuse behind bars. *Victimization of the Elderly and Disabled, 15*(5), 67–80.

Cook-Daniels, L. (2017). Coping and abuse inside the family and out: LGBT and/or male victims of elder abuse. In X. Dong (Ed.), *Elder abuse research, practice and policy* (pp. 541–553). Switzerland: Springer.

De Vries, B., & Gutman, G. (2016). End–of-life preparations among LGBT older adults. *Generations-Journal of the American Society on Aging, 40*(2), 46–48.

DeLiema, M., Gassoumis, Z., Homeier, D., & Wilber, K. (2012). Determining prevalence and correlates of elder abuse using promotores: Low income immigrant Latinos report high rates of abuse and neglect. *Journal of the American Geriatrics Society, 60*(7), 1333–1339.

DeLiema, M., Homeier, D., Anglin, D., Li, D., & Wilber, K. (2016). The forensic lens: Bringing elder neglect into focus in the emergency department. *Annals of Emergency Medicine, 68*(3), 371–377.

DeLiema, M., Navarro, A., Enguidanos, S., & Wilber, K. (2015). Voices from the frontlines: Examining elder abuse from multiple professional perspectives. *Health and Social Work, 40*, e15–e24.

Department of Health and Human Services, & Centers for Medicare and Medicaid. (2015). *Elder abuse in Indian country.* Retrieved from https://www.cms.gov/Outreach-and- Education/American-Indian-Alaska-Native/AIAN/Downloads/Elder_Abuse_Lit_Review.pdf.

Dong, X. (2014). Elder abuse: Research, practice, and health policy. The 2012 GSA Maxwell Pollack award lecture. *The Gerontologist, 54*(2), 153–162.

Dong, X., Simon, M., Fulmer, T., Mendes de Leon, C., Hebert, L., Beck, T., … Evans, D. (2011). A prospective population-based study of differences in elder self-neglect and mortality between black and white older adults. *Journals Of Gerontology Series A: Biomedical Sciences and Medical Sciences, 66A*(6), 695–704.

Evans, C., Hunold, K., Rosen, T., & Platts-Mills, T. (2017). Diagnosis of elder abuse in U.S. emergency departments. *Journal of the American Geriatrics Society, 65*, 91–97.

Frazao, S., Correia, A., Norton, P., & Magalhaes, T. (2015). Physical abuse against elderly persons in institutional settings. *Journal of Forensic and Legal Medicine, 36*, 54–60.

Gallione, C., Dal Molin, A., Cristina, F., Ferns, H., Mattioli, M., & Suardi, B. (2017). Screening tools for identification of elder abuse: A systematic review. *Journal of Clinical Nursing, 26*, 2154–2176.

Gibbs, L. (2014). Understanding the medical markers of elder abuse and neglect: Physical examination findings. In L. Gibbs, & L. Mosqueda (Eds.), *Clinics in geriatric medicine medical implications of elder abuse and neglect* (pp. 687–712). Philadelphia: Elsevier.

Goergen, T., & Beaulieu, M. (2013). Critical concepts in elder abuse research. *International Psychogeriatrics, 25*, 1217, 128.

Griffin, l (1999). Elder maltreatment in the African American community: You just don't hit your momma!!! In T. Tatara (Ed.), *Understanding elder abuse in minority populations* (pp. 27–48). Philadelphia: Taylor & Francis.

Heisler, C. (2017). Elder abuse forensics: The intersection of law and science. In X. Dong (Ed.), *Elder abuse research, practice and policy* (pp. 387–416). Switzerland: Springer.

Hoover, R., & Polson, M. (2014). Detecting elder abuse and neglect: Assessment and intervention. *American Family Physician, 89*, 453–460.

Hornyak, B. (n. d). AoA and the Aging Network. Retrieved from HYPERLINK "http://longtermcarescorecard.org/ ~ /media/files/publications/blog/2011/oct/hornyakaoa.pdf" /o "http://longtermcarescorecard.org/ ~ /media/files/publications/blog/2011/oct/hornyakaoa.pdf" http://longtermcarescorecard.org/ ~ /media/files/publications/blog/2011/oct/hornyakaoa.pdf.

Howard, L. (2014). Does government oversight improve access to nursing home care? longitudinal evidence from US counties. *Inquiry: The Journal of Health Care Organization, Provision, and Financing, 51*, 1–12.

Jackson, S. (2017). Adult protective services and victim services: A review of the literature to increase understanding between these two fields. *Aggression And Violent Behavior, 34*(May), 214–227.

Kim, K., & Peterson, B. (2014). *Aging behind bars trends and implications of graying prisoners in the federal prison system* (p. ii). Urban Institute.

Lee, Y., Kaplan, C., & Perez-Stable, J. (2014). Elder mistreatment among Chinese and Korean immigrants: The roles of sociocultural contexts on perceptions and help-seeking Behaviors. *Journal of Elder Abuse and Neglect, 26*(3), 244–269.

Lee, H., & Lightfoot, E. (2014). Culture as a risk factor in perceiving and responding to elder mistreatment. *Journal of Aggression, Maltreatment and Trauma, 23,* 5–19.

Littlefield, D. (Oct 7, 2014). *Caregiver convicted of murder for money.* The San Diego Union-Tribune. Retrieved from http://www.sandiegouniontribune.com/news/courts/sdut-caregiver-guilty-murder-denise-goodwin-2014oct07-story.html.

Meyer, K., Yonashiro-Cho, J., Gassoumis, Z., Mosqueda, L., Han, S., & Wilber, K. (2017). What can elder mistreatment researchers learn about primary prevention from family violence intervention models? *The Gerontologist, 00*(0), 1–9.

Mosqueda, L., Burnight, K., & Liao, S. (2005). The life cycle of bruises in older adults. *Journal of the American Geriatrics Society, 53,* 1339–1343.

Murphy, K., Waa, S., Jaffer, J., Sauter, A., & Chan, A. (2013). A literature review of findings in physical elder abuse. *Canadian Association of Radiologists Journal, 64,* 10–14.

Mysyuk, Y., Westendor, R., & Lindenberg, J. (2016). How older persons explain why they became victims of abuse. *Age and Aging, 45,* 695–702.

Namboodri, B., Rosen, T., Dayaa, J., Bischof, J., Ramadan, N., Patel, M., … Platts-Mills, T. (2018). Elder abuse identification in the pre-hospital setting: An examination of state emergency medical services protocols. *Journal of the American Geriatrics Society, 66*(5), 962–968.

The National Resource Center on LGBT Aging. (n.d.). Retrieved from https://www.lgbtagingcenter.org/index.cfm.

Nerenberg, L., Davies, M., & Navarro, A. (2012). In pursuit of a useful framework to champion elder justice. *Generations-Journal of the American Society on Aging, 36*(3), 89–96.

Palmer, M., Brodell, R., & Mostow, E. (2013). Elder abuse: Dermatologic clues and critical solutions. *Journal of the American Academy of Dermatology, 68,* 37–42.

Paranjape, A., Corbie-Smith, G., Thompson, N., & Kaslow, N. (2009). When older African American women are affected by violence in the home. *Violence Against Women, 15*(8), 977–990.

Peak, T., Ascione, F., & Doney, J. (2012). Adult protective services and animal welfare: Should animal abuse and neglect be assessed during adult protective services screening? *Journal of Elder Abuse and Neglect, 24,* 37–49.

Phillips, L., & Ziminski, C. (2012). The public health nursing role in elder neglect in assisted living facilities. *Public Health Nursing, 29,* 499–509.

Snyder, J., & Benson, w. (2017). Adult protective services and the long-term care Ombudsman program. In X. Dong (Ed.), *Elder abuse research, practice and policy* (pp. 317–342). Switzerland: Springer.

Sonntag, H. (2017). Medicine behind bars: Regulating and litigating prison healthcare under state law forty years after Estelle v. Gamble. *Case Western Reserve Law Review, 68*(2), 603–649.

Stetson Law. (2016). *Mandatory reporting statutes for elder abuse.* Retrieved from http://www.stetson.edu/law/academics/elder/ecpp/media/Mandatory%20Reporting%20 statutes%20for%20Elder%20Abuse%202016.pdf.

Straus, M. (1987). *The conflict tactics scales and its critics: An evaluation and new data on validity and reliability.* New Hampshire University, Durham. Family Research Lab.

Tatara, T. (1989). Toward the development of estimates of the national incidence of reports of elder abuse based on currently available study data. In R. Filinson, & S. Ingman (Eds.), *Elder abuse: Practice and policy* (pp. 153–165). New York: Human Sciences Press.

Wiglesworth, A., Austin, R., Corona, M., Schneider, D., Liao, S., Gibbs, L., & Mosqueda, L. (2009). Bruising as a marker of physical elder abuse. *Journal of the American Geriatrics Society, 57,* 1191–1196.

Wolfenson, D. (2017). The risks to LGBT elders in nursing homes and assisted living facilities and possible solutions. *Tulane Journal of Law and Sexuality, 26,* 123–131.

World Health Organization. (2017). *Elder abuse.* Retrieved from http://www.who.int/mediacentre/fatsheets/fs357/en/.

Yonashiro-Cho, J., Meyer, K., & Wilber, K. (2017). The aging network. In X. Dong (Ed.), *Elder abuse research, practice and policy* (pp. 297–315). Switzerland: Springer.

Further Reading

Elder Abuse Prevention Unit. (2014). *Neglect.* Retrieved from https://www.eapu.com.au/elder-abuse/neglect.

Tatara, T. (Ed.). (1999). *Understanding elder abuse in minority populations.* Philadelphia: Taylor & Francis.

United Nations Economic Commission for Europe. (2014). *Policy brief abuse of older persons.* Retrieved from http://www.unece.org/fileadmin/DAM/pau/age/Policy_briefs/ECE-WG-14. pdf.

3

DEMENTIA AND MEMORY DISORDERS IN ABUSE IN THE ELDERLY

Patricia M. Speck,[1] Rita A. Jablonski[2]

[1]School of Nursing, Department of Family, Community, & Health Systems, University of Alabama at Birmingham, Birmingham, AL, United States;
[2]School of Nursing, Department of Adult Chronic and Continuing Care, University of Alabama at Birmingham, Birmingham, AL, United States

CHAPTER OUTLINE
Introduction   56
Case 1   57
  Discussion   57
Case 2   57
  Discussion   57
The First Evaluation: Is It Neurodegeneration or Other Illness?   58
Case 1 Review   59
  Discussion   59
Case 2 Review   60
  Discussion   60
Elder Maltreatment, Memory Disorders, and Dementia   60
Case 1 Resolution   61
  Discussion   61
Case 2 Resolution   61
  Discussion   61
Elder Maltreatment and Alzheimer's Dementia   61
Case 3   63
  Discussion   64
Vascular Dementia   64
Case 4   65
  Discussion   66

Elder Abuse. https://doi.org/10.1016/B978-0-12-815779-4.00003-3

Case 5 66
Discussion 67
Frontotemporal Dementia 67
Case 6 68
Discussion 69
Dementia with Lewy Bodies 69
Case 7 70
Discussion 70
Mixed Dementia and Overlapping Presentations 71
Stages of Dementia and Risk for Abuse 71
Mild Stage 71
Case 8 72
Discussion 73
Moderate Stage 73
Nurse Case 9 73
Discussion 74
Severe Stage 75
Case 10 75
Discussion 75
Care Transitions 76
Assisted Living Facilities 76
Nursing Homes 77
Case 11 78
Discussion 78
Conclusion 79
References 80
Further Reading 83

Introduction

Although each type of dementia has unique primary or presenting features, the overall trajectory remains the same: consistent cognitive and functional decline until the person with dementia is completely dependent on others for care. The average period from diagnosis to death is 8–10 years, although brain changes may precede clinical manifestations by 20 years or more (Alzheimer's Association, 2018a, 2018b). The combination of dependence on others and progressive loss of cognitive abilities creates situations where the person with dementia may engage in verbally and physically assaultive behaviors toward caregivers. Conversely, the presence of dementia, regardless of type, increases the risk for formal or informal caregiver abuse and financial exploitation (Fang & Yan, 2018; McCausland, Knight, Page, & Trevillion, 2016; Tronetti, 2014).

Case 1

Gladys, a 62-year-old, calls the police because her checkbook is missing. She is a community-dwelling older person who retired from teaching in her 50s.

Discussion

If Gladys' home has no signs of forced entry and she does not report that there was someone in her home, law enforcement may briefly assist Gladys with the search for her checkbook, especially if they do not have another call. In this case, Gladys admits she is having trouble remembering where she puts things. If Gladys has children close by, law enforcement may request that Gladys give them permission to call the adult child to inquire about her memory. In this case, the children report that their mother, in the recent past, misplaced other items, only to be found later in odd places. Law enforcement may speak to the child about getting Gladys evaluated by the primary care provider. Persons with early dementia are often aware of their memory decline. Some hide the memory decline and others are open to the decline, trying to control it using notes or scraps of paper, and resistance to the notion that they need support. Either way, the discussion with family and caretakers starts years and sometimes decades before total dependence is necessary.

Case 2

Ruby, a 70-year-old, heard a knock on the door and opened it. A woman asked for a drink of water. When Ruby turned around, the woman pushed her way into the house. Ruby resisted and was pushed backward onto her couch. She called the police, who responded a few minutes later, but the woman was gone.

Discussion

In this case, there were no signs of forced entry, and Ruby cannot tell if anything is missing. The officers direct Ruby to her bedroom jewelry box and ask her if anything was missing; she reported her rings were gone, but she could not describe what they looked like. Ruby admits that she sometimes misplaces her jewelry only to find it later somewhere else in the house. Ruby called her child and asked them to come over. The child spoke to the police and described the jewelry. The child planned to

Table 3.1 Memory Loss and Cognitive Impairment.

Definitions

Memory loss and cognitive impairment are often used interchangeable but reflect different levels of brain defects.

Memory: Refers to the ability to retrieve or recall information.

Cognition: Refers to the sum total of all thinking skills; cognition involves memory, executive, and visual-spatial judgment, language production and understanding, concentration, and attention (Eshkoor, Hamid, Mun, & Ng, 2015).

Cognitive impairment: It is characterized by deficiencies in any singular or multiple cognitive domains.

• **Mild Cognitive Impairment:** The subjective and objective recognition of deficiencies in one or more cognitive domains without loss of independent social or occupational functioning (Alzheimer's Association, 2018a, 2018b; Langa & Levine, 2014).

Dementia: It is an overarching clinical term that describes a progressive decline in both cognitive and functional abilities resulting from neurodegeneration (Bang, Spina, & Miller, 2015; Kirshner, 2014).

come to Ruby's home after work but could not leave until then without losing income. After the police left, Ruby cannot find her purse, which is common for victims needing to recall the location of items while in a stress response (Table 3.1).

The First Evaluation: Is It Neurodegeneration or Other Illness?

Any memory disorder complaint requires thorough clinical evaluations. The first step is a comprehensive physical examination to determine if reversible metabolic problems are causing the cognitive impairments. Common health problems that impair cognition include hypothyroidism, sleep apnea, renal disease, liver disease, alcoholism, depression, anemia, delirium, and vitamin insufficiencies such as cyanocobalamin (vitamin B12) (Galvin, Sadowsky, & NINCDS-ADRDA, 2012; McKhann et al., 2011). Laboratory tests such as metabolic panels, complete blood counts, thyroid-stimulating hormone levels, liver function tests, and vitamin levels form the foundation of these evaluations (Galvin et al., 2012). Pharmacologic agents that are associated with cognitive problems include anticholinergics (Fox et al., 2011) and benzodiazepines (Galvin et al., 2012).

Following an assault, or in these cases an assault and robbery, the older person's stress response, also known as allostatic load, has the capacity to impact immediate memory (Henckens, Hermans, Pu, Joels, & Fernandez, 2009) and result in the elders' deaths (Henckens et al., 2009; McEwen & Seeman, 1999). Some elders with support experience heart rate variability and anxiety; others with high Adverse Childhood Experiences (ACEs) scores, as well as lifelong chaotic experiences such as family violence or abject poverty, turn to tried-and-true behavioral modifications to control the vagal nerve response of heart tone and anxiety following a stress (McEwen & Seeman, 1999). Alcohol use increases for some following trauma if used previously to uncouple the vagal nerve stimulus of anxiety from the cardiac tone response (Reed, Porges, & Newlin, 1999). With longstanding comorbidities from a lifetime of stress and recent trauma, disease exacerbation with hospitalizations of elders following physically stressful events increases, as does death (Anda et al., 2009; Dong & Simon, 2015; Friedman, Avila, Rizvi, Partida, & Friedman, 2017). Coercion, dependence, and dejection predict death for some, where social and family support can mitigate symptoms and improve recovery (Schofield, Powers, & Loxton, 2013).

Case 1 Review

Discussion

The role of the primary care provider is to comprehensively evaluate Gladys. The laboratory provides clues for the cause of memory decline and in Gladys' case; her thyroid-stimulating hormone level was high, indicating inadequate circulating levels of thyroid hormone. This medical condition is easily corrected with medication. However, the medication administration needs several days to reach a therapeutic level, requiring some support with independent community dwelling. Once the diagnosis is complete, a medical and social intervention plan is developed to help maintain Gladys' independence as long as possible, but also to protect Gladys from harm. In this case, Gladys' child was present and assisting Gladys in making decisions about her safety. These plans need collaboration with the family. It is also time to initiate the Power of Attorney and Living Will directives for future unplanned events, such as forgetting to take the medication. The local senior citizen's legal services are available to Gladys and her child.

Case 2 Review

Discussion

Ruby's child reported that after she quit drinking alcohol, her laboratory levels were now normal, but her forgetfulness is worsening. The family completed the formal paperwork with the help of local senior citizen's legal services when she was hospitalized about a year ago, in preparation for continued cognitive decline; however, she resisted moving from her home to live with her child. The child reported to the health-care provider that Ruby had been the victim of a crime and was now having more difficulty remembering how the assailant gained access to the inside of her home and how she was injured during the event. The child reported that Ruby resumed drinking since the break-in. The health-care provider, with Ruby's permission, alerted the local community resource group about the crime and requested they work with Ruby and her child to develop a safety plan for Ruby.

Elder Maltreatment, Memory Disorders, and Dementia

Mild cognitive impairment (MCI) (Table 3.1) is defined as the subjective or objective recognition of deficiencies in one or more cognitive domains without loss of independent social or occupational functioning (Alzheimer's Association, 2018a, 2018b; Langa & Levine, 2014). Two predominant subtypes of MCI are *amnestic* or *nonamnestic.* Amnestic MCI is characterized by new difficulties with recall abilities; recent conversations are forgotten, or appointments are missed. Persons with nonamnestic MCI demonstrate new problems with judgment, visual perception, or completing complex tasks but do not demonstrate recall problems (Alzheimer's Association, 2018a, 2018b; Eshkoor et al., 2015; Langa & Levine, 2014). MCI may be a harbinger for Alzheimer's dementia or another type of dementia; MCI may also be an indication of a reversible medical problem (Langa & Levine, 2014).

Screening tools can be used to detect MCI. The Montreal Cognitive Assessment (MoCA) is superior to the Mini-Mental State Exam (MMSE) for detecting MCI (Langa & Levine, 2014). Scores of 25 out of 30 have a sensitivity of 80%—100% and a specificity of 50%—76% (Langa & Levine, 2014). Copies of the MoCA, along with directions for administration, can be found at www.mocatest.org.

Formal neuropsychological testing is preferable for more detailed information about which cognitive domains demonstrate deficits.

Case 1 Resolution

Discussion

Once it was discovered that Gladys had hypothyroidism and required medication, her child was instructed to observe her taking the medication over a couple of weeks and to keep a log of her improvement. Gladys was glad to help but discounted that she needed her child's supervision while taking her medication. In her case, the demonstrated MCI is amnesic, where Gladys' recall ability reflects a new difficulty with short-term memory formation and therefore memory recall, a symptom demonstrated earlier to her children and the reason for supervision of medication administration.

Case 2 Resolution

Discussion

Ruby had a diagnosis of nonamnesic MCI. She opened the door because her judgment about safety was diminished. Had this situation occurred prior to Ruby's cognitive impairment, she would have used the door's peephole to visually appraise the visitor prior to opening the door. In this case, she opened the door without thinking about the potential for danger. She recalled that her son told her to never open the door and when he arrived, he seemed irritated with her disobedience. This is an opportunity to reeducate him about her diagnosis symptoms. Ruby did recall the events of the assault and robbery and verbalized that she was assaulted. She could not recall how the assailant gained access to the inside of her house or how the police got to her, confirming the symptom of short-term memory deficit (Table 3.2).

Elder Maltreatment and Alzheimer's Dementia

Nearly six million people who reside in the United States have a diagnosis of Alzheimer's dementia (AD) (Alzheimer's Association, 2018a, 2018b). A significant number of elders with AD are victims of maltreatment, which affects their emotional well-being, leading

Table 3.2 Types of Dementia.

Alzheimers Dementia
Vascular Dementia
Dementia with Lewy Bodies
Frontotemporal Dementia (FTD)
- Behavior Variant FTD
- NonFluent Primary Progressive Aphasia (PPA)
    - Nine nonfluent PPA
- Semantic Variant Primary Progressive Aphasia

to possible depression, inadequate feelings, self-loathing, and lowered self-esteem (Vandeweerd, Paveza, & Fulmer, 2006). As a result, family distress increases, and the elder experiences reduction in quality of life and functioning (Vandeweerd et al., 2006). The elder with AD experiences difficulties adjusting to their home environment, such as not remembering to eat or to clean after toileting, due to diminishing cognition and increasing health problems. Immunologic dysfunction and disease development may occur, which result in increased mortality (Vandeweerd et al., 2006). In AD, β-amyloid accumulates outside of neurons, forming plaque (Hugo & Ganguli, 2014). Plaque occurring between synapses prevents chemicals from being exchanged between the neurons, causing cell death (Alzheimer's Association, 2018a, 2018b). Abnormal accumulations of the tau protein occur inside the neuron; as tau builds up it folds upon itself, creating fibrillary tangles. These intracellular tangles result in neuronal death because the tangles interfere with normal cellular functions (Alzheimer's Association, 2018a, 2018b). As neurons die, the brain tissue atrophies. The atrophy of brain tissue can be seen on magnetic resonance imaging (MRI) and usually affects the hippocampus and temporal–parietal areas (Hugo & Ganguli, 2014).

AD that occurs before age 65 is called early-onset or young-onset (Alzheimer's Association, 2018a, 2018b). There is a subset of early-onset AD that is due to mutations of the amyloid precursor protein on chromosome 21, the Presenilin I gene on chromosome 14, and the Presenilin II gene on chromosome 1 (Hugo & Ganguli, 2014). AD that occurs after age 65 is known as late-onset AD. Mutations of the apolipoprotein E gene (ApoE), where one or both of the epsilon allele pairs are an allele

4, are thought to increase the risk of AD. The current thinking is that the homozygous pairing of two allele 4s may result in both an earlier presentation of AD symptoms and a more rapid cognitive and functional decline (Verghese, Castellano, & Holtzman, 2011).

Early signs and symptoms include short-term memory loss that evolves into difficulty performing executive tasks such as balancing bank statements and paying bills (Hugo & Ganguli, 2014). As more neurons die, cognitive and functional abilities are lost in the reverse order of their attainment: instrumental activities of daily living become impaired, followed by activities of daily living. Persons with AD may become more combative and refuse care. The person will ultimately require complete care and be unable to walk or swallow as the disease progresses.

Case 3

Gayle was a vibrant and active 70-year-old accountant retiree who volunteered annually to help elders complete their tax returns. About 3 years earlier, the volunteer coordinator noted that Gayle was spending an inordinate amount of time "just looking" at the computer, rather than completing tax returns. The coordinator called Gayle frequently, but within the year, when Gayle failed to volunteer to help during tax season, the coordinator never mentioned the volunteer activity again. Gayle had a long-term relationship with her partner who was verbally abusive. Neighbors complained that they heard yelling each evening coming from their household over the last year, and eventually their concern resulted in a police report. When the police arrived and saw the home, they called the Adult Protective Services (APS) worker to investigate and determine if Gayle is safe in her home with her partner. They recognized that Gayle's partner also had diminished physical abilities and their home was uninhabitable. Gayle's partner was directed toward assisted living but refused to leave the home, even if the current home was in an uninhabitable condition. Gayle was hospitalized for evaluation after the incident. The provider found that Gayle was malnourished and had difficulty eating. She was frail and needed assistance with mobility. On discharge, Gayle was placed in a nursing home Eby her child. Within 2 months, Gayle failed to recognize her child and her long-time partner. Gayle's child placed her on hospice care. Gayle continued to refuse food and made utterances that she wanted to die. Severely malnourished and dehydrated, Gayle died from a septic urinary tract infection within 3 months of admission. Gayle's first AD symptoms had appeared a little over 3 years earlier.

Discussion

Gayle's case is classic AD, with symptoms appearing years earlier, and in her case is classified as late-onset AD because of her age. Her symptoms appeared as an inability to perform executive function math with tax returns, a familiar lifelong activity. She was aware of the memory deficit and developed work-arounds for important activities, until she couldn't any longer due to her AD progression. With previous head injuries from the abusive partner, there was concern in the early AD diagnosis that these contributed to the findings. In addition, Gayle had a history of treatment for depression. The depression from domestic violence (DV) and emotional abuse contributed to Gayle's current state of health, which also contributed to her rapid demise. Gayle's partner refused to leave an uninhabitable house, a decision protected by the US Constitution and her right to self-determination, until a competency hearing took away her rights. Until the courts remove capacity and give decision-making to a guardian, everyone has the right to self-determination, even if choosing to live in, what others think is an uninhabitable or unsafe place.

Vascular Dementia

Currently considered the second most common form of dementia in the United States, Vascular dementia (VaD) comprises up to 20% of dementia diagnoses (Hugo & Ganguli, 2014; Rizzi, Rosset, & Roriz-Cruz, 2014) (Table 3.2). Overt VaD often presents immediately after a major stroke; up to 65% of all stroke survivors develop some level of cognitive impairment, with one-third of these cases meeting criteria for dementia (Black, 2011). Head injury, such as contra coupe with arterial sheering or intracranial ruptures, results in focal injury with specific deficit expression of tinnitus, absent olfactory capacity, and motion and balance deficits, among others, that leads to global injury to the elder (Joshi, Thomas, & Sorenson, 2012; "Stroke by strangulation," 1981; Vilke & Chan, 2011; YadollahiKhales, Ghorbani, & Borhani-Haghighi, 2015). Strangulation also results in global injury, leading to capillary rupture and global brain anoxia. Both head injury and strangulation promote the same cascade of small vessel disease (Campbell et al., 2018). Comorbid diseases, such as hypertension, diabetes mellitus, and autoimmune diseases, compound small vessel disease in the brain (de Haan, Nys, & Van Zandvoort, 2006; Hinckley, 2009). Covert cardiovascular disease, also known as small vessel disease or white matter disease, also contributes to VaD (Black, 2011; Iadecola, 2013). Hypertension, especially when combined with diabetes, results in endothelial wall damage, with clotted arterioles and venules as the body attempts to heal the damage (Hilgeman et al., 2014). Clotted arterioles result in hypoperfusion and infarcts; obstructed venules prevent drainage and the removal of harmful β-amyloid and tau proteins (Hilgeman et al., 2014). Obstructed arterioles and venules also result in leaking vessels and microbleeds (Black, 2011; Verghese et al., 2011).

The signs of VaD are dependent on the size and areas of the brain compromised by hypoperfusion, infarcts, and microbleeds. Hemiparesis or hemiplegia, plus receptive or expressive aphasia, may occur secondary to a large artery occlusion; the deficits are highly brain-site dependent. There may be an acute cognitive decline following a major stroke, which then stabilizes and plateaus. In persons with covert cardiovascular disease, VaD may manifest as a very gradual decline in a stepwise fashion (Hugo & Ganguli, 2014). Deficits are usually observed in the cognitive domains of attention and executive functions, accompanied by difficulty with ambulation and mood or personality changes (Hugo & Ganguli, 2014). Depression and awareness of deficits are common with VaD (Black, 2011; Hugo & Ganguli, 2014). As VaD progresses, loss of cognitive and functional abilities follows the AD pattern, resulting in complete dependence on others for care.

Case 4

Daryl is a 38-year-old single executive who had a stroke following an incident of DV, within the 3 weeks following her mother's death. Daryl's ACE score was eight out of a maximum score of 10, indicating significant childhood exposure to adverse events, and she reports that the most stressful event in her childhood was placement in juvenile detention facilities following the arrest of her parents. Her parents were jailed for drug crimes and during their incarcerations, Daryl spent her time in the library after school to avoid returning to the juvenile detention facility. She petitioned the court for emancipation when she was 16 year old, and she then entered college. She matriculated and received a graduate degree in business and became an executive for a large multinational business by the time she was 22 year old.

By all accounts, she is very successful. However, she is diagnosed with lupus, which is a stress-related disease. She and her boyfriend fight over her mother, who is "the ex-con." Daryl wanted her mother to come live with her once she is released from prison, but the boyfriend did not want the mother in their home. The boyfriend and Daryl then got into a fight, which led to the boyfriend strangling Daryl. The boyfriend then left and Daryl's mother came to live in her home. Her mother's release was predicated on receiving treatment for cancer, but she died soon after her release and the boyfriend returned to the home to live with Daryl. Her father remains incarcerated, and Daryl has not had any contact with him since childhood. Daryl and her boyfriend got into another fight and he strangled her again, but this time to unconsciousness. She woke and saw her face was bloodied, bruised, and swollen, and so she went to the emergency department. An extensive workup revealed that Daryl had a stroke, which was focal, but the entire cranium was filling with subdural bleeds. Daryl was hospitalized.

Discussion

Daryl not only has documented injury from strangulation, but she has comorbidities that accelerate her demise. Her recovery is dependent on the size and areas of the brain compromised by hypoperfusion, infarcts, and microbleeds, and consequently, she remained hospitalized and then was discharged to a rehabilitation center. Law enforcement arrested the boyfriend for attempted murder, and he is now incarcerated. Fast forward to retirement age, Daryl retired from her executive position because her lupus worsened, and she could no longer tolerate the high pressure due to chronic depression and awareness of her intellectual deficits since the strangulation incident. She was disabled and applied for government assistance. Five years after the last strangulation incident, Daryl died from complications of her progressive small vessel disease and inflammatory lupus disease. The prosecuting attorney understood the relationship between intentional injury and subsequent death and considered charging the ex-boyfriend with second-degree murder.

Case 5

Mac was an 80-year-old active retired male with years of hypertension and diet-controlled diabetes, who walked 5 to 6 miles each day. He took medications to lower his blood pressure. His systolic blood pressure was perpetually high, and at age 75, his heart began to skip beats. This caused him to pass out, and he had to have a pacemaker placed. As he received a pacemaker, he complained of symptoms of memory loss, which was a direct result of his heart disease and high blood pressure. However, Mac was determined to regain his youth and prided himself on his tolerance for walking long distances. One day while on a walk, he was approached by two males who demanded his money. He doubled his fist and hit one of them in the face but fell when he turned to run away. The robbers then beat him with baseball bats. The workup at the hospital discovered a contra coup brain injury related to the impact of the bat, a fractured skull over the frontal lobe, and a fractured hand, elbow, and knee cap. He had multiple bruises on his head and back, but also on his arms and hips.

Discussion

Mac had little memory of the assaultive event over the course of his hospitalization. He did not remember that his wallet had $20 that was found in the trash of a neighbor's home. He also could not identify the men who assaulted him. The focal injury on the frontal lobe reduced his capacity for executive function tasks, and his past slow global demise from hypertension and diabetes accelerated over the next 2 years, likely due to healing of the injury. He was discharged to rehabilitation where he regained use of his limbs, but now he needed a walker resulting from the brain contra coup due to the fall. Mac was a hearty man in good shape at the time of the assault, regaining some of the lost executive function, but was now dependent on his family for care. The robbers were finally caught after they killed two elderly persons using the same robbery modus operandi, and they were sentenced to life in prison. Details from Mac's case were used during sentencing to demonstrate the callousness of the assaults, but his case was not prosecuted because he was unable to identify the males. Had Mac died, his case would have been presented for prosecution and the facts presented in his absence. The US Constitution's Confrontation Clause of the Sixth Amendment guarantees that defendants have the right to face their accuser, a clear gap in justice for elders with memory problems.

Frontotemporal Dementia

Frontotemporal dementia (FTD) involves the neurodegeneration and atrophy of the frontal and temporal lobes where signs and symptoms vary according to the location of atrophy (Table 3.2).

The mean age of FTD diagnosis is 58, with onset occurring in persons as young as 30 years of age (Waldo, 2015). FTD has three distinct subtypes representing the presentation: behavioral variant FTD (bvFTD), nonfluent primary progressive aphasia (NF), and semantic variant primary progressive aphasia (SV).

bvFTD: Sixty percent of FTD follows the behavioral variant pattern. The personality changes occur in a gradual and subtle manner, marked by increasing levels of impulsivity, disinhibition, lack of insight, lack of empathy, and distractibility (Waldo, 2015). As the disease progresses, there is usually disinterest in personal hygiene, hyperorality, and apathy. Persons with early bvFTD do well on screening tools, such as the MMSE or MoCA, because forgetfulness is not an initial presenting symptom. As the dementia progresses, memory problems emerge, accompanied by gait disturbances and functional decline. Speech difficulties and swallowing problems also occur (Bott, Radke, Stephens, & Kramer, 2014; Kirshner, 2014; Laforce, 2013; Waldo, 2015). Ultimately, the person with bvFTD becomes completely dependent on others for care.

NF: The initial presentation is difficult, effortful speech coupled with word-finding and agrammatism, causing inability to construct a sentence. As the disease progresses, behavioral symptoms similar to bvFTD are observed, and a similar trajectory of decline is followed (Bott et al., 2014; Kirshner, 2014; Laforce, 2013; Waldo, 2015).

SV: In SV, speech is fluid but empty: the flow, rhythm, and syntax are preserved, but the ability to properly employ nouns diminishes (Bott et al., 2014; Kirshner, 2014; Laforce, 2013; Waldo, 2015). Semantic paraphasias, or noun substitutions, occur; for example, nonspecific nouns such as "thing" or "it" may replace specific nouns such as "car" or "table." Memory loss and functional decline occur until the person is completely dependent on others for care.

Case 6

Larry is a 60-year-old man, dependent on his parents for care since his diagnosis of FTD. APS recommended engaging Larry in the community services agency activities to reduce caregiver stress. The bus picks up Larry, who is now in a wheelchair, every week day and takes him to the community center for a variety of dependent-care activities. His mother packs him a bag with a change of clothes, wipes, and medication. Male volunteers take care of his hygiene and toileting, changing his clothing when necessary. On this particular day, another male walked in on Larry and the volunteer assigned to Larry in the changing room. The volunteer had Larry's penis exposed and was performing fellatio on Larry. Larry pointed to his penis and said, "it, it, it."

Discussion

Persons dependent on others for their care have special protections, and when abuses occur, such as sexual assault, there is mandatory reporting to law enforcement and APS. In an agency such as a community center, there may also be other investigators from state agencies who evaluate the institution according to the state standards for the particular type of institution. In Larry's case, his parents should have been called as soon as possible. Larry should also be taken for an acute medical forensic evaluation. The police and APS will interview Larry and the witness. The forensic nurse in sexual assault care will collect a medical legal history of the event, the patient's medical history, and complete an assessment of capacity, as well as document the findings. The legal competency paperwork should travel with Larry and his parents who are responsible for his well-being. After the collection of evidence from his anus, genitalia, mouth, and other areas suspected of oral contact, Larry will be offered treatment according to the Centers for Disease Control and Prevention (CDC) guidelines for Sexually Transmitted Infections (STI) (2015). The parents, as custodial and court-appointed guardians, receive anticipatory guidance from the forensic nurse in preparation for follow-up with instructions for care. The advocate speaks to the parents about the prosecutorial processes and becomes the bridge between systems for Larry and his guardians. The multi-disciplinary team will meet to discuss the outcomes of evidence analysis and the progress of the case. In this case, the volunteer at the community center was charged with aggravated rape of a dependent person, and the forensic and laboratory discovered the assailant's saliva on Larry's breasts, penis, and anus. The accused pled guilty and is currently serving several concurrent sentences for his crimes.

Dementia with Lewy Bodies

Dementia with Lewy Bodies (DLB) presents with a unique, fluctuating pattern of deficits. Family members will describe variations in memory performance, speech coherence, attention, and concentration (McKeith et al., 2017) (Table 3.2). Excessive daytime sleepiness and episodes of intermittent unresponsiveness are also reported and may become mistaken for syncope or a transient ischemic attack (Aarsland, 2016; Ajon Gealogo, 2013; McKeith et al., 2017; Walker, Possin, Boeve, & Aarsland, 2015). Posttraumatic stress disorder (PTSD) may mimic DLB, especially in veterans of foreign wars who have seen combat, leading to sleep disorders, particularly nightmares (Leskin, Woodward, Young, & Sheikh, 2002; Levin & Nielsen, 2007). The reports from veterans on triggering is by one of the five senses, which are sight, smell, touch, hearing, or taste, which results in panic and not anxiety, unique to the veteran (Leskin et al., 2002). Bedpartners of veterans or DLB may report that the person "acts out" their dreams during sleep (Levin & Nielsen, 2007), a parasomnia known as rapid eye movement sleep behavior disorder. This parasomnia often predates other DLB signs (McKeith et al., 2017). Detailed visual hallucinations occur with DLB. Parkinsonism features also develop, such as bradykinesia, tremors, and rigidity.

Persons with Parkinson disease may develop dementia, but this is not DLB. In Parkinson disease dementia, the person has Parkinsonian symptoms for two or more years before developing dementia. In DLB, the cognitive symptoms precede the movement disorders (Ajon Gealogo, 2013). The trajectory for DLB is one of progressive cognitive and functional decline until the person is completely dependent on others for care.

Case 7

Lon is a 75-year-old Vietnam veteran who has fitful sleeping habits, which occasionally result in injury to his partner during his sleep. They have a California king-sized bed and the wife puts pillows between them. Family is concerned that Lon is violent and being protected by his wife. Together, they make an appointment for an evaluation of his worsening symptoms. The analysis showed he had significant cardiovascular plaque disease but does not have other symptoms indicating DLB, although this is likely due to war trauma and PTSD.

Discussion

Commonly, veterans have PTSD, particularly those in combat theater. The key for discovering the diagnosis is monitoring the symptoms. Leskin et al. (2002) reported that patients diagnosed with PTSD/panic disorder reported a significantly greater proportion of nightmare complaints (96%) and insomnia (100%). Two primary approaches to PTSD sleep problem treatment include pharmacotherapy and psychotherapy (Gehrmann, Gerlinde, & Ross, 2016). Little is known about the efficacy of using both approaches concurrently, but the preferred treatment for PTSD is cognitive behavioral therapy.

Mixed Dementia and Overlapping Presentations

A person with dementia may have two or more coexisting pathologies. The most common combination is AD and VaD. AD and DLB pathologies may also present concurrently. Some individuals with AD will also have VaD and DLB. As people age, the probability of having a mixed dementia increases (Alzheimer's Association, 2018a, 2018b). There is also overlap between many of the dementias. For example, there is a frontal variant of AD in which the initial presentations include behavioral symptoms or executive dysfunctions (Kirshner, 2014). Parkinsonism can occur in bvFTD and NF, even though DLB rarely occurs with FTD (Alzheimer's Association, 2018a, 2018b; Waldo, 2015).

Stages of Dementia and Risk for Abuse

The progression of all dementias can be described using the mild, moderate, and severe staging approach originally developed for use with AD (Alzheimer's Association, 2018a, 2018b). Some resources reference the "seven stages of dementia." These seven stages are an adaptation of Reisberg and colleagues' Global Deterioration Scale (Reisberg, Ferris, De Leon, & Crook, 1982). One of the authors has used the Global Deterioration Scale in her research but finds the scale unhelpful in clinical practice when discussing the progression of dementia with families. People with dementia often span two or three of the scale's categories, which causes families and clinicians to under- or overestimate the severity of the dementia.

Mild Stage

The mild stage of dementia is characterized by the ability to independently perform activities of daily living but requiring assistance with more complex instrumental activities of daily living. As persons with dementia progress through the mild stage, they become more dependent on others for completion of the instrumental activities of daily living. Persons in the mild stage may be able to drive, especially in familiar areas; independently shop and cook; and, depending on the occupation, work. Persons in the mild stage may begin to require assistance with paying bills, especially if bill paying is done electronically. They may also need assistance with complex activities such as assembling paperwork for tax preparation. A person with bvFTD, however, may be discouraged from driving if the impulsivity manifests as road rage. Likewise, a person with bvFTD may also require financial supervision because of impulsive buying sprees.

Repetition, or repeatedly restating the same information, often surfaces in MCI but increases in frequency during the mild stage of dementia. Formal and informal caregivers may respond by telling the person with dementia that he or she "already said that." Or, in the case of repetitive questioning, formal and informal caregivers may respond with annoyance or anger. Person with dementia often lack awareness of their deficits, a phenomenon known as *anosognosia,* meaning they "forget that they forgot." Because of the anosognosia, persons with dementia frequently react to accusations of repetition with their own annoyance and anger. Additionally, persons with dementia in the mild stage begin forgetting the location of familiar objects, such as house and car keys, and may begin to exhibit paranoia. Forgetting is different from misplacing. A person who misplaces keys can retrace his or her steps and locate them. Persons with mild dementia may be unable to retrace their steps and may not experience recall when they find the missing object. Without this interim memory, persons with dementia may conclude that someone is hiding their possessions. The combination of anosognosia and paranoia creates fear on the part of persons with dementia, who may become accusatory and even verbally abuse to those closest to them.

Case 8

Frances is an 80-year-old retired shopper who believes that her former husband is in her assisted living apartment, stealing her money. She can fix her meals, clean her apartment, wash her clothes, gather with her friends, and make plans to go on outings offered by the volunteers at the facility. Her son tells his mother that her ex-husband is dead, and he could not be stealing her money; Frances tells her son that he is a liar and working with the ex-husband to take her money. The son is very frustrated but understands that her dementia will include him eventually in the paranoid accusations.

Discussion

Formal and informal caregivers often attribute intentionality to the dementia-related behaviors: "He or she is doing this on purpose." Unique aspects of certain dementias inadvertently support this attribution of intentionality. For example, a caregiver faced with the fluctuating cognition observed in LBD may errone-ously conclude that the person with dementia is "faking it" because they have excellent memory of events long ago. Many family members believe the person with dementia's memory is excellent because of their ability to recall distant events with great detail and clarity. On the other hand, a family member of someone with bvFTD may find it difficult to understand that the personality changes are due to neurodegeneration and may accuse the person with dementia of "being a jerk." The attribution of intentionality, combined with the verbally and sometimes physically abusive behavior from the person with dementia, lays the beginning foundation for responding with verbal and possibly physical abuse from the caregiver who is reacting to a perceived intentional attack from the person with dementia.

Moderate Stage

The moderate stage of dementia is marked by difficulty with per-forming instrumental activities of daily living, such as shopping, managing finances, preparing meals, and beginning difficulties with activities of daily living. Some clinicians further subdivide the moderate stage into early-moderate and late-moderate, but there are no clear definitions or consensus regarding these delineations. The person in the moderate stage should not be living alone.

As the person with dementia requires more assistance with activities such as bathing and dressing, care refusal behaviors may be more evident. The neurodegenerative changes affect threat perception. That is, persons in the moderate stage of dementia may begin to perceive helping activities as intrusions or even as assaults (Jablonski, Therrien, & Kolanowski, 2011).

Nurse Case 9

Lilly is an 85-year-old retired secretary and a devoutly religious woman. Her husband died 25 years ago, and she lives alone in the home they bought when she first married. She had eight children and the youngest daughter is in charge of caring for her mother. On this particular day, the youngest daughter was unable to come to Lilly's house to care for her mother, and she asked her sister, a nurse, to help. The nurse sister took a rare vacation day. When she arrived at her mother's home, Lilly was unkempt, sitting on the couch covered in dried feces, still in her nightgown that was covered in food drippings. Her hair was unkempt. The nurse called her younger sister to see if this is a new state for her mother, thinking she might have had a stroke. The younger sister said, "Lilly doesn't want anything done, so I just feed her, give her the medicine, and leave." The nurse sister called APS for help.

Discussion

When refusals occur, the caregiver is placed in a difficult position. If the caregiver chooses to avoid conflict or confrontation by allowing the person with dementia to remain in the same soiled clothes or abstain from bathing, the caregiver may be accused of neglect. In this case, the daughter who is a nurse was unaware of the situation and called for help from APS. After APS left, the nurse daughter was successful in getting her mother into the shower, where she washed her hair, scrubbed her nails, and assisted in cleaning dried feces off her mother. She also started the washing machine. It is not uncommon for an older person to fear falling in the tub and may put the bathing off if there is no help, even if it affects their health. When the caregiver attempts to force the person with dementia to engage in self-care activities, the caregiver may be accused of physical abuse. Sometimes, even with supervision and help, the elder slips in the bath or slides to the floor, which results in grab marks on the arm. Bruising is related to age, medication, and significant pressure to prevent a fall. Sometimes, frail adults with friable skin tear when grabbed. Precautions in fall prevention, such as grab bars, nonslip flooring, and other devices, are a strategy for safety of all older persons. If Lilly and her family cannot afford the house structural changes, there are community volunteers who could help. The elder, like Lilly, who enters the moderate stage of dementia and remains a community dweller without supervision puts care providers at risk of accusations of neglect, particularly if the older person enters late-stage moderate dementia and wanders. In this case, home health was employed to assist the youngest daughter with light laundry, bathing, and meals, and a sitter was hired to watch Lilly. However, Lilly "eloped," wandered away, and fell. She tripped in a pothole in the street and broke her hip. She said she was walking to church. It was very cold, and she had on light clothes. Neighbors found her, and she was hospitalized. The sitter was washing clothes, and unaware she was gone. On discharge, Lilly was admitted to a nursing home, wheelchair bound, protesting her move to the nursing home. However, her children petitioned court for a sibling to be named guardian of Lilly, and the Judge granted guardianship to the eldest son, an attorney, who signed the papers to admit her to the nursing home. The family declined to charge the sitter with neglect and endangerment.

Severe Stage

Persons in the severe stage require continuous verbal cueing or outright physical assistance with all activities of daily living. They are incontinent of bowel and bladder. The ability to speak in a logical and coherent fashion is gone; if speech is present, it may be nonsensical or unintelligible. The ability to understand speech is also lost. Caregivers' best communicate often with gestures and pantomime. The person loses voluntary motor function, becoming bedridden. The ability to swallow is also lost.

Case 10

Mary is a 65-year-old female with severe-stage dementia, who lives at the county nursing home. Mary requires full care, has no teeth, and is diapered, requiring baby food or liquid nutrition. She is unable to speak but responds positively to her niece, who is visited twice a year by APS. Mary's guardian is her niece who transports her to her home every weekend. On this particular weekend, the niece hears a noise from Mary's room and walks in on her new boyfriend, caught with his penis in Mary's mouth. Mary is blue, gasping for air. The niece calls the police, who call the forensic nurse, and the boyfriend is arrested.

Discussion

Care-resistant behavior can persist in the severe stage, but the weakening of voluntary movements may make the behavior less difficult to manage. In Mary's case, she was unable to resist the assault, and the boyfriend did nothing to protect Mary's airway, creating a hypoxic event. Mary recovered and did not resist the forensic nurse's care. Mary's niece commented it was good to have help of her boyfriend on the weekends, but she was very disappointed in his behavior. The caregiver may be physically overwhelmed by the amount of care that the person with dementia requires at this point. The potential for neglect is significant at this stage. Mary's niece wanted to drop charges against her boyfriend, and when made aware, APS restricted Mary's activities with her niece and labeled her a passive perpetrator, unable to protect Mary from those who would do her harm. Mary died 10 months later at the nursing home from fulminant Hepatitis B, caught after the oral assault despite having up-to-date immunizations. When in doubt, the CDC STI recommendations for postassault care should be consulted. The case went forward, and the boyfriend was found guilty of second-degree murder because he knew he was a chronic carrier of hepatitis and was sentenced to 10 years in prison.

Care Transitions

The decision to move the person with dementia out of the home and into some type of facility is most affected by the caregiver's ability to provide necessary care. Some caregivers are able to afford personal care aids or sitters, which may delay placement. Medicaid may subsidize in-home care for persons who meet nursing home eligibility requirements; these programs vary from state to state. If in-home care is not a viable option, either for financial reasons or care needs, the person with dementia may be placed in an assisted living facility or a nursing home.

Assisted Living Facilities

Assisted living facilities are generally described as congregate residential settings that provide 24-hour supervision, at least two meals daily, and an array of personal and health-related services (Gimm, Chowdhury, & Castle, 2016). They became popular in the late 1990s as alternatives to traditional nursing home care and were marketed for people who needed some support but who did not require the level of care offered by nursing homes (Steinhauer, 2001, p. 1). Since their inception, assisted living facilities have expanded their levels of care. For example, 59% of assisted living facilities provide skilled nursing services, defined as medical activities that must be legally performed by a registered or licensed practical nurse (Harris-Kojetin et al., 2016). Assisted living facilities are rapidly replacing nursing homes as the preferred setting for residential long-term care for persons with dementia. Nationally, one million older adults reside in one of the 30,200 assisted living facilities; comparatively, 1.7 million older adults reside in any of the 15,600 nursing homes (Harris-Kojetin et al., 2016). Assisted living beds outnumber nursing home beds in the Midwest region of the United States, a trend that is predicted to occur nationally (Harris-Kojetin et al., 2016). Unlike nursing homes, assisted living facilities are not certified by Medicare but are licensed by individual states; thus, there are no consistent requirements for the quantity and quality of caregiving personnel. The prevalence of persons with dementia residing in these facilities has been reported to range from 42% by staff report to 89% from a diagnosis supported by cognitive testing (Samus et al., 2013; Zimmerman, Sloane, & Reed, 2014). In some states, such as Alabama, the prevalence may be much higher because assisted living facilities that provide care to persons with dementia must be licensed as special care assisted living facilities, or SCALFs.

Nursing Homes

Nursing homes are certified by the Centers for Medicare and Medicaid Services, meaning that they are subject to federal oversight. The Code of Federal Regulations Section 42 provides extensive directives regarding nearly every aspect of nursing home care, from the qualifications of licensed administrators to the height of commodes. Nursing homes also receive annual inspections from surveyors who evaluate compliance with the federal regulations. Facilities found to deviate from the regulations face significant monetary penalties.

Nursing homes that provide posthospital care, such as physical therapy, occupational therapy, and wound care, receive reimbursement from Medicare for up to 100 days, as long as the person receiving the care is showing progress toward specified goals. Once the person is no longer eligible for the Medicare benefit, the individual is responsible for paying the nursing home costs. Medicaid will pay for nursing home care if the person meets explicit financial criteria.

Section 483.12 of the Code of Federal Regulations addresses the responsibility of nursing homes to protect their residents from abuse, neglect, and exploitation (CFR §483.21). Facilities are responsible for investigating and reporting all allegations of abusive conduct. Furthermore, facilities cannot employ individuals who have engaged in past incidents of abuse, neglect, mistreatment of residents, or misappropriation of their property. Dementia and abuse prevention training are two mandatory topics that must be provided annually to nursing assistants working in nursing homes.

The Department of Health and Human Services recognizes that many nursing home residents have likely experienced past trauma and stress. The Centers for Medicare and Medicaid services have mandated that all facilities include trauma-informed care practices by November 2019 (CFR §483.21). Health is intrinsically linked to trauma and stress, where trauma-informed care principles provide a "universal precautions assumption" that all have some level of trauma and stress. Health-care systems serving elderly are now mandated to plan quality systems and procedures based on trauma-informed care and safe environments, defined as care that minimizes trauma and stress triggers and retraumatization (Substance Abuse and Mental Health Services Administration, 2014).

Case 11

Helen is an 80-year-old female with severe Alzheimer's disease, newly admitted to the nursing home. During the initial care-planning conference, Helen's son tells the team that he was no longer able to care for his mother because she became highly agitated around dusk. Using the term "sun downing," Helen's son describes daily events that include sobbing, constant movement around the house, attempts to leave the house, and several episodes of his mother locking herself in the main bathroom. Helen ultimately becomes combative and hits and kicks her son when he tries to help her get ready for bed.

Discussion

The Director of Nursing asks Helen's son about DV. The son relates that Helen's first husband, his natural father, was an alcoholic. The son recalls that his father often returned home from work in the evening, drunk, and would often yell and scream at both of them. As Helen's son is speaking, he suddenly recalls that Helen would tell him to hide in a bedroom closet while she tried to reason with his father. Helen's first husband died when the son was 6 years old; Helen later remarried a kind gentle man who ultimately adopted Helen's son. The Director of Nursing tells the team that Helen is most likely "moving backward in time" and reexperiencing past traumatic events. The goals for her care will include "derailing" the memories and avoiding triggers, such as darkened rooms and shadows, loud noises, and threatening frontal assault positions by care providers. The team assembles a trauma-informed care plan. This plan includes directing Helen to one of the brightly lit, but less busy social rooms every afternoon at 3 p.m. They also decide to use strategies that reduce threat perception, a problem additionally exaggerated in persons with dementia (Jablonski et al., 2011). These strategies include approaching at an angle, at or below eye level; assessing responses to gentle touch; and using gestures and pantomime in addition to short, one-step, respectful requests. For example, saying things such as "come with me please," versus saying the command "come with me to go to the bathroom." Care refusals are common in persons with dementia (Jablonski-Jaudon, Kolanowski, Winstead, Jones-Townsend, & Azuero, 2016) and may be even more prevalent in persons with past histories of trauma who may equate necessary personal care with sexual or physical assaults. Additional strategies to prevent and reduce care refusals include chaining, where the clinician begins the task and has the person with dementia complete it; bridging, where the person with dementia holds an object related to the care being provided to tap into procedural memories; and distraction or redirection (Jablonski et al., 2011; Jablonski-Jaudon et al., 2016). Additional strategies and information can be found at www.makedementiayourbitch.com. The physical and occupational therapy director decides to schedule her for late afternoon physical therapy and occupational therapy activities to avoid her from being triggered by the usual before-supper lull. The activity director notes in Helen's chart that she will be included in post-supper activities that include music or other creative activities to serve as pleasant redirections. Helen's late afternoon and early evening periods of agitation and fighting slowly decrease and eventually disappear, and she no longer is suspicious of the staff when they approach her.

Conclusion

Older adults with cognitive impairments are especially vulnerable to abuse and other forms of maltreatment because their concerns may not be addressed or believed. This chapter provided information about the current state of the science regarding patient presentations and evolutions of the four most common types of dementia: AD, VaD, DLB, and FTD. The case exemplars offered opportunities to apply this new knowledge to situations where abuse, maltreatment, and neglect occurred. In the future, graduate forensic nurses, a rapidly growing specialty, will respond with nurse practitioners, clinical specialists, and administrators in the geriatric specialty. They will dovetail their geriatric expertise in normal aging, palliative care, and hospice nursing and forensic nursing education to respond to the growing numbers of elders with dementia at risk for maltreatment, and this new coupling of professional expertise will produce better solutions for the most vulnerable elders affected by dementia and memory disorders.

References

Aarsland, D. (2016). Cognitive impairment in Parkinson's disease and dementia with Lewy bodies. *Parkinsonism and Related Disorders, 22*(Suppl. 1), S144–S148. https://doi.org/10.1016/j.parkreldis.2015.09.034.

Ajon Gealogo, G. (2013). Dementia with Lewy bodies: A comprehensive review for nurses. *Journal of Neuroscience Nursing, 45*(6), 347–359. https://doi.org/10.1097/JNN.0b013e3182a3ce2b.

Alzheimer's Association. (2018a). 2018 Alzheimer's disease facts and figures. *Alzheimer's and Dementia, 14*(3), 367–429.

Alzheimer's Association. (2018b). *Mild cognitive impairment*. Retrieved from https://www.alz.org/dementia/mild-cognitive-impairment-mci.asp#about.

Anda, R. F., Dong, M., Brown, D. W., Felitti, V. J., Giles, W. H., Perry, B. D., ... Dube, S. R. (2009). The relationship of adverse childhood experiences to a history of premature death of family members. *BMC Public Health, 9*(106). https://doi.org/10.1186/1471-2458-9-106.

Bang, J., Spina, S., & Miller, B. L. (2015). Frontotemporal dementia. *The Lancet, 386*(10004), 1672–1682. https://doi.org/10.1016/s0140-6736(15)00461-4.

Black, S. E. (2011). Vascular cognitive impairment: Epidemiology, subtypes, diagnosis and management. *The Journal of the Royal College of Physicians of Edinburgh, 41*(1), 49–56. https://doi.org/10.4997/JRCPE.2011.121.

Bott, N. T., Stephens, A., Black, M. L., & Kramer, J. H. (2014). Frontotemporal dementia: Diagnosis, deficits and management. *Neurodegenerative Disease Management, 4*(6), 439–454. https://doi.org/10.2217/nmt.14.34.

Campbell, J. C., Anderson, J. C., McFadgion, A., Gill, J., Zink, E., Patch, M., ... Campbell, D. (2018). The effects of intimate partner violence and probable traumatic brain injury on central nervous system symptoms. *Journal of Women's Health, 27*(6), 761–767. https://doi.org/10.1089/jwh.2016.6311Bla (15409996).

Centers for Disease Control and Prevention [CDC]. (2015). Sexually transmitted diseases treatment guidelines, 2015. *Morbidity and Mortality Weekly Report Recommendations and Reports, 64*(3). Retrieved from https://www.cdc.gov/std/tg2015/tg-2015-print.pdf.

De Haan, E. H., Nys, G. M., & Van Zandvoort, M. J. (2006). Cognitive function following stroke and vascular cognitive impairment. *Current Opinion in Neurology, 19*(6), 559–564.

Dong, X., & Simon, M. A. (2015). Elder self-neglect is associated with an increased rate of 30-day hospital readmission: Findings from the Chicago health and aging project. *Gerontology, 61*(1), 41–50. https://doi.org/10.1159/000360698.

Eshkoor, S. A., Hamid, T. A., Mun, C. Y., & Ng, C. K. (2015). Mild cognitive impairment and its management in older people. *Clinical Interventions in Aging, 10*, 687–693. https://doi.org/10.2147/cia.s73922.

Fang, B., & Yan, E. (2018). Abuse of older persons with dementia: A review of the literature. *Trauma, Violence, and Abuse, 19*(2), 127−147. https://doi.org/10.1177/1524838016650185.

Fox, C., Richardson, K., Maidment, I. D., Savva, G. M., Matthews, F. E., Smithard, D., ... Brayne, C. (2011). Anticholinergic medication use and cognitive impairment in the older population: The medical research council cognitive function and ageing study. *Journal of the American Geriatrics Society, 59*(8), 1477−1483. https://doi.org/10.1111/j.1532-5415.2011.03491.x.

Friedman, L. S., Avila, S., Rizvi, T., Partida, R., & Friedman, D. (2017). Physical abuse of elderly adults: Victim characteristics and determinants of revictimization. *Journal of the American Geriatrics Society, 65*(7), 1420−1426. https://doi.org/10.1111/jgs.14794.

Galvin, J. E., Sadowsky, C. H., & NINCDS-ADRDA. (2012). Practical guidelines for the recognition and diagnosis of dementia. *The Journal of the American Board of Family Medicine, 25*(3), 367−382. https://doi.org/10.3122/jabfm.2012.03.100181.

Gehrmann, P., Gerlinde, H., & Ross, R. (2016). PTSD and sleep. In M. J. Friedman (Ed.), *Vol. 27. PTSD research quarterly* (pp. 1−7). Veteran's Administration.

Gimm, G., Chowdhury, S., & Castle, N. (2016). Resident aggression and abuse in assisted living. *Journal of Applied Gerontology.* https://doi.org/10.1177/0733464816661947, 733464816661947.

Harris-Kojetin, L., Sengupta, M., Park-Lee, E., Valverde, R., Caffrey, C., Rome, V., & Lendon, J. (2016). Long-term care providers and services users in the United States: Data from the national study of long-term care providers, 2013-2014. *Vital Health Statistics 3,* (38), 1−105, 10-12.

Henckens, M. J., Hermans, E. J., Pu, Z., Joels, M., & Fernandez, G. (2009). Stressed memories: How acute stress affects memory formation in humans. *Journal of Neuroscience, 29*(32), 10111−10119. https://doi.org/10.1523/jneurosci.1184-09.2009.

Hilgeman, M. M., Allen, R. S., Snow, A. L., Durkin, D. W., DeCoster, J., & Burgio, L. D. (2014). Preserving identity and planning for advance care (PIPAC): Preliminary outcomes from a patient-centered intervention for individuals with mild dementia. *Aging and Mental Health, 18*(4), 411−424. https://doi.org/10.1080/13607863.2013.868403.

Hinckley, J. (2009). Clinical decision-making for stroke and aphasia in the older adult. *Perspectives on Gerontology, 14*(1), 4−11.

Hugo, J., & Ganguli, M. (2014). Dementia and cognitive impairment: Epidemiology, diagnosis, and treatment. *Clinics in Geriatric Medicine, 30*(3), 421−442. https://doi.org/10.1016/j.cger.2014.04.001.

Iadecola, C. (2013). The pathobiology of vascular dementia. *Neuron, 80*(4), 844−866. https://doi.org/10.1016/j.neuron.2013.10.008.

Jablonski-Jaudon, R. A., Kolanowski, A. M., Winstead, V., Jones-Townsend, C., & Azuero, A. (2016). Maturation of the mouth intervention: From reducing threat to relationship-centered care. *Journal of Gerontological Nursing, 42*(3), 15−23. https://doi.org/10.3928/00989134-20160212-05. quiz 24-15.

Jablonski, R. A., Therrien, B., & Kolanowski, A. (2011a). No more fighting and biting during mouth care: Applying the theoretical constructs of threat perception to clinical practice. *Research and Theory for Nursing Practice, 25*(3), 163−175.

Jablonski, R. A., Therrien, B., Mahoney, E. K., Kolanowski, A., Gabello, M., & Brock, A. (2011b). An intervention to reduce care-resistant behavior in persons with dementia during oral hygiene: A pilot study. *Special Care in Dentistry, 31*(3), 77−87. https://doi.org/10.1111/j.1754-4505.2011.00190.x.

Joshi, M., Thomas, K. A., & Sorenson, S. B. (2012). "I didn't know i could turn colors": Health problems and health care experiences of women strangled by an intimate partner. *Social Work in Health Care, 51*(9), 798–814. https://doi.org/10.1080/00981389.2012.692352.

Kirshner, H. S. (2014). Frontotemporal dementia and primary progressive aphasia, a review. *Neuropsychiatric Disease and Treatment, 10*, 1045–1055. https://doi.org/10.2147/NDT.S38821.

Laforce, R., Jr. (2013). Behavioral and language variants of frontotemporal dementia: A review of key symptoms. *Clinical Neurology and Neurosurgery, 115*(12), 2405–2410. https://doi.org/10.1016/j.clineuro.2013.09.031.

Langa, K. M., & Levine, D. A. (2014). The diagnosis and management of mild cognitive impairment: A clinical review. *Journal of the American Medical Association, 312*(23), 2551–2561. https://doi.org/10.1001/jama.2014.13806.

Leskin, G. A., Woodward, S. H., Young, H. E., & Sheikh, J. I. (2002). Effects of comorbid diagnoses on sleep disturbance in PTSD. *Journal of Psychiatric Research, 36*(6), 449–452.

Levin, R., & Nielsen, T. A. (2007). Disturbed dreaming, posttraumatic stress disorder, and affect distress: A review and neurocognitive model. *Psychological Bulletin, 133*(3), 482–528. http://dix.doi.org/10.1037/0033-2909.133.3.482.

McCausland, B., Knight, L., Page, L., & Trevillion, K. (2016). A systematic review of the prevalence and odds of domestic abuse victimization among people with dementia. *International Review of Psychiatry, 28*(5), 475–484. https://doi.org/10.1080/09540261.2016.1215296.

McEwen, B. S., & Seeman, T. (1999). Protective and damaging effects of mediators of stress. Elaborating and testing the concepts of allostasis and allostatic load. *Annals of the New York Academy of Sciences, 896*, 30–47.

McKeith, I. G., Boeve, B. F., Dickson, D. W., Halliday, G., Taylor, J. P., Weintraub, D., … Kosaka, K. (2017). Diagnosis and management of dementia with Lewy bodies: Fourth consensus report of the DLB consortium. *Neurology, 89*(1), 88–100. https://doi.org/10.1212/wnl.0000000000004058.

McKhann, G. M., Knopman, D. S., Chertkow, H., Hyman, B. T., Jack, C. R., Jr., Kawas, C. H., … Phelps, C. H. (2011). The diagnosis of dementia due to Alzheimer's disease: Recommendations from the National Institute on Aging-Alzheimer's association workgroups on diagnostic guidelines for Alzheimer's disease. *Alzheimer's and Dementia, 7*(3), 263–269. https://doi.org/10.1016/j.jalz.2011.03.005.

Reed, S. F., Porges, S. W., & Newlin, D. B. (1999). Effect of alcohol on vagal regulation of cardiovascular function: Contributions of the polyvagal theory to the psychophysiology of alcohol. *Experimental and Clinical Psychopharmacology, 7*(4), 484–492.

Reisberg, B., Ferris, S., De Leon, M., & Crook, T. (1982). The global deterioration scale for assessment of primary degenerative dementia. *American Journal of Psychiatry, 139*, 1136–1139.

Rizzi, L., Rosset, I., & Roriz-Cruz, M. (2014). Global Epidemiology of Dementia: Alzheimer's and Vascular Types. *BioMed Research International, 8*. https://doi.org/10.1155/2014/908915.

Samus, Q. M., Onyike, C. U., Johnston, D., Mayer, L., McNabney, M., Baker, A. S., … Rosenblatt, A. (2013). 12-month incidence, prevalence, persistence, and treatment of mental disorders among individuals recently admitted to assisted living facilities in Maryland. *International Psychogeriatrics, 25*(5), 721–731. https://doi.org/10.1017/S1041610212002244.

Schofield, M. J., Powers, J. R., & Loxton, D. (2013). Mortality and disability outcomes of self-reported elder abuse: A 12-year prospective investigation. *Journal of the American Geriatrics Society, 61*(5), 679–685. https://doi.org/10.1111/jgs.12212.

Steinhauer, J. (2001, Febuary 12). *As assisted living centers boom, calls for regulation are growing.* The New York Times.

Stroke by strangulation. (1981). *Emergency Medicine, 13*, 126–127 (00136654).

Substance Abuse and Mental Health Services Administration. (2014). *SAMHSA's concept of trauma and guidance for a trauma-informed approach.* HHS Publication No. (SMA) 14-4884. Rockville, MD: Substance Abuse and Mental Health Services Administration. Retreived from https://store.samhsa.gov/system/files/sma14-4884.pdf.

Tronetti, P. (2014). Evaluating abuse in the patient with dementia. *Clinics in Geriatric Medicine, 30*(4), 825–838. https://doi.org/10.1016/j.cger.2014.08.010.

Vandeweerd, C., Paveza, G. J., & Fulmer, T. (2006). Abuse and neglect in older adults with Alzheimer's disease. *Nursing Clinics of North America, 41*(1), 43–55. https://doi.org/10.1016/j.cnur.2005.09.004. v-vi.

Verghese, P. B., Castellano, J. M., & Holtzman, D. M. (2011). Apolipoprotein E in Alzheimer's disease and other neurological disorders. *The Lancet Neurology, 10*(3), 241–252. https://doi.org/10.1016/s1474-4422(10)70325-2.

Vilke, G. M., & Chan, T. C. (2011). Evaluation and management for carotid dissection in patients presenting after choking or strangulation. *Journal of Emergency Medicine, 40*(3), 355–358. https://doi.org/10.1016/j.jemermed.2010.02.018 (0736-4679).

Waldo, M. L. (2015). The frontotemporal dementias. *Psychiatric Clinics of North America, 38*(2), 193–209. https://doi.org/10.1016/j.psc.2015.02.001.

Walker, Z., Possin, K. L., Boeve, B. F., & Aarsland, D. (2015). Lewy body dementias. *The Lancet, 386*(10004), 1683–1697. https://doi.org/10.1016/s0140-6736(15)00462-6.

YadollahiKhales, G., Ghorbani, A., & Borhani-Haghighi, A. (2015). Tinnitus 3 years after strangulation. *The Journal of Nervous and Mental Disease, 203*(2), 154–155. https://doi.org/10.1097/NMD.0000000000000253.

Zimmerman, S., Sloane, P. D., & Reed, D. (2014). Dementia prevalence and care in assisted living. *Health Affairs (Millwood), 33*(4), 658–666. https://doi.org/10.1377/hlthaff.2013.1255.

Further Reading

Dong, X., & Simon, M. A. (2013). Association between elder self-neglect and hospice utilization in a community population. *Archives of Gerontology and Geriatrics, 56*(1), 192–198. https://doi.org/10.1016/j.archger.2012.06.008.

4

INTERPERSONAL VIOLENCE AND THE ELDERLY

Kathleen Thimsen

Goldfarb School of Nursing at Barnes Jewish College, St Louis, MO, United States

CHAPTER OUTLINE
The Elderly and Interpersonal Violence   85
Risk Factors   86
Elder Abuse and Violence: The Role of Relationships   90
    Power and Privilege   90
    Caregiver Role Change   91
Case Study 1   92
    Health-Care Providers   93
Case Study 2   94
    Care Provider   95
    Burden and Fatigue Driven Violence   97
Case Study 3   97
    Cyclical Violence   98
Unintentional Elder Abuse and Violence   99
    Resources and Health Literacy Gaps   99
      Case Study 4   99
Prevention and Advocacy   100
References   103

The Elderly and Interpersonal Violence

Interprofessional providers serving the elder population play a role in the underreporting for a variety of reasons. Lack of knowledge, inadequate training, and the deficits of skills and culturally competent attitudes among professionals only potentiates the underidentification of abuse. Missed opportunities to identify and respond to victims are often overlooked due to knowledge

Elder Abuse. https://doi.org/10.1016/B978-0-12-815779-4.00004-5

of risk factors, indicators, and trends, which predisposes a victim to further abuse and potential fatality.

Typically, victims of elder abuse are most often being identified in encounters that the victim presents with overt signs of abuse and violence that are severe in nature (Laumann, Leitschand & Waite, 2008). The need to advance identification and appropriateness of response includes education that increases the knowledge, along with training that demonstrates skills and changes attitudes that include age bias or ageism-rooted responses.

Projections of the growth of elders in society predict the edge of the Baby Boomer generation, now past 70 years of age. The next two decades will see that the number of persons who are aged 70 and older increases by 28 million. This projection represents that the number of elder baby boomers will grow, and the share of the population in this age group will be 18% of those aged 65 and older by over by the year 2030 (Colby & Ortman, 2014).

The incidence and prevalence of violence is significantly un-identified and underreported according to numerous reports and statistics (Aciermo, Hernandez-Tejada, Muzzy, & Steve, 2009; Aciermo et al., 2010; Administration on Aging, 1998; Amstadter et al., 2011a, 2011b; Castle, 2011; Dong & Simon, 2013a, 2013b). It has been estimated that the incidence of elder abuse has a variance in reporting along with a wide range of signs and symptoms that result in reporting and subsequent investigations. The Department of Justice Report on Elder Abuse (2010) stated the incidence rate to be from 1% to 7% of all cases of abuse that are reported. Studies looking at epidemiologic aspects of elder abuse project the prevalence rate to be more realistically 25%–29% of vulnerable adults over the age of 65 years of age (Amstadter et al., 2011a, 2011b). The data that are collected have only included abuse cases that involved significant physically overt signs and symptoms of injury, trauma, and fatalities that are in reality, homicides (Drake, Pickens, Wolf, & Thimsen, 2018). There are also recent discussions about gaps in investigations that are mistaken for age-related conditions or disease-based signs and symptoms. These types of cases are often dismissed as age-related conditions that require skilled geriatric assessments to demonstrate the patient scenario meet the federal definition of neglect or abuse.

Risk Factors

Vulnerability was the single most predicative indicator of potential for abuse. Vulnerability and subsequent abuse commonly result from a life history of physical, emotional, psychological, domestic abuse, long-term dysfunctional relationships, immobility, and increased dependence on others for activities of daily living and support (Dong 2014). As functional decline, loss of mobility and abilities to perform activities of daily living decrease, so does vulnerability. Elders who have been victims of violence and abuse as children or in interpersonal relationships across the life span have increased risk for elder abuse.

Quality of life in the elderly is severely impacted by abuse according to Friedman, Avila, Shah, Tanouye, and Joseph (2014). The quality of life impact is rooted in the form of the actual type of abuse that is being perpetrated. Emotional and psychological abuse further jeopardizes the independence of the elder by diminishing or dhumanizing them. Psychological retraumatization causes additional injury to the self-image and self-esteem of the elders, which increases the depth of dependency that often creates a vicious cycle of abuse. Emotional or psychological abuse is commonly the catalyst that perpetuates and gives rise to the escalation of violence and abuse that continues the cycle of violence (Baker et al., 2009).

Physical, sexual, and financial abuse increases in intensity over the time the abuse is perpetrated. As the abuse escalates, so does the need for access to health care and elder advocacy. The discussion by Dong et al. includes the use of health-care access through emergency departments (EDs) and hospitalization of abused elders (Dong et al., 2013a; Dong et al., 2013b). The ED utilization rate for victims of elder abuse poses four times greater incidence than health-care access and encounters for nonabused elders (Dong & Simon, 2013a, 2013b).

Difficulties arise in accurate identification of elder abuse victims because of age-related physiologic changes and comorbid conditions found in any person over the age of 65 who presents for health or medical care. The symptoms related to abuse are often not considered as signs of abuse. Instead they are a sign, symptom, or complication of aging. The need for improving differential diagnosis related to elder abuse, aging, and comorbidities is critical to the identification of potential, suspected, or actual abuse.

The actual prevalence of elder violence and related abuse cases is unknown for a variety of reasons (Aciermo et al., 2010). Cases of elder abuse and violence are reported 1 out of every 14 cases (Cannell et al., 2014; Cooper et al, 2008). The literature is severely lacking in information on the clinical indicators of elder abuse, violence, or mention of violence that can be differentiated from manifestations of comorbidities and age-related physiologic changes (Brozowski & Hall, 2010; Cronholm, Ismailji & Mettner, 2013; Dong 2014; Policastro & Payne, 2014; Shugarman et al., 2003). US Census (2014) data show that 96.8% of the elder population, those aged 65 and older, or 44.7 million people lived independently in a private home. Persons of that same age living in a group environment, such as in senior housing, and assisted living and supportive living environments numbered 1.5 million with 1.2 million residing in a nonskilled, custodial nursing home. Place of residence is significant in cases of elder abuse. Caspi (2018) studied the incidence of elder abuse cases to be highest in assisted living and long-term care settings. Given that the senior living industry is growing, assisted living and supportive living environments need to meet future demand, and corresponding prevention strategies will need to be studied and advanced.

Elder persons seldom self-report their own cases of abuse and violence. Self-reported abuse commonly is not how a victim is identified. The result of the deficit in self-reporting presents additional dangers, as the individual remains in the abusive situation without remedy or rescue. Victims of elder abuse presenting to the ED for care with the chief complaint of urinary tract infection, altered mental status, and/or respiratory issues that are the result of neglect and abuse are treated and returned to the same environment where the abuse was being perpetrated in up to 78% of the cases (Dong & Simon, 2013a, 2013b). In elders who age in place or live in a home of an adult child or close relative, abuse often goes unidentified due to the social beliefs and acceptance of "what occurs in the privacy of one's home" is private. Elder persons or observers may be hesitant to report historic or present maltreatment due to the subject being an embarrassment. Consequences of reporting or coming forward carry the fear of punishment, loss of freedom, or loss of independence.

As the cases of abuse and violence are on the rise, a newly identified cause of injury has identified the issue of patient-on-patient or elder-on-elder acts of violence being perpetrated. The increase in diagnosed dementia cases and the need for structured living environments conducive to memory-impaired care report a rise in resident-to-resident violence (Caspi, 2018; Teresi et al., 2013).

Health-care professionals are among the disciplines that play a role in the underreporting. There is a deficit in knowledge and inadequate training of all disciplines involved in providing care and services, along with investigations of substandard care and the perpetration of harm to seniors. In settings that have limited access to trained professionals or licensed staff, the problem is magnified due to the limited insight and care management knowledge, along with strategies required to identify, respond, and ultimately report deficits in care. This predisposes a victim to being identified only in situations where signs of abuse and violence are blatant, obvious, and severe in nature (Laumann, Leitschand, & Waite, 2008). The utilization rate of services for victims of elder abuse and violence poses a four times greater incidence than health-care access and encounters for nonabused, violence-affected elders of the same age group (Dong & Simon, 2013a, 2013b).

Difficulties arise in accurate identification of elder abuse and violence victims because of age-related physiologic changes and comorbid conditions found in any person over the age of 65 seeking health or medical care. The symptoms related to abuse and violence are often not considered as being abuse or violence related. Instead, they are thought to be signs, symptoms, or complications of aging. The need for differential diagnosis related to elder abuse and violence, aging, and comorbidities is critical to the identification of potential, suspected, or actual abuse and violence.

An issue that exacerbates identifying elder mistreatment and violence is a knowledge deficit related to the elder abuse and violence. Published education and training programs addressing this problem have been identified in reviews of the literature discussing the five types of violence against the elderly, along with the behaviors of perpetrators that may be seen during a healthcare encounter. The types of elder maltreatment described in the published training programs include emotional, psychological, physical, sexual, financial, and self-neglect. The literature, in this book and elsewhere, also lists common signs and symptoms identified in victims of elder abuse and violence.

The existing clinical gaps in the published education and training relate to the need for improved recognition and advancement of knowledge in differentiating the signs, symptoms, and behavioral indicators to the possible etiology of abuse and violence. The need for progressive and in-depth understanding of geriatric physiology that may be influenced by comorbidities, chronic conditions, or genetic predisposition calls for deeper inquiry and dissemination. Normal aging does present increases in vulnerability and the potential for elder victimization. It is common that perpetrators of elder violence and abuse may become serial abusers as they are often a trusted family member, caregiver, or another senior living in the same residential environment. Additional gaps exist in care, treatment, planning, and protecting of suspected victims, as well as safeguarding the patient at the time of care when transitioning from home to nursing facility or hospital. Elder abuse and violence can exist in the privacy of a person's home or in assisted living and nursing homes (American College of Emergency Physicians, 2013; Fulmer et al., 2003; Fulmer, Paveza, Abraham, & Fairchild, 2000) and has been identified to be on the rise nationally. These types of cases better identify interpersonal violence that occurs as the result of behavioral predisposition to violence or cognitive impairment that exacerbates the potential for carrying out acts of trauma and the resulting injury or death.

Other contributing factors to underidentification and underreporting that are key to understanding the disparities between other vulnerable populations and the elderly arise from the concept of ageism. The term was coined in 1968 by Robert Butler MD, who was an early advocate for aging and was the founding director of the National Institute on Aging (Columbia Aging, n.d.).

The term *vulnerable* has definitions and implications based on known risk factors for abuse and violence prevalent across the life continuum. Vulnerabilities increase with dependence, frailty, and increased needs for basic care needs, food, water, safety, shelter, and preventative strategies to address risks. In addition to the known risk factors, research has identified the contribution of prior trauma, violence, and abuse contributing to the potential for victimization late in life (Santos, Nunes, Kislaya, Gil, & Ribeiro, 2018; Van der Kolk, 1994) The perpetration of generational violence is a known risk factor, yet social and medical histories fail to address it in assessment, planning, and prescribing care and treatment for the most at-risk persons.

Elder Abuse and Violence: The Role of Relationships

Power and Privilege

The relationships formed in families are foundational to the evolution of the relationship over the life span. Relationships between parent and child form the attachment, as well as the child's orientation, beliefs, values, and moral underpinnings for a lifetime. The brain's development involves the building blocks, known as neurons, which create the network links that create systems. This system is how the brain regulates functions. This network spans simple to complex functions. There is sequencing of the functional development that associates prior events to future development and function. Chronic exposure to prolonged traumatic experiences and toxic stress has been shown to alter brain development and function, which causes long-term effects on physical and mental health, as well as behaviors (Cook, Spinazzola, Ford, & Lanktree, 2005). Neuron development that is imprinted by a parent or authority figure who exerts power and control creates the regulation and interactions that frames the relationships and dynamics that are formed for a lifetime. Although in traditional, caring, and loving homes, this is cohesive with the expectations and beliefs about what is normal and acceptable for relationships, behaviors, and social interaction.

In familial circumstances in which the parent–child dynamics are maladaptive and nonnurturing, such as in forms of interpersonal violence seen in domestic abuse, child abuse, and sexual abuse, the child's neural development is negatively impacted. The neural development creates the individual's response to social encounters and day-to-day life in ways that are not conducive or commiserate with social norms. Rather, the maladaptive behaviors and associated family dysfunction are often reenacted (Chamberlain, 2009; Cook et al., 2005).

As the child develops and has increased social interactions, the behaviors and feelings of the lived experience become destructive and problematic. As individuals continue along the life span, power is viewed as the privilege that comes with being an adult or authority figure. This presents the potential for continuing generational dysfunction and the perpetration of cyclical violence (Poole Heller, 2000).

Caregiver Role Change

In familial relationships, especially in society today, the potential for elder abuse will increase as the population of baby boomers grows the older spectrum of the population. Estimates project that by 2029, the cohort of persons aged 65 and older will comprise 20% of the nation's population (Colby & Ortman, 2014).

As the population ages, the potential for increased dependence on others for assistance, housing, care, and financial support rises. Estimates of the aging population outliving their retirement, savings, and investments are high (C-span.org, 2008). The needs of the population will call on families to assist, if not become primary caregivers to their parents. Although many families might be equipped physically and financially, the psychological realities are often not considered. The strain of additional responsibilities of providing care for one's parent or possibly both parents is much more than a reversal of roles. The toll of an adult often 24/7 demands may be manageable for a short period of time without respite. However, caregiver burden is experienced by even the most loving, nurturing, and caring families. In cases of families or caregivers with a history of abuse or trauma, the capacity to manage the burden without violence and abuse poses a challenge. Dysfunctional children, who are now the adult and primary caregivers, often are faced with caring for someone who may have not been nurturing or caring and who had unhealthy relationships with the now caregiver child or children. In many cases, resentment, revenge, and guilt play into the power and privilege dynamic.

Case Study 1

D.H. was a 69-year-old widow and mother of three grown children. The children were in the legal profession and viewed themselves as loving, caring, and nurturing. D.H. had a history of depression, anger, and withdrawal from social engagement for many years. She had been widowed since the age of 50. Her husband had been an attorney and was highly respected in the community before his death. D.H. had been diagnosed with Lewy body dementia. Over the course of 5 years, she became unsafe to live alone. One of her daughters, T.S., moved into her home to assume supervision of her mother. As the dementia accelerated, and the decline in cognitive and physical function advanced, T.S. began to resent D.H. and would "lose her cool." After 4 months of living 24/7 with D.H. and her paranoia, demands, and expressions of anger directed at T.S., the situation became volatile. D.H. demanded that T.S. leave her home and never come back or speak to her again. Feeling helpless and abandoned, T.S. sought help from a crisis line therapist. She expressed thoughts of killing her mother and verbalized there had been numerous times she pushed, yelled, or slapped her mother. She was remorseful and guilt-ridden. The therapist asked how she was feeling after disclosing the homicidal thinking. T.S. responded, saying that she felt "like I did when I was little."

A social worker was brought into the situation that resulted in an evaluation with diagnostics and included a neuropsychological exam that revealed severe atrophy of the temporal lobes of the brain and severe psychosis. A life planner was consulted and worked with the three children to aid in the decision-making process of placement in a nursing facility. When T.S. was asked about her childhood, she and her siblings recalled a life of the mother being absent emotionally, depressed, and withdrawn. D.H. had physically slapped, pushed, and kicked the two daughters. The son recalled that his mother was emotionally absent but had never hurt or yelled at him. The role of power and privilege was imprinted on the children and sadly was cycled back to them being in power and having the privilege of perpetrating that violence they had learned during childhood back onto their mother. The reversal in role extended privilege with the power to care for D.H. As T.S. experienced being poorly nurtured as a child, she now had the power to visit the same on her mother. Perhaps, the extreme stress of the caregiving exacerbated the recycling of the violence, or possibly the change in the power of position created the need for T.S. to be the caregiver with albeit limited caregiver and coping skills, along with dysfunctional views of how to be a nurturing, appropriate, and informed caregiver.

Health-Care Providers

Much has been written on the topic of patient-centered care in health care. This concept involves including the patient in the discussion of findings, treatment options, and expectations so that the patient and significant others can make informed decisions. Studies that address disparities in health care are beginning to address the costs associated with end-of-life care in the elderly. As briefly defined earlier, Dr. Butler defined ageism as the bias shown toward persons over the age of 65. Ageism can be applied to many aspects of the lived experience. Employment practices that prevent a person in the elder age bracket from getting a job, requiring mandatory retirement age, or imposing performance expectations that are more rigorous than those for other age groups or any situation where a person is being overtreated or undertreated for medical issues based on age are examples of common acts of ageism.

In health care, diagnosis and associated treatments may be withheld due to age. In other cases, overtreatment occurs with extensive surgeries being performed on an aged person who has no potential for improved quality of life or better prognosis. Prescribing medications that have no significant benefit because risk outweighs benefit is also a form of overtreatment. These health-care practices are based on ageism and in many cases become neglectful or abusive. Another example often perpetrated by health-care professionals and others is to decide a course of care for the patient without disclosure, discussion, or in some cases without consent.

Case Study 2

Dr. W. was an 81-year-old, retired, orthopedic surgeon and emeritus professor of an Ivy League school of medicine. Dr. W. experienced a fall while trail hiking. He sustained a fractured femur and was hospitalized. During his hospitalization of 5 days, he complained of pain in his lower legs and the back of his head for 3 days before his discharge. Neither interventions were put into place to address the pain nor were any assessments entered into the record. On admission to a rehabilitation facility, the nurse assessed a pressure ulcer to Dr. W.'s occipital region that measured 3×4 inches with a black covering obscuring visualization of the wound depth or tissue involvement. No lower extremity vascular assessments, such as capillary refill and pulse checks, were carried out. On day three of the rehabilitation admission, Dr. W's heels were noted to be bruised and mushy. By day six, the heels were noted to be black with odorous dark brown exudate. On day 10, Dr. W. was sent to the ED and diagnosed with arterial compromise, although no diagnostic testing was ordered to be performed to confirm the diagnosis. Dr. W. had no history of vascular disease before this admission. Dr. W's three sons were notified of the need for bilateral below-the-knee amputation the following morning. One of the sons was a vascular surgeon who lived out of state. On arrival to the hospital, he observed his father's condition and began to ask questions. During morning rounds, the attending physician who had trained under Dr. W. 20 years before announced the need for the amputation. Conversation between the attending physician and the attending orthopedic surgeon uncovered that no vascular testing had been ordered for Dr. W. and that his diagnosis was based on appearance without evidence of arterial disease. The physician demanded that diagnostic testing be done before any permission for surgery would be executed. Appropriate testing was ordered and carried out. The results of the examinations determined that Dr. W. had significant ulcerations to both heals with calcaneus involvement, and further exams revealed osteomyelitis of both heels. The testing results did not show any evidence of arterial involvement, rather they were pressure sores consistent with being left in the supine position, without an appropriate turning schedule and no pressure relieving devices being ordered. The amputations were not performed. Appropriate treatment and therapy plans were put into place with the wounds projected to heal over the following 6 months.

Two of Dr. W's sons were attorneys, who felt the need to address the lack of discussions in their father's care, treatments, and undiagnosed condition that could have ultimately resulted in bilateral amputations. A complaint was filed with the state health and human services department for investigation of abusive practices related to Dr. W's care in the hospital and nursing home and by the health-care professionals involved in his care. Over the course of 10 months, it was determined that Dr. W. was a victim of elder abuse by negligent attention to complaints of pain, lack of assessments, and recommendation for a life-altering surgical procedure that was unnecessary and not validated by diagnostic testing.

During the investigations, conferences, and depositions, there were numerous comments and testimony that showed ageism was at the root of the provision of care and orders related to treatments and interventions. Examples of comments included the following: "A lot of elderly complain of pain but don't actually have pain," "He never said his heels hurt so why would we look at them"? and "Older people get wounds, there's not a lot you can do about it." The most critical of statements was made by the attending surgeon, who said "Look, he had a great life and was my mentor, but he was old and his life was pretty well over. That's why I recommended an amputation, not having wounds to take care of would make his life better." Sadly, the case had an unfortunate, yet common, outcome. The jury decided that the attending surgeon had made a good point when stating that Dr. W. was elderly and had a very good life. They did not understand that in health care, there are standards of care and practice that are in place regardless of age. The standard of care that is provided to a 20-year-old person is the same standards to be used in the elderly related to assessment, diagnosis, and options for treatment. The defense team never brought up or asked about the quality of life that Dr. W. was living before the fracture. One week before the fall, Dr. W. had completed a marathon and had completed top of his class for age 65 and older. By the time the case was finished in court, Dr. W. was 86 years old and was training for a senior triathlon in New Mexico. He never had the amputations.

Care Provider

The literature on abuse addresses the increased risks associated with loss of independence and function. The systematic decline potentiates the vulnerabilities of the aged. Adaptations and the need for resources need to be identified and deployed. Caregiver services are called on to provide the supervision of care and ultimate authority over the life of the elder. Caregivers may serve in several capacities. Persons residing in their own home or apartment may have intermittent caregivers who operate on a schedule of agreed-upon visits that have specific needs and goals identified by a health-care professional, typically a registered nurse. This type of caregiver performs specific functions that might include bathing; ambulation or aiding transfer from bed to commode or to a chair or wheelchair; help with meals; laundry; and cooking. Another type of caregiver is a direct employee of the person being cared for. In this scenario, the menu of services and schedule for care is determined by the client. The types of care and services might include those as noted above, as well as providing transportation and assistance in setting up appointments, shopping for food, clothing, picking up medications at the pharmacy, accompanying the person to appointments, and help with bill paying. This type of caregiver is often not trained in safety or in appropriateness of what to observe or how to communicate with family or physician. This level of caregiver may also be unknowledgeable or untrained in skills related to ambulation, feeding, appropriate food preparation, hydration, medication safety, turning and positioning, or fall precautions emergency preparedness.

Facility or assisted living caregivers may be trained in basic care, but the need for specific geriatric care is vital to the well-being of the senior. The elderly may have changes in taste, smell, and swallowing that should be reported to appropriately address the cause. There should be best practice approaches and interventions employed by the health-care providers to address these changes. Persons with dementia often have challenges in walking down a hall with patterned floor tiles, as the dark-colored tile variant is perceived as a "hole" that may cause them to stop and not proceed beyond or seek ways to avoid or detour around. Physiologic changes experienced across the aging spectrum often include the idea that the person is becoming stubborn, manipulative, aggressive, and uncooperative, when in fact there are rationale and very real explanations of these behaviors. Caregivers not trained with a geriatric focus may become frustrated and angry with the person, resulting in yelling, screaming, making derogatory, or threatening remarks, as well as being insulting and speaking in infantile tone or language. Psychological abuse is one of the most common types of abuse and is the gateway to other forms of abuse and violence. Psychological and physical abuse is not mutually exclusive but rather frequently occurs as "hand and glove." Examples include caregivers who threaten withholding food or care if the elder does not do what they are being told to do, debasing, gaslighting, or derogatory language that is accompanied by pushing, shoving, slapping, or grabbing, which may be the course of action used by the abusive caregiver to prompt the person to comply with instructions. As the caregiver's patience decreases and the burden or frustration increases, so does the escalation of violence.

Burden and Fatigue Driven Violence

Often reference is made of caregiver burden that can be a contributor to elder abuse. This type of violence occurs in circumstances in which a caregiver is primarily responsible for the oversight and the provision of the elder's needs on a 24/7 basis. When this level and high acuity of care is ongoing and without relief or respite, the caregiver may become angry, overwhelmed, or depressed, resulting in emotional outbursts with escalation to physical abuse (Etters, Goodall & Harrison, 2008).

Caring for an ill or frail individual may appear to be straightforward. Caregivers, while having loving intention, may not realize or fathom the complexity of the care that is or will be needed. As the need for more involved care occurs, so does the training, skills development, higher level of medical supplies and equipment, caregiver respite, evaluation for transition to a higher level of supportive care, and other resources. Given increasingly complex service needs, caregivers attempt to provide the highest and best level of care they have the capacity to perform. Sadly, the elder being cared for may still suffer injury. These types of injury or premature death often mimic conditions resulting from neglect or abuse, when in fact these are symptoms of caregiver deficits in the knowledge or skills necessary to ensure safe and appropriate care (Adelman, Tmanova, & Delgado, 2014).

Case Study 3

L.M. was caring for her husband O.M. in their home. Both were 88 years old. O.M. was frail after radical surgery for advanced lung cancer and radiation treatments. O.M. had declined significantly over the 4 months since completing the therapy. He would sleep most of the day and then roam at night. L.M. attempted to care for the home, cook, and do laundry during the day but also experienced periods of interrupted sleep due to O.M.'s roaming. They had no children and had spent 72 years caring for each other. They were both survivors of the Holocaust, having met at Auschwitz. As O.M.'s health declined due to his advanced cancer, L.M. began to withdraw, cry, and became angry. The periods of depression became more frequent and more intense. When O.M. eventually became bedfast and could no longer get out of bed or attend to his activities of living, the burden became too great for L.M. to deal with. There came a time when O.M. had been in bed, unattended for 4 days, and declined to a health state that required emergency medical services. On admission to the ED, the two elders were both in severely poor states of health. Their case was reported to the Adult Protective Services (APS) as self-neglect. They both also had significant signs and symptoms of dehydration, sleep deprivation, and no nutritional intake for the 4 days before the intervention. O.M.'s physical appearance suggested severe neglect as he was soiled and found to have six severe advanced pressure ulcers. His labs revealed toxic levels of acetaminophen. He also was diagnosed with Fournier's gangrene.

L.M. became conscious and alert and found herself in a situation of being accused of abusing her husband. She was devastated and guilt-ridden. Sadly, O.M. had become septic and died after a week in the hospital. L.M. became withdrawn and was told she needed to go to a nursing home, as she was incompetent. She related to the social worker and APS investigator that she had done the best that she could. She also explained that she had given Tylenol PM to help O.M. sleep at night and not during the day. Despite her attempts to inform and clarify the living situation, a court-appointed guardian was assigned. The plan was for her to be transferred to a nursing facility. The evening before the transfer, L.M. was found dead in the bathroom from suicide by hanging. She left a lucid note that was detailed and explicit about the circumstances and the unmet needs that she and O.M. knew they had but did not know what resources might have been available. It also included critical aspects of the couple's beliefs that they did not want to burden anyone and, more importantly, they had survived what they thought to be worse during the Holocaust.

Cyclical Violence

Serial abuse and violence can occur both in a person's home by either a familial or paid caregiver or in long-term care and assisted living residential settings. Serial and cyclical violence is perpetrated on the most frail and vulnerable of elders. Persons receiving care from a family member who was a victim of abuse as a child, and is now in the role of a caregiver, may experience the caregiver opportunity to punish the senior for past indiscretions of abuse by enacting similar or identical violence committed against them in past years.

Elders who are institutionalized or living in assisted or supported housing may be faced with caregivers employed by the facility that was neglected or abused in their childhoods. The caregivers may perform acts of violence and abuse that are unintentional, given their personal histories. They may also be purposefully harming the elder or using the violence to entertain or support other types of crimes.

APS received a complaint by several families of residents in a long-term care facility. The investigation revealed violations that placed the residents in imminent danger for harm. Consultants were brought into the setting to address the specifics of care violations. The wound specialist was seeing residents to perform initial assessments and plans of care. Some of the residents that were listed to be evaluated were not found in their assigned rooms. After the fifth resident was not found, the wound consultant asked where they were. A newer staff member took the consultant aside and told her that illegal activities were being transacted on the fourth floor, where there were no residents assigned since the APS investigation. He advised that it was not safe to go to that floor. The consultant called law enforcement and reported the concerns. On arrival and investigation, it was found that the fourth floor was being used for illegal activities of selling drugs and guns and using the elders as subjects of prostitution and sadomasochism.

Unintentional Elder Abuse and Violence

Resources and Health Literacy Gaps

Case Study 4

R.C., a 65-year-old paraplegic, was being cared for by his 85-year-old mother. R.C. had been living with his mother for 14 years since his spinal cord injury from a motor vehicle accident. APS requested a consultation on a report of potential adult abuse. According to the report, there was loud yelling and arguing that was getting more frequent coming from the mobile home the two shared. The mother would leave the home for long periods of time and return with a few groceries once a week. R.C. also was frequently hospitalized for urosepsis and pressure ulcers. On the last admission to the hospital, R.C.'s weight had declined by 40 pounds in a 3-month period, indicating starvation by clinical standards. Laboratory findings revealed altered values indicating anemia, malnutrition, dehydration, and infection. His labs results were as follows: hemoglobin 5.6, hematocrit 21.4, prealbumin 8, albumin 1.8, BUN 56, creatinine 4.2, and white blood cells 27,000. The electronic health record (EHR) trend report was instrumental in identifying the trajectory of R.C.'s decline. An in-home assessment was requested as R.C. and his mother refused a nursing home referral. The evaluation revealed a clean, well-maintained home environment, with limited food and no medical equipment except a wheelchair that was donated to R.C. but not measured for his body type or weight. The wheels were noted to need repairs. R.C.'s mother admitted that she could not lift R.C. out of bed, which resulted in him staying in bed 24/7. R.C. was severely depressed and withdrawn, which was compounded by his bedroom having no windows and no television. For entertainment, R.C. listened to a radio.

It was decided to provide as much reeducation and training to R.C. and his mom about his condition and on procedures and techniques that were necessary to appropriately and safely give R.C. independence and provide his mother some reduction in burden. R.C.'s mother was also shown how to insert the indwelling Foley catheter using sterile technique and was given resources to order and obtain the sterile equipment and supplies for the indwelling catheter. R.C. and his mother were also shown the proper procedure to follow when inserting the catheter. R.C. felt comfortable in performing his own catheterizations and performed the skill appropriately on a teach-back session. Arrangements for meals on wheels were initiated, and a custom wheelchair was ordered.

APS agreed to a 3-month trial of the at-home plan and interventions. On reevaluation, R.C. had not had a urinary tract infection, no antibiotic use, had gained 20 pounds, was getting himself out of bed and into his wheelchair every day, and was going outside. He had taken up the hobby of building model ships and eventually helped in preparing meals for himself and his mother. Although outwardly the situation appeared to be neglect, in actuality, it was knowledge deficits and limited access to resources.

Prevention and Advocacy

As the number of society's baby boomers explode, the senior segment of the population who are the face of aging will forever be changed (Chism, 2013). With boomers having been a generation known for advocacy and driving demand, the industries serving seniors will be challenged to improve access, quality, and innovative ways to address the continuum of aging.

Prevention begins with awareness in society. The movement by the American Association of Retired Persons (AARP) has led the way since its inception in 1958. AARP was instrumental in proposing and achieving senior discounts well before discounts were a trend. Today, AARP leads the way in advocacy, travel, insurance coverage, education, legislative platforms, community-based, and internet resources specifically focused on the elder population.

Advocacy must continue as a preventative measure. Health and human services in each state have APS and serve as the mechanism for Ombudsman programs and leading investigations in reported cases. Criteria assigned to a case being determined to be elder abuse needs review and revision with advances in the science of aging and differential assessments and evaluations of reports. Training of all personnel involved with investigating, following up on reports, pursuing charges, and seeking safe harbor for abuse victims is severely lacking. With the new knowledge of the physiology of aging, as well as the methods and means of perpetration of all forms of abuse, along with recognizing trauma's long-term impact on relationships, health and ultimately daily life, early identification and mitigation of injury, and potentially death will be achievable.

Screenings for elder abuse and all forms of violence need additional research. Prevention, identification, and appropriate best practices for response need testing and validation with wide dissemination of standards across the nation. Currently, each state has its own version of criteria and follow-up procedures. This makes it difficult for persons being taken across state lines for care, or for those moved to different jurisdictions that are not consistent with each other, to communicate concerns and repeat offenders. The American College of Emergency Physicians issued geriatric guidelines that created standardization of evidence-based geriatric care in the ED. Elder abuse was not included in the guidelines due to the limitation of available validated screening instruments specific to the ED (American College of Emergency Physicians, 2013) Many of the high-risk indicators and medical and hospitalization history, along with diagnostic trends of biologic markers, are housed in the EHR. As clinics are acculturated to the EHR, the ability and capacity to mine data to inform a clinical provider cues to potential problems or concerns such as abuse will evolve.

Many industries including the community service organizations, utility companies, banks, and residential care sites that serve the elderly have developed practices to identify and report circumstances that meet indicators for abuse relative to that specific business. The development of policies, procedures, protocols, and referral pathways should be implemented across social intersections and disciplines to ensure timely and appropriate placement of the senior.

Aging in place has created demand for alternate living environments that are conducive to privacy, social stimulation, and engaging activities for mind, body, and spiritual stimulation with at move away from institutionalizing and warehousing of elders. Assisted living and supportive living environments provide an alternative to living alone. Having proximity to others in a social context decreases isolation, depression, and other conditions associated with self-neglect and elder suicide. The assisted living movement has certainly created alternatives to institutionalization. Programs such as the Green House Project and the creation and growth of retirement communities especially designed for an aging generation have already began the evolution of changing the face of the elderly. Self-contained communities have flourished in many areas of the country to meet the needs of a very active and healthy segment of society.

The needs of the aging population that have been addressed in the past require a new lens to evaluate efficacy and efficiency. Many gaps in care practices and needs are going unmet, for much of the population. Seniors living independently outnumber those who live in assisted living or nursing homes. Those elders need additional services and products to improve the quality of life and longevity. The need for focused training and education that includes geriatric, population-based competencies, and best practice with standardization across care settings should be implemented to appropriately and safely address gaps in the elder market and industries. Adaptive devices, telehealth, and accessibility options for home, mobility, and function are widely marketed and growing in consumer demand. Specialists in physical, occupational, speech, audiology, and vision are especially trained in evaluations and therapeutic interventions that improve the quality of life and social engagement of the elder population. Smart homes and smart devices can markedly improve the potential for seniors to age in place and maintain independence for as long as safely possible.

Life Care Planners and geriatric care managers have increased awareness and advocacy of the multiplicity of senior needs, available solutions, and alternatives. The growth of the field of elder law signals the need for expertise in guiding legal decisions and identification of senior needs for life planning and end-of-life decisions before the need arises. The financial service industry has also produced some interesting products to assist seniors living on fixed incomes, or who are close to outliving their retirement savings.

The elder care industry has tremendous opportunities for growth with additional quality of life improvements that would markedly add to the ability of seniors to age in place safely. Having programs that can provide respite for families rendering 24/7 care will be in demand. Employee and staff programs focused on compassion fatigue and debriefing after critical incidents are already showing promise for improving the quality of care and the satisfaction of the employees. Creating evidence based, objective assessment and survey queries would markedly improve outcomes of investigations. The variance of evaluation, assessment and investigations of elder injuries and deaths calls for improved mechanisms aimed at objective markers and findings. The development of such instruments would greatly improve the rigor of elder abuse case investigations while minimizing bias or subjective findings that have proven to fail elders who have been abused, injured or who have died. The competencies and associated protocols and practices will be critical in safeguarding the aged. Improving identification with differential diagnosis and developing policies that address the barriers and obstacles to reporting, and ensuring safe harbor for elder abuse victims post-discharge, will greatly impact the quality of life for future generations.

References

cC-span.org. (July 18, 2008). *Outliving retirement savings [video file]*. Retrieved from https://www.c-span.org/video/?206198-3/outliving-retirement-savings.

Aciermo, R., Hernandez, M. A., Armstadter, A. B., Resnick, H. S., Steve, K., & Muzzy, W. (2010). Prevalence and correlates of emotional, physical, sexual, and financial abuse and potential neglect in the United States: The national elder mistreatment study. *American Journal of Public Health, 100*(2), 292–297.

Aciermo, R., Hernandez-Tejada, M., Muzzy, W., & Steve, K. (2009). *The national elder mistreatment study (2264560)*. Washington, DC: Government Printing Office.

Adelman, R. D., Tmanova, L. L., & Delgado, D. (2014). Caregiver burden: A clinical review. *Journal of the American Medical Association, 311*(10), 1052–1060. https://doi.org/10.1001/jama.2014.304.

Administration on Aging. (1998). *The national elder abuse incidence study: Final report (final report-online)*. Washington, DC: Government Printing Office.

American College of Emergency Physicians. (2013). *Geriatric emergency department guidelines [practice guidelines]*. Irving, TX: Author.

Amstadter, A. B., Cisler, J. M., McCauley, J. L., Hernandez, M. A., Muzzy, W., & Aciermo, R. (2011a). Do incident and perpetrator characteristics of elder mistreatment differ by gender of the victim? Results from national elder mistreatment study. *Journal of Elder Abuse and Neglect, 23,* 43−57.

Amstadter, A. B., Zajac, K., Strachan, M., Hernandez, M. A., Kilpatrick, D. G., & Aciermo, R. (2011b). Prevalence and correlates of elder mistreatment in South Carolina: The South Carolina elder mistreatment study. *Journal of Interpersonal Violence, 26,* 2947−2972.

Baker, M. W., Lacroix, A. Z., Wu, C., Cochrane, B. B., Wallace, R., & Woods, N. F. (2009). Mortality and risk associated with physical and verbal abuse in women aged 50−79. *Journal of the American Geriatrics Society, 57*(10), 1799−1809.

Brozowski, K., & Hall, D. R. (2010). Aging and risk: Physical and sexual abuse of elders in Canada. *Journal of Interpersonal Violence, 25,* 1183−1199.

Cannell, M. B., Manini, T., Spence-Almaguer, E., Maldonado-Molina, M., & Andrensen, E. (2014). U.S. population estimates and correlates of sexual abuse in community dwelling older adults. *Journal of Elder Abuse and Neglect.* https://doi.org/10.1080/08946566.2013.879845.

Caspi, E. (2018). The circumstances surrounding the death of 105 elders as the result of resident to resident incidents in dementia long-term care homes. *Journal of Elder Abuse and Neglect,* 1−25. https://doi.org/10.1080/08946566.2018.1474515.

Castle, N. (2011). Nursing home deficiency citations for abuse. *Journal of Applied Gerontology, 30,* 719−743.

Chamberlain, L. B. (2009). The amazing teen brain: What every child advocate needs to know. *Child Law Practice, 28*(2), 17−24. Retrieved from www.practicenores.org/v17n2/brain.html.

Chism, R. W. (June 6, 2013). *Ageism, myths and new beginnings [Blog post].* Retrieved from http://changingaging.org/blog/ageism-myths-and-new-beginings/.

Colby, S. L., & Ortman, J. M. (2014). *The baby boomer cohort in the United States: 2012-2060 [fact sheet].* Retrieved from census.gov https://www.census.gov/prod/2014pubs/p25-1141.pdf.

Columbia Aging. (n.d.). Retrieved from https://aging.columbia.edu/about/robert-butler.

Cook, A., Spinazzola, P., Ford, J., & Lanktree, C. (2005). Complex trauma in children and adolescents. *Psychiatric Annuals, 35*(5), 390−398.

Cooper, Selwood, & Livingston. (2008). The prevalence of elder abuse and neglect: A systematic review. *Age and Ageing, 37,* 151, 16.

Cronholm, P. F., Ismailji, T., & Mettner, J. (2013). Academy on violence and abuse: Highlights of proceedings from the 2011 conference, "Toward a New Understanding". *Trauma, Violence and Abuse, 14,* 271−281.

Department of Justice. (2010). *Report on elder abuse.* Retrieved from www.justice.gov.

Dong, X. (2014). Elder abuse: Research, practice, and health policy. The 2012 GSA Maxwell Pollack lecture. *The Gerontologist, 54*(2), 153−162.

Dong, X., & Simon, M. (2013a). Association between elder abuse and use of ED: Findings from the Chicago health and aging project. *American Journal of Emergency Medicine, 31,* 693−698.

Dong, X., & Simon, M. (2013b). Elder abuse as a risk factor for hospitalization in older persons. *JAMA Internal Medicine, 173,* 911−917.

Drake, S. A., Pickens, S., Wolf, D. A., & Thimsen, K. (2018). Improving medicolegal death investigative gaps of fatal elder abuse. *Journal of Elder Abuse and Neglect,* 1−10. https://doi.org/10.1080/08946566.2018.1537017.

Etters, L., Goodall, D., & Harrison, B. (2008). Caregiver burden among dementia patient caregivers: A review of the literature. *Journal of the American Academy of Nurse Practitioners, 20*(8). https://doi.org/10.1111/j.1745-7599.2008.00342.x.

Friedman, L. S., Avila, S., Shah, M., Tanouye, K., & Joseph, K. (2014). A description of cases of severe physical abuse in the elderly and 1-year mortality. *Journal of Elder ABuse and Neglect, 26*(1), 1–11. https://doi.org/10.1080/08946566.2013.780944.

Fulmer, T., Firpo, A., Guadagno, L., Easter, T., Kahan, F., & Paris, B. (2003). Themes from grounded theory analysis of elder neglect assessment by experts. *The Gerontologist, 43*(5), 745–752.

Fulmer, T., Paveza, G., Abraam, I., & Fairchild, S. (2000). Elder neglect assessment in the emergency department. *Journal of Emergency Nursing,* 436–443.

Jackson, S. L., & Haefmeister, T. E. (2013). *Understanding elder abuse: Research in brief (NCJ 241731).* Retrieved from U.S. Department of Justice.

Laumann, E. O., Leitsch, S. A., & Waite, L. J. (2008). Elder mistreatment in the United States: Prevalence estimates from a nationally representative study. *Journal of Gerontology: Series B Psychological Sciences and Social Sciences, 63,* S248–S254.

Policastro, C., & Payne, B. K. (2014). Assessing the level of elder abuse knowledge pre-professionals possess: Implications for the further development of university curriculum. *Journal of Elder Abuse and Neglect, 26,* 12–30. https://doi.org/10.1080/08946566.2013.784070.

Poole Heller, D. (2000). *Speaking the unspeakable: An exploration of the dynamics of sadistic and non-sadistic sexual and physical violence.* Retrieved from healingtraumacenter.com.

Santos, A. J., Nunes, B., Kislaya, I., Gil, A. P., & Ribeiro, O. (2018). Older adults' emotional reactions top elder abuse: Individual and victimization determinants. *Health and Social Care in the Community,* 1–12. https://doi.org/10.1111/hsc.12673.

Shugarman, L. R., Fries, B. E., Wolf, R. S., & Morris, J. N. (2003). Identifying older people at risk for abuse during routine screening practices. *Journal of the American Geriatrics Society, 51*(1), 24–31.

Teresi, J. A., Ramirez, M., Ellis, J., Silver, S., Boratgis, G., Kong, J., … Lachs, M. S. (2013). A staff intervention targeting resident to resident elder mistreatment (R-REM) in long term care increased staff knowledge, recognition and reporting: Results from a cluster randomization trial. *International Journal of Nursing Studies, 50*(5), 644–656. https://doi.org/10.1016/j.ijnurstu.2012.10.010.

Van der Kolk, B. A. (1994). The body keeps score: Memory and the evolving psychobiology of posttraumatic stress. *Harvard Review of Psychiatry, 1,* 253–265.

5

WOUND IDENTIFICATION AND PHYSICAL ABUSE

Patricia M. Speck,[1] Diana K. Faugno,[2] Melanie Gibbons Hallman[3]

[1] School of Nursing, Department of Family, Community & Health Systems, University of Alabama at Birmingham, Birmingham, AL, United States;
[2] Eisenhower Medical Center, Rancho Mirage, CA, United States;
[3] Family, Community, and Health Systems, University of Alabama at Birmingham School of Nursing, Birmingham, AL, United States

CHAPTER OUTLINE
Introduction   108
Definitions   109
The Integument   109
Skin Anatomical Structures and Aging Influence   110
Impact of Aging on Integument   111
Trauma and Older Age   112
Skin Injury and Overlapping Phases of Healing   114
Healing Phases   119
Definitions of Injury Terms   121
Field Triage Decision Schema   127
Intentional Injury in Older Persons   129
Case Presentations   131
     Case 1: Unintentional Injury With Comorbidities   131
     Case 2: Intentional Injury With Comorbidities   132
     Case 3: Intentional Injury From Neglect   133
Summary   134
References   135

Elder Abuse. https://doi.org/10.1016/B978-0-12-815779-4.00005-7

Introduction

Injury in older persons is often unseen by health care providers (HCPs), but when elders present to emergency departments for injury, the cause of the injury is frequently unknown. When the cause and manner of cutaneous manifestations are unknown, providers are often faced with completing a barrage of tests to confirm common reasons for appearance of integument changes, such as disease or injury. The common differentials include falls, urinary tract infection, dehydration, and anemia manifested as a low red blood cell count, which can be brought on by bleeding in the bowel or by other causes. Other differentials include pneumonia, heart problems such as atrial fibrillation, stroke, including ministrokes that do not cause weakness on one side, and other potential causes for a fall. When not witnessed, and health symptoms are not obvious, the default diagnosis is dependent on the known comorbidities.

Intentional injury in older populations is not screened and not recognized unless obvious. Typically, physical assault of elders includes hitting, slapping, pinching, or sticking the older person with an object, as well as the use of either chemical or binding restraints, or neglect, which is tantamount to failing to provide daily needs (Young, 2014). In obvious physical abuse, most providers know that the injury is intentional, but they are reticent to report because the older person denies the cause. Consequently, elder abuse is vastly underreported (Clarysse, Kivlahan, Beyer, & Gutermuth, 2018; Pavlik, Hyman, Festa, & Dyer, 2001; Pillemer & Finkelhor, 1988; Young, 2014). The estimates are that "approximately 1 in 10 Americans aged 60 years and over have experienced some form of elder abuse. Some estimates range as high as 5 million elders who experience abuse each year. One study estimated that only 1 in 14 cases of abuse is reported to authorities" (National Council on Aging, 2018). Although there are several kinds of abuse, such as emotional, financial, and verbal, the detectable areas of physical abuse, neglect, and mistreatment will be the subject of this chapter. Physical manifestations of elder abuse include bruises, pressure marks, broken bones, abrasions, and burns. Documenting the history of the injury and describing the injury is the first step in establishing the cause and manner of the finding. Especially in elder maltreatment, due diligence requires a differential diagnosis necessary to rule out the variety of comorbid contributions to integument changes, including postmortem changes (Lachs & Pillemer, 1995; Lofaso & Rosen, 2014).

Definitions

The Centers for Disease Control and Prevention (CDC) reports that "elder abuse is an intentional act, or failure to act, by a caregiver or another person in a relationship involving an expectation of trust that causes or creates a risk of harm to an older adult" (2018). The CDC defines an older adult as someone over the age 60. Forms of elder abuse include:

Physical Abuse: The intentional use of physical force that results in acute or chronic illness, bodily injury, physical pain, functional impairment, distress, or death. Physical abuse may include, but is not limited to, violent acts such as striking with or without an object or weapon, hitting, beating, scratching, biting, choking, suffocation, pushing, shoving, shaking, slapping, kicking, stomping, pinching, and burning. For the purposes of this chapter, physical abuse is addressed from injury through the healing process or death.

Sexual Abuse or Abusive Sexual Contact: Sexual abuse in the elderly produces injury, which is covered in Chapter 6. These acts qualify as sexual abuse if they are committed against a person who is not competent to give informed approval.

Neglect: Serious risk of compromised health and safety can be due to failure by a caregiver or other responsible person to protect an elder from harm. Neglect is also seen as the failure to meet an elder's essential needs such as medical care, nutrition, hydration, hygiene, clothing, basic activities of daily living, or shelter. Examples include not providing adequate nutrition, hygiene, clothing, shelter, or access to necessary health care or failure to prevent exposure to unsafe activities and environment (Center for Disease Control and Prevention, 2018b).

The Integument

The rapidity of the aging process, now thought to be a function of environmental and genetic influences, varies greatly (Genes and Disease, 1998a). The purpose of the chapter is to address the fundamentals of normal integument throughout the aging process, as well as injury and healing processes in older persons. When known, authors disclose the cause and manner of injury and the underlying medical conditions that influence injury severity.

The integument system, also known as the skin, is the largest organ in human beings. Functions involve excreting wastes, regulating temperature, and preventing dehydration by controlling the level of perspiration (Informed Health Online, 2009). The skin is waterproof and protects from infection (Takeo, Lee, & Ito, 2015). The skin is made of water, proteins, lipids, minerals, and chemicals. There are also sensory receptors woven throughout the underlying matrix, which sense pain, sensations, and pressure. The differentiation of cells in the skin layers creates a waterproof barrier via keratin, structures with fibrous protein, adipose made of fat and lipids, and chemicals and minerals such as sodium, potassium, and others. Hair and the hair follicle, which exist in the dermal layer, function to protect from the sun, keep a person warm, and secrete sebum oils and melanin. This influences the color of the skin, along with carotene and hemoglobin (Seifert, Monaghan, Voss, & Maden, 2012). Additionally, skin stores water, fat, glucose, and vitamin D3, all necessary for the functions of the skin—to provide protection from bacteria, viruses, and other microbes (Broughton, Janis, & Attinger, 2006). As the integument ages, the rapidity of cell division, metabolic activity, circulation, response to lowered hormones, and muscle strength decreases (Wilkinson & Hardman, 2017). With older persons, the dermis has underlying matrix that loses elasticity due to loss of capillary flow, hormones, and other elements necessary for healing, as well as capacity for regeneration, which results in delayed wound repair. Additionally, fat reduction in the dermal and subcutaneous layers of the integument, through a reduction in the number and size of cells, promotes loss of form, contributing to thinning of the hypodermis and sagging of the integument (OpenStax College, 2018; Takeo et al., 2015; Wilkinson & Hardman, 2017).

Skin Anatomical Structures and Aging Influence

Epidermis: The result of decreased mitosis in the *stratum basale* is thinner epidermis (OpenStax College, 2018; Takeo et al., 2015).

Dermis: Elasticity and resilience in the dermal layers reflects an inability of dermal regeneration, resulting in slower healing. A result of changes in collagen and elastin production in the dermis, along with weakening muscles under the skin, results in sagging skin an inability to retain moisture (OpenStax College, 2018; Takeo et al., 2015) and promotes intolerance to cold.

Hypodermis: The fat stores in the hypodermis lose structure with redistribution of adipose, contributing to thinning (OpenStax College, 2018; Takeo et al., 2015).

Accessory structures: Accessory structures have less circulation and result in thinning hair and nails and dry skin due to reduced sebum and sweat. A lack of sweat causes intolerance to extreme heat, and the inactivity of melanocytes and dendritic cells results in pale skin and lower immunity (OpenStax College, 2018; Takeo et al., 2015).

Glands: The basic physiology of fluid production, defined by mechanism, is a function of secretory glands, drainage, or discharge. The location of *secretory glands* varies depending on the type of integument layer, whether skin or mucous membrane, or dorsal surfaces of the hand or foot. Glands include, but are not limited to, salivary in the mouth; tear ducts in the eyes; cerumen within the ear canal; sweat and sebum for the skin; insulin in the pancreas; gall in the gall bladder; and mucous-producing glands in the nasal membrane, anal canal, or vulva, such as Bartholin's, Skene's, vaginal, cervix, and others (Genes and Disease, 1998b).

Drainage: Drainage reflects the type of fluid released following injury to tissue, and color reflects the response to injury. For instance, blood or blood products are drainage and include serous, sanguineous, seropurulent, and purulent, where each color represents a specificity to the stage of healing and influence of pathogens, important to those tracking acquired infections (Horan, Andrus, & Dudeck, 2008).

Discharge: Discharge is a mixture of secretory fluid, drainage, and cells. Areas where discharge may be present, such as the vagina or nose, may or may not be infectious (Johnson, 2018).

Impact of Aging on Integument

Older persons have comorbid disorders that create complex analysis for wound healing delay. Table 5.1 lists some elements that delay wound healing in older persons.

Fluid production also diminishes with aging (Takeo et al., 2015). The capacity for fluid production, whether secretory, drainage, or discharge, diminishes, resulting in caking of the sloughing tissue when fluid is present. For example, urine on the vulva creates caking of shedding tissue in crural folds of the labia minora or coronal smegma-like caking under the foreskin. Caking of tissue in these folds has potential to cause injury through the mechanism of continuous moisture to the area, resulting in anastomosis, including labial or vulvar adhesions, or adhesion of foreskin to corona and glans (LeLievre, 2000). If diapered, moisture next to the skin of an older person causes the skin to swell initially and then break down in a contact dermatitis. This is a predictable outcome of the moisture exposure; the process is more rapid in older persons, where skin barriers are less protective (Larner, Matar, Goldman, & Chilcott, 2015; LeLievre, 2000). The knowledge

Table 5.1 Elements Delaying Wound Healing in Elders.

Local Factors	Systemic Factors
Ischemia	Age and gender
Oxygenation	Obesity
Increased skin tension	Smoking
Poor surgical apposition	Malnutrition
Wound dehiscence	Deficiency of vitamins and trace elements
Poor venous drainage	Immunocompromised conditions: cancer, radiation therapy, AIDS
Presence of foreign body and foreign body reactions	Medications: glucocorticoid steroids, non-steroidal anti-inflammatory drugs, chemotherapy
Continued presence of microorganisms infection	Inherited neutrophil disorders, such as Leukocyte adhesion deficiency Impaired macrophage activity (malakoplakia)
Excess local mobility, such as over a joint	Sex hormones
	Stress

Table edited for presentation. Grey, J. E., Enoch, S., Harding, K. G. (2006). Wound assessment. British Medical Journal (Clinical research ed.), 332(7536), 285–288. https://doi.org/10.1136/bmj.332.7536.285.

about fluid breakdown process is from parallel medical examiner literature that describes stages in moisture exposure conditions. *Washerwoman Syndrome* describes "hand which are immersed in water for extended periods of time, causing swelling, then wrinkling, and eventual breakdown of the underlying structures of the integument" (US Legal Inc., 2016), and while this is also a postmortem finding, it parallels the findings in living persons' integument moistened for prolonged periods of time. Fig. 5.1 demonstrates the three layers of the integument, each with function and structure.

Trauma and Older Age

Persons older than 55 years of age are at increased risk of death from trauma. However, HCPs have difficulty in the recognition of intentional injury. Red flags include cutaneous clues, patterned shapes and distribution, differing ages of injury, blunt traumas, parallel injuries, and alopecia (Clarysse et al., 2018). When controlling for race, comorbidities, and insurance status, increasing age was associated with increased mortality from injury (MacKenzie et al., 2006). One-year mortality rates of traumatized younger

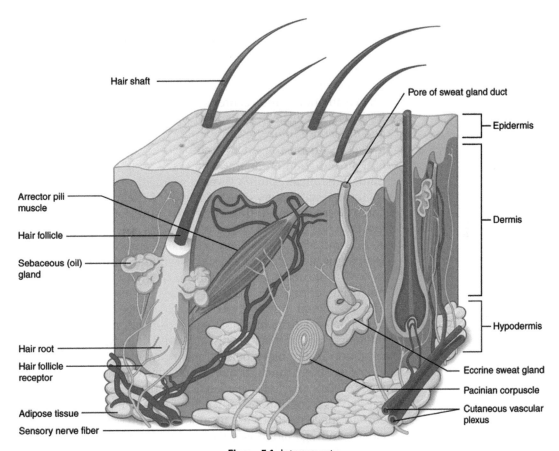

Figure 5.1 Integument.

persons aged 18–54 were 6.9% following trauma and 32.2% for persons 75–84 years, where each year after age 65 corresponded to an increase of 6.8% in mortality (Grossman, Miller, Scaff, & Arcona, 2002). Another case–control study reported that when death was the outcome, younger victims had higher Injury Severity Scores than older trauma victims (Morris, MacKenzie, & Edelstein, 1990; Ong et al., 2009). When traumatized, victims develop comorbidities associated with the trauma and have poor outcomes. For example, a study of the National Trauma Data Base demonstrated differences in age groups: 24% of trauma patients 50–64 years and 33% of trauma patients 65 and older developed comorbidities associated with the Injury Severity Score at the time of trauma (McGwin, MacLennan, Fife, Davis, & Rue, 2004). Prospectively in New Zealand, a study looking at age and Injury Severity Score found comorbid outcomes increased with age: 40% by age 61 and 50% by age 80 (Tan, Ng, & Civil, 2004). Recently, another study found advancing age with a decrease in trauma alert level resulted in an increase in mortality (Earl-Royal, Shofer, Ruggieri, Frasso, & Holena, 2016).

Questions arise as to the adequacy of emergency medical service and nontrauma center personnel to recognize severe injury in elderly. For instance, a Pennsylvania study of trauma patients 65 and older with Injury Severity Scale scores of greater than 15 were less likely to be triaged to trauma centers than their less than 65-year-old counterparts at 36.6% and 47.0%, respectively, even though the mean trauma severity score was 19.3 in older persons at nontrauma centers (Lane, Sorondo, & Kelly, 2003). These outcomes were similar to those found in a previous study with those less than 65 compared with those persons aged 65 years and older at 15% and 56%, respectively (Zimmer-Gembeck et al., 1995). The evaluation of anatomic, physiological, and comorbid conditions as well as location and mechanism of injury identification does not occur during the triage of older persons following trauma. The additional training necessary to triage correctly includes detection of deficits in physiological reserves, medication use and influence, and impact of disease over time with the comorbid condition in the older person, not to mention the rapid decline following severe injury, usually unrecognized (Paranitharan & Pollanen, 2008). An extensive analytical literature review revealed that age acts as a continuous rather than dichotomous variable, where current triage methods are insufficient to predict serious injury in elders, and age alone is associated with poor outcomes (Jacobs et al., 2003). Considering injury severity was not validated in older persons; significant adjustments for older persons is necessary (Sattin, 2002). Hence, advanced age lowers the threshold for triage directly to a trauma center. A retrospective cohort study of 33,298 injured adults 65 years or older experiencing multiple trauma mechanisms demonstrated existing current national triage guidelines are insufficient as the current study using "the alternative triage guidelines identified more high-risk patients than current guidelines, [presenting] … the opportunity to improve early clinical management to reduce morbidity and mortality among patients with specific injury patterns" (Newgard et al., 2016, p. 23).

Skin Injury and Overlapping Phases of Healing

The phases of healing following injury includes hemostasis as clot formation; inflammation, which debrides injured tissue;

proliferation as epithelization; fibroplasia; angiogenesis; and maturation manifested as collagen formation with tight cross-links to other collagen, with protein molecules increasing the tensile strength of the scar (Broughton et al., 2006).

Vasoconstriction: The moment an injury occurs, the body responds with predictable phases. Within moments of the injury, platelets aggregate and release cytokines, chemokines, and hormones. The intimal layer of the capillaries vasoconstricts due to the vasoactive mediators epinephrine, norepinephrine, prosta-glandins, serotonin, and thromboxane and causes temporary blanching of the wound. The first color of wound margins is white. The primary plug forms because the exposed subendothelium has collagen and tissue factor, which activates platelet aggregation, and leads to clot formation. The exposed collagen surfaces activate and cause platelets to aggregate and attach. Collagen acti-vation creates an environment for platelets to degranulate and release chemotactic and growth factors, such as platelet-derived growth factor (PDGF), proteases, and vasoactive agents such as serotonin and histamine. The initial vasoconstriction period lasts no longer than 10−15 minutes (Simon, Moutran, & Romo, 2018).

Inflammation: After the vasoconstriction phase, the inflamma-tion phase is marked by a persistent period of vasodilation, hence why some injuries persist in bleeding after initially stopping. This phase is mediated by histamine, prostaglandins, kinins, and leuko-trienes. Vasodilation is necessary to expose the wound to increased blood flow, which brings necessary inflammatory cells and factors that fight infection and debride the wound of devitalized tissue. The sensation of pain is a result of pH alterations secondary to tissue demise and bacterial degradation, edema, and subsequent tissue hypoxemia caused by vasoconstriction or pressure on vital capillaries from swelling at the site of injury (Simon et al., 2018).

The process of coagulation creates a scab, activates thrombin, and facilitates migration of inflammatory cells to the site of injury by relaxing intimal layers of capillaries and vessels, thereby increasing vascular permeability. By this mechanism, factors and cells necessary for healing flow from the intravascular space into the extravascular space, resulting in swelling. One factor is plasminogen, which is converted to plasmin, a potent enzyme that aids in cell lysis, and is necessary to clean the wound for healing (Simon et al., 2018).

The cellular aspect of the inflammatory phase occurs within hours of injury and consists of migration of cells, including neutrophils, macrophages, and lymphocytes. Neutrophils are the predominant cell type for the first 48 hours after injury but are not necessary to heal the wound. They cleanse the wound site of bacteria and necrotic matter, releasing inflammatory mediators and bactericidal oxygen free radicals. Macrophages are necessary to phagocytose debris and bacteria, which is essential in the early phases of wound healing. They also secrete collagenases and elastases, which break down injured tissue and release cytokines. In addition, macrophages release PDGF, an important cytokine that stimulates the chemotaxis and proliferation of fibroblasts and smooth muscle cells. Finally, macrophages secrete substances that attract endothelial cells to the wound and stimulate their proliferation to promote angiogenesis. When these cells are absent, fibroplasia and granulation tissue formation are impaired, and the overall rate of wound healing is delayed. T lymphocytes are another cell that migrates into the wound during the inflammatory phase, approximately 72 hours after an injury. T lymphocytes are attracted to the wound by the cellular release of interleukin-1, which also contributes to the regulation of collagenase. Lymphocytes secrete lymphokines such as heparin-binding epidermal growth factor and basic fibroblast growth factor. Lymphocytes also affect cellular immunity and antibody production (Broughton et al., 2006; Simon et al., 2018). It is important that the provider is able to distinguish between inflammation from injury and inflammation from infection noted in Fig. 5.2.

Proliferation: Formation of granulation tissue is central to the proliferative phase. Granulation formation occurs 3—5 days following injury and dovetails with the inflammatory phase when wounds are large, healing by secondary intention. Granulation tissue includes inflammatory cells, fibroblasts, and neovasculature, which forms new capillaries and vessels in a matrix of fibronectin, collagen, glycosaminoglycans, and proteoglycans (Broughton et al., 2006; Simon et al., 2018, May 24).

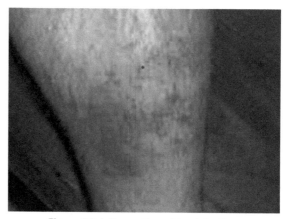

Figure 5.2 Inflammation of leg infection.

Epithelialization: The epithelialization process begins within hours of tissue injury. Epidermal cells at the wound edges undergo structural changes, allowing them to detach from their connections to other epidermal cells and to their basement membrane. Epidermal cells secrete collagenases that break down collagen and plasminogen activator, which stimulates the production of plasmin. Plasmin promotes clot dissolution along the path of epithelial cell migration. Migrating epithelial cells interact with a provisional matrix of fibrin cross-linked to fibronectin and collagen. Fibronectin seems to promote keratinocyte adhesion to guide these cells across the wound base. Intracellular actin microfilaments are formed, allowing the epidermal cells to creep across the wound surface. As the cells migrate, they dissect the wound and separate the overlying eschar from the underlying viable tissue.

In superficial wounds, such as wounds due to laser resurfacing, dermabrasion, and chemical peel treatments, adnexal structures such as sebaceous glands and hair follicles contribute to reepithelialization. Accidental separation yields a webbing appearance that exposes the viable tissues. Epithelialization is necessary for the formation of epithelium over a denuded or anoxic surface. Health by secondary intention involves the migration of cells at the wound edges over a distance of less than 1 mm, from one side of the incision to the other. Incisional wounds are epithelialized within 24–48 hours after injury. When epithelialization is complete, there is restoration of the linkages to the basement membrane with new desmosome attachments to other epidermal cells and new hemidesmosome linkages to the basement membrane.

Wounds in moist environments demonstrate a faster and more direct course of epithelialization. Occlusive and semiocclusive dressings applied in the first 48 hours after injury may maintain tissue humidity and optimize epithelialization. Studies demonstrate occlusive dressings in the form of silicone sheeting, or other similar forms of dressing, limit epidermal inflammatory factors that contribute to epidermal hyperplasia by restoring barrier function and increasing skin hydration (Broughton et al., 2006; Simon et al., 2018).

Fibroplasia: The fibroblast is necessary for the formation of granulation tissue. Fibroblasts are responsible for the production of collagen, elastin, fibronectin, glycosaminoglycans, and proteases. Inflammation cells decrease in the wound, whereas fibroblasts grow in number. Therefore, the demand for the inflammatory phase disappears and the chemotactic factors are no longer produced, and those already present are inactivated. Fibroplasia, like other phases, overlaps as the wound heals. Fibroplasia begins

3–5 days after injury and may last as long as 14 days or longer in older persons. Skin fibroblasts and mesenchymal cells differentiate to perform migratory and contractile capabilities. Fibroblasts migrate and proliferate in response to fibronectin, PDGF, fibroblast growth factor, transforming growth factor, and C5a. Fibronectin serves as an anchor for the myofibroblast as it migrates within the wound (Broughton et al., 2006; Simon et al., 2018).

Proliferation: Collagen synthesis and deposition is necessary during the proliferative phase to form tensile strength in wound healing in general. Collagen is rich in hydroxylysine and hydroxyproline moieties, which enables it to form strong cross-links. The hydroxylation of proline and lysine residues depends on the presence of oxygen, vitamin C, ferrous iron, and α-ketoglutarate. Deficiencies of oxygen caused by obesity, poor circulation, or tissue injury, and vitamin C deficiencies caused by poor nutrition or metabolization, result in underhydroxylated collagen, less capable of forming strong cross-links and, therefore, are more vulnerable to breakdown (Simon et al., 2018, May 24; Timms, 2011).

Collagen synthesis begins approximately 3 days after injury and may continue at a rapid rate for approximately 2–4 weeks. Collagen synthesis occurs in the presence of collagenases and other factors that destroy old collagen throughout the process of generating new collagen. Approximately 80% of the collagen in normal skin is type I collagen; the remaining is mostly type III. In contrast, type III collagen is the primary component of early granulation tissue and is abundant in embryonic tissue. Collagen fibers deposit in a framework of fibronectin, which is essential to collagen formation, where experimental wounds depleted of fibronectin demonstrate decreased collagen accumulation (Broughton et al., 2006; Simon et al., 2018, May 24).

Procollagen forms when collagen exists in the extracellular space, which is then separated from its terminal segments and called tropocollagen. Tropocollagen aggregates with other tropocollagen molecules to form collagen filaments. Filament, fibril, and fiber formation occur in a matrix gel of glycosaminoglycans, hyaluronic acid, chondroitin sulfate, dermatan sulfate, and heparin sulfate, all produced by fibroblasts. Intermolecular cross-links make collagen fiber stable and resistant to destruction. Age, tension, pressure, and stress affect the rate of collagen synthesis.

Present in smaller amounts is elastin, a structural protein with random coils allowing for stretch and recoil properties of the skin. Elastin diminishes in older persons, resulting in "tenting" of skin, beginning in hands and eventually in all integument areas. The coiling is useful in determining dehydration in younger persons, but not so much with older persons. Different is wound contraction, defined as the centripetal movement of wound edges, which facilitates closure and begins concurrently with collagen synthesis. Contraction is maximal at 5–15 days after an injury. Contraction results in wound size reduction. The maximal rate of contraction is 0.75 mm/d and depends on the degree of tissue laxity and shape of the wound. Loose tissues contract more than tissues with poor laxity, and square wounds tend to contract more than circular wounds. Wound contraction depends on the myofibroblast located at the periphery of the wound, its connection to components of the extracellular matrix, and myofibroblast proliferation. Radiation and drugs, which inhibit cell division, delay wound contraction. Contraction does not seem to depend on collagen synthesis. Although the role of the peripheral nervous system in wound healing is not well delineated, recent studies suggest that sympathetic innervation affects wound contraction and epithelialization through unknown mechanisms. Contraction is not contracture, which is a pathologic process of excessive contraction that limits motion where the cause is excessive wound pressure (Broughton et al., 2006; Simon et al., 2018).

Maturation: The maturation phase depends on continued collagen synthesis in the presence of collagen destruction. Collagenases and matrix metalloproteinases in the wound assist removal of excess collagen while synthesis of new collagen persists. Tissue inhibitors of metalloproteinases limit these collagenolytic enzymes, so that a balance exists between formation of new collagen and removal of old collagen. During maturation, collagen remodeling becomes increasingly organized. Fibronectin gradually disappears, and hyaluronic acid and glycosaminoglycans are replaced by proteoglycans. Type III collagen is replaced by type I collagen. Water from edema is resorbed from the scar. These events allow collagen fibers to lie closer together, facilitating collagen cross-linking and ultimately decreasing scar thickness. Intra- and intermolecular collagen cross-links result in increased strength. Remodeling begins approximately 21 days after injury, when the net collagen content of the wound is stable. Remodeling continues indefinitely (Broughton et al., 2006; Simon et al., 2018, May 24).

Healing Phases

The tensile strength of a wound is a measurement of its load capacity per unit area. The bursting strength of a wound is the force required to break a wound regardless of its dimension. Bursting strength varies with skin thickness and healing phase. For example, it is easier to break a wound within a couple of days, opposed to breaking a wound at 2 months. Peak tensile strength of a wound occurs approximately 60 days after injury. A healed wound only reaches approximately 80% of the tensile strength of unwounded skin.

Cytokines emerge as important mediators of wound healing events. By definition, a cytokine is a protein mediator, released from various cell sources, which binds to cell surface receptors to stimulate a cell response throughout the healing phases.

Fibroblast growth factor is a mitogen for mesenchymal cells and an important stimulus for angiogenesis. Fibroblast growth factor is a mitogen for endothelial cells, fibroblasts, keratinocytes, and myoblasts. This factor also stimulates wound contraction and epithelialization and production of collagen, fibronectin, and proteoglycans.

PDGF is released from the alpha granules of platelets and is responsible for the stimulation of neutrophils and macrophages, as well as for the production of transforming growth factor-β. PDGF is a mitogen and chemotactic agent for fibroblasts and smooth muscle cells and stimulates angiogenesis, collagen synthesis, and collagenase. Vascular endothelial growth factor is similar to PDGF, but it does not bind the same receptors. Vascular endothelial growth factor is mitogenic for endothelial cells and plays an important role in angiogenesis.

Transforming growth factor-β is released from the alpha granules of platelets and has been shown to regulate its own production in an autocrine manner. This factor is an important stimulant for fibroblast proliferation and the production of proteoglycans, collagen, and fibrin. The factor also promotes accumulation of the extracellular matrix and fibrosis. Transforming growth factor-β has been demonstrated to reduce scarring and to reverse the inhibition of wound healing by glucocorticoids.

Tumor necrosis factor-α is produced by macrophages and stimulates angiogenesis and the synthesis of collagen and collagenase. Tumor necrosis factor-α is a mitogen for fibroblasts.

Aged persons have thinning integument, less circulatory capacity, and comorbidities affecting nutrition absorption and healing time. Thinning integument includes all three major layers of the integument, as well as the reduction of circulatory support for the tissue. The result is more serious injury with minor insult and longer healing times. Some phases may be skipped, such as inflammation. For the provider assessing skin injury, these slower and diminished processes need consideration when treating an older person's injury (Broughton et al., 2006; Simon et al., 2018).

Definitions of Injury Terms

Abrasion: A skin wound caused by tangential trauma when the skin contacts a resistant object or surface with sufficient force. In lay terms, it is often referred to as a scrape or scratch. Abrasions may be small, such a skinned knee, or large, as seen in "road rash," and can involve different degrees of epidermal and dermal tissue loss. Different types of abrasions include scrape or brush, collar, linear, imprint, grazed, friction, and patterned.

Laceration: A soft tissue injury characterized by tearing or splitting of the tissues. It results from blunt forces, such as ripping, crushing, overstretching, pulling, bending, or shearing. Lacerations are more specifically described based on their anatomical location and appearance, for example, the older person's laceration on the hand or knee, as shown in Figs. 5.3 and 5.4, respectively.

Bruise, Contusion, Ecchymotic Spread: A bruise, also known as a contusion, is a leakage of blood from damaged vessels into tissues and is always the result of trauma. The amount of force differs with each developmental phase and comorbidity. Bruises may be superficial or deep or a combination of the two. It may be painful with swelling and locally be warm to touch due to the inflammatory phase of healing. To distinguish the size,

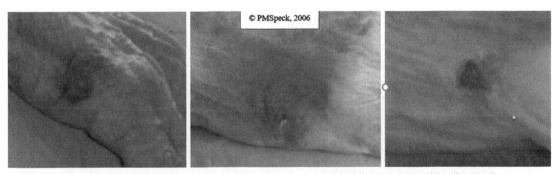

© PMSpeck, 2006

Figure 5.3 Laceration from bump on bedrail in nonagenarian person, highlighting delayed healing in phases over a 3-month time period.

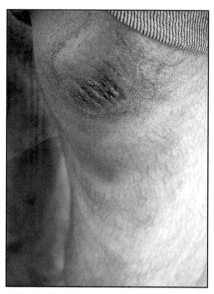

Figure 5.4 Combined abrasion, contusion, and laceration of the knee.

palpate the area if the skin is intact. A bruise results from a simple bumping into furniture or dropping something with weight onto fleshy portions of the integument. Without an alternate light source, bruises are hard to distinguish in persons with darker skin. To distinguish natural melanin deposits from bruises, it is important to understand that bruises resolve, usually within weeks. The bruise is also initially white due to hemostasis, turns red to blue to purple quickly, and progresses through resolving colors of yellow and green to brown, eventually turning to light brown as it fades away. Fig. 5.5 demonstrates the phases of a bruise and healing.

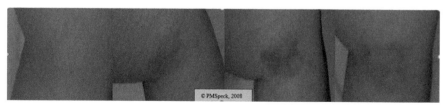

Figure 5.5 Contusion (bruise) stages of healing.

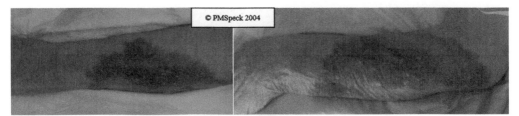

© PMSpeck 2004

Figure 5.6 Hematoma following injury, with ecchymotic spread.

Contusions of muscle, soft tissue, and internal organs results from direct, blunt, compressive force that causes blood vessels, such as the capillaries, to rupture in space. Following the initial phase of vasoconstriction, blood leaks into the surrounding soft tissue in the healing phase of vasodilation.

A *subdermal hematoma* is a collection of blood in the skin, often clotted, bulging, or mass-like. The capillary fragility is in the epidermis and dermis, as well as in the subcutaneous tissue. A hematoma is not the same as a bruise, although a hematoma may be found within a bruise. The most common cause of a hematoma is injury or trauma to the deeper capillary or blood vessels. Following injury that results in a hematoma, ecchymotic spread occurs from a gravitational pull of blood products through the layers of tissue and ultimately reveals an absence of discoloration, also called sparing, at the point of injury that may reveal the shape of impact. Fig. 5.6 demonstrates subdural hematoma and subsequent ecchymotic spread.

Ecchymosis and *ecchymotic spread* are terms used to describe an irregularly formed blue or purplish patch of blood under the epidermal skin or mucous membranes, caused when blood extravasates into the tissue between the epidermis and dermis, varying in size between millimeters to centimeters. Ecchymosis may be a result of trauma, but often in older persons, it follows a superficial sheering movement of epidermal and dermal layers, such as a scratch.

Petechiae: Tiny round purple spots less than 3 mm due to bleeding between the epidermis and dermal layers of skin are identified as petechiae. The causes include trauma, blood clotting disorders, or a result of change in circulatory pressures as seen in strangulation (McQuown et al., 2016; Pritchard, Reckdenwald, & Nordham, 2017; Zilkens et al., 2016). A petechia, plural petechiae,

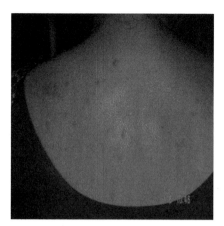

Figure 5.7 Petechiae.

is a small 1–2 mm red or purple spot on the skin, caused by a minor capillary pressure from strangulation creates a "freckled" appearance. In an unconscious strangulation patient, massive capillary ruptures coalesce in a florid appearance. Petechiae refer to one of the three descriptive types of bleeding into the skin differentiated by size, the other two being purpura and ecchymosis, demonstrated in Fig. 5.7.

Purpura: Purpura occurs when small blood vessels burst, causing blood to pool under the skin. This can create purple spots on the skin that range in size from small dots to large patches. Purpura spots are generally benign, but may indicate a more serious medical condition, such as a blood clotting disorder.

Burn: Tissue injury caused by heat, fire, caustic chemical agents, friction, electricity, or electromagnetic energy. Burns are categorized based on the severity of tissue injury: superficial (first degree), partial thickness (second degree), and full thickness (third degree) (Berry & Mancini, 2018).

Classification of Burns: A classification of burns exists for rapid communication about the severity of the burn and addresses the thickness of the burn. In older persons, the burns are likely to rapidly penetrate the epidermis and dermis, resulting in the exposure of the subcutaneous tissue of a third-degree burn. The rapidity of affecting deeper layers is directly related to the thinning of the dermal collagen structures as persons age. The classification follows in Fig. 5.8–5.13.

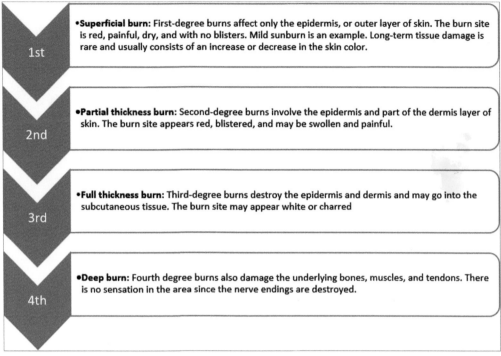

1st
•**Superficial burn:** First-degree burns affect only the epidermis, or outer layer of skin. The burn site is red, painful, dry, and with no blisters. Mild sunburn is an example. Long-term tissue damage is rare and usually consists of an increase or decrease in the skin color.

2nd
•**Partial thickness burn:** Second-degree burns involve the epidermis and part of the dermis layer of skin. The burn site appears red, blistered, and may be swollen and painful.

3rd
•**Full thickness burn:** Third-degree burns destroy the epidermis and dermis and may go into the subcutaneous tissue. The burn site may appear white or charred

4th
•**Deep burn:** Fourth degree burns also damage the underlying bones, muscles, and tendons. There is no sensation in the area since the nerve endings are destroyed.

Figure 5.8 Burn classification edited for presentation (Center for Disease Control and Prevention, 2019).

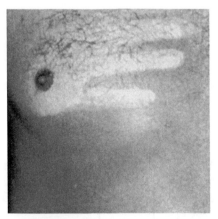

Figure 5.9 First-degree burn.

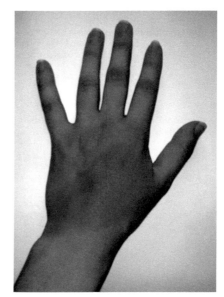

Figure 5.10 Partial thickness burn.

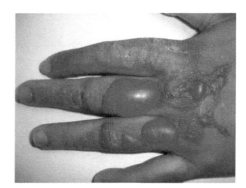

Figure 5.11 Second and third-degree burns of hand.

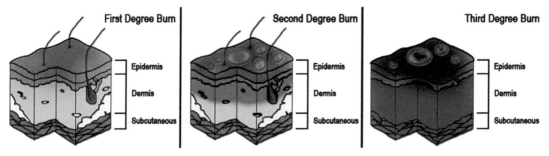

Figure 5.12 Demonstration of burn thickness and injury to integument structures.

Hematoma greater than 3 mm: A localized, swollen mass of extravasated blood that is relatively or completely confined within a subdermal or subcutaneous space.

Erythema: Redness of the skin due to capillary dilation that is a nonspecific sign for inflammation, irritation, and/or injury. Common terminology is redness.

Avulsion, cut, incision: Forcible tearing away of an anatomical structure or tissue by way of traumatic or surgical means. Avulsions may be described as full thickness with a complete loss of dermis, such as when subcutaneous fat is visible, or partial thickness with loss of epidermis where the underlying dermis is visible.

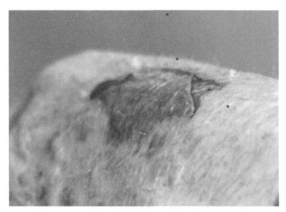

Figure 5.13 Avulsion flap of tissue on hand.

Field Triage Decision Schema

The CDC published the schema for evaluating injury, with data that support a lack of referral of older persons to trauma centers. The referral deficit is thought to be related to a lack of awareness in first responders about the fragility of older persons to minor trauma, as well as a rapid decline of older persons with unrecognized early shock. Fig. 5.14 is the consensus algorithm for field evaluation of trauma.

Table 5.2 reflects the Abbreviated Injury Scale, useful for first responders when predicting survivability of older persons. Note the lower score applies in elder injury.

Fig. 5.15 is a pictorial depiction of zones of coagulation in the first stages of healing following injury. Failure of the wound to coagulate can be due to medication, the wound being too large to coagulate, or other influences. This causes fluid loss in an older person, whose healthy hydration index is narrow, as compared with a younger person. Consequently, minor losses of fluid may have major impact, where early shock occurs not with increasing heart rate where normal is 90 beats per minute (BPM) but falls

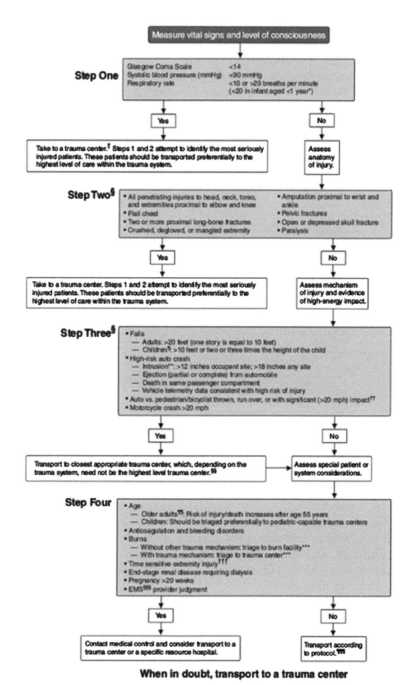

Figure 5.14 Field triage decision schema. From https://www.cdc.gov/mmwr/preview/mmwrhtml/rr6101a1.htm#Fig2.

Table 5.2 Abbreviated Injury Scale (AIS).

AIS Score	Injury
1	Minor
2	Moderate
3	Serious
4	Severe
5	Critical
6	Lethal[a]

[a]Although a perfect linear correlation with an AIS of 6 and mortality does not exist, survivability is unlikely; for older persons, a lower score, e.g., 4, may also be lethal.
CDC https://www.cdc.gov/mmwr/preview/mmwrhtml/rr5801a1.htm.

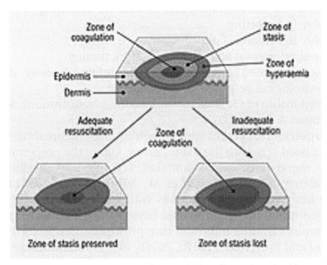

Figure 5.15 Injury depth and zones of coagulation. Reproduced with permission from Hettiaratchy, S., Dziewulski, P. (2004). Pathophysiology and types of burns. *BMJ, 328,* 1427.

into normal range for healthy persons around 60 BPM, predictive of poor outcomes for the older frail person.

Intentional Injury in Older Persons

The majority of the chapter covered injury without discussing intent. The next part of this chapter focuses on intentional bruising and injury from "physical violence, meaning acts carried out with the intention of causing physical pain or injury," (Lachs & Pillemer, 1995, p. 437) with comprehensive coverage of sensory issues, psychological responses, mental and physical functioning, as well as reporting delays and relationships to offenders. The study of elder abuse historically focused on neglect, which is underreported and misunderstood (Dong, 2012; Dong et al., 2009; Lachs, Williams, O'Brien, Pillemer, & Charlson, 1998). The most common physically violent acts toward elderly persons include "slapping, hitting, and striking with objects," which frequently results in bruises, sprains, abrasions, fractures, burn, or other wounds (O'Malley, O'Malley, Everitt, & Sarson, 1984, p. 437). Bruising studies describe injury patterns in intention injury as a marker for suspecting abuse (Wiglesworth et al., 2009; Ziminski, Wiglesworth, Austin, Phillips, & Mosqueda, 2013). Important is recognizing that suspicion followed by comprehensive evaluation and detection does not guarantee successful prosecution, which is elusive (Navarro et al., 2016). Seven barriers to the assessment of elder abuse are identified and include the following:

1. Delay in reporting
2. Delay in evidence collection
3. Impaired mental and/or physical functioning
4. Assessing intentional bruising and injury, sensory deficits, psychological response of the victim and
5. Relationship of victim to offender (Burgess, Commons, Safarik, Looper, & Ross, 2007).

Perpetrators: Persons who perpetrate elder maltreatment must have trusted access to the older person. Often, the perpetrator is a family member or other caretaker, regardless of dwelling and dependency location (Speck et al., 2014). Perpetrators of elder abuse have various presentations with commonalities, providing an opportunity for creating macrosystem approaches to prevention through trauma informed care principles (Center for Disease Control and Prevention, 2018a, 2018b; Center for Substance Abuse Treatment, 2014). Common is the presence of the following:

- Current diagnosis of mental illness
- Current abuse of alcohol
- High levels of hostility
- Poor or inadequate preparation or training for caregiving responsibilities
- Assumption of caregiving responsibilities at an early age
- Inadequate coping skills
- Exposure to abuse as a child (Center for Disease Control and Prevention, 2018a, 2018b)

Other characteristics include mental health diagnosis, with possible substance abuse, hostility, inadequate preparation to care for the older person, and caregiving at a young age. Also associated are history of child abuse and inadequate coping skills (Center for Disease Control and Prevention, 2018a, 2018b).

Case Presentations

The following cases demonstrate the difficult physical injury presentations of elder maltreatment faced by the Coordinated Community Response Teams (CCRT) in communities throughout the United States. The pseudo cases are the culmination of the author's forensic nursing experiences working on CCRTs that span collectively over 100 years.

Case 1: Unintentional Injury With Comorbidities

Margie was in her late 80s and enrolled in hospice for cancer. On this day, Bea, her care provider, was transferring her into the shower from a wheelchair. Margie became limp after standing, which can happen due to a positional change in posture from sitting to standing, and Bea grabbed her upper arm to prevent Margie from falling to the floor. As a result of Bea's reflexive grab, the upper arm had skin tearing, specifically an avulsion, which is not uncommon in Margie's condition. Although the event was not witnessed, Bea reported the incident rapidly, and the hospice nurse responded on the same day to document and assess the event and create a plan of care. Bea apologized profusely to Margie's daughter. The family wanted Bea to remain the personal care provider to avoid Margie's confusion with changes in routine care providers.

It is not uncommon for frail elders with comorbid conditions to experience unintentional integument injury. In Margie's case, she experienced long-term medication use for eczema and arthritis, which are treated using cortisone prescribed from the 1950s through the 1980s. She remained on a small dose, related to chronic use, due to inadequate secretion of ACTH and suppression of the hypothalamic adrenal axis through negative feedback. The steroid use may be related to injury healing as her injury took 6 months to fully heal. The family struggled to prevent skin injuries associated with the disease and dying process.

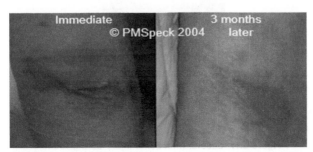

Figure 5.16 Case 1. Unintentional injury to fragile skin, affected by long-term steroid use.

Case 2: Intentional Injury With Comorbidities

Dwayne was an elderly male who was working in the garden when he was attacked by drug-seeking neighbor adolescents. He had early memory decline but continued to drive and exercise daily. While on his daily walk, three adolescent males approached him, demanding his money. He refused and was beaten with a small baseball bat. The adolescents took $20. The medical workup identified multiple facial and skull fractures, and Dwayne had little memory of the event. Dwayne was unable to identify his assailants, which is not uncommon following traumatic brain injury for any person. However, the risk to elders following traumatic head injury is persistent and decreases the capacity for short-term memory, causing physiological changes that overwhelm fragile systems in older populations. Although Dwayne did survive for almost a year, his family complained he had a precipitous decline in his memory and his personality during his recovery, needing dependent care. The loss of independence places significant burden on families not prepared for care of a dependent older person following trauma.

The adolescent males were eventually caught after murdering two other older persons using the same small baseball bat and were sentenced to short terms for aggravated assault and robbery. The prosecution failed to charge the males with murder because the males did not have premeditated intent to kill, only to rob. Failure of prosecutors to recognize assault on an older person leads to subsequent health decline and death from injuries sustained during the assault and denies justice to the elder, their families, and the community (Figs. 5.16 and 5.17).

© Speck, 1994

Figure 5.17 Case 2. Intentional injury during robbery.

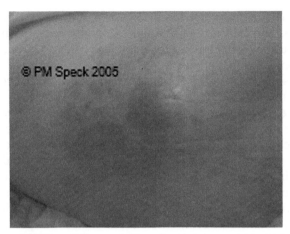

Figure 5.18 Case 3. Demonstration of early integument breakdown.

Case 3: Intentional Injury From Neglect

Sophia was in her early 80s, living with her son, who was disgusted by Sophia's continued physical demise, particularly with the new episodes of fecal incontinence. In response, Sophia's son isolated her in the closet in the garage with an outside door and a small window. He took away her underwear, placed a bucket in the closet, and told her to lay down on a plywood bed covered with a shower curtain. He told her to stay there until she could hold her bowels. When her neighbors heard her screaming for help, they called the police. The police found the closet door locked, and they broke the lock to find Sophia sitting in feces on the plywood board, crying. Her hip had some early breakdown as demonstrated in Fig. 5.18.

An ambulance arrived, and the medical technicians transferred Sophia to the emergency department. The physician admitted Sophia to the hospital for malnutrition and dehydration. She quickly returned to health following management of her admitting diagnoses, stabilizing the comorbid disease states of diabetes, hypertension, and heart disease. When her son explained that "she was crazy" and had screaming fits, her doctor told him he would prescribe her medication and sent her home with the son.

Several months later, neighbors complained they had not seen Sophia lately. The next visit by Adult Protective Services (APS) found Sophia in the locked garage closet again, but this time, she was no longer moving, was in a flimsy nightgown, laying in feces, and her mental capacity for communication was minimal. Police were called again, and Sophia went by ambulance to the hospital emergency department. APS petitioned the court on Sophia's behalf. Her injuries included malnutrition, elevated hemoglobin A1C, falling blood pressure, and decreasing kidney function. She had a decubitus ulcer on the bony prominences of her buttock and elbow. When stable, Sophia was sent to rehabilitation, where she died.

The son had a history of alcoholism and admitted to locking his mother in the closet to keep her quiet. He also admitted that when she experienced fecal incontinence, he cleaned her with the hose before he brought dinner to her in the closet. He put a local heater in the closet to keep the area warm and bragged that he washed the area twice every day. He resisted putting Sophia in the nursing home because he relied on her check for their food. Law enforcement arrested Sophia's son for neglect and told the prosecutor that the son's actions contributed to Sophia's death. However, when the son told the prosecutor to call their physician to make a statement, the physician told the prosecutor that she was in poor health with multiple comorbidities and anything could have contributed to her death, and followed up with, "I've known this family for over 45 years, and there is not a finer family or son." The prosecutor declined to bring charges.

The son fits the profile of a person at risk of perpetrating elder maltreatment. However, the system failed to protect Sophia from abysmal and neglectful treatment, and these authors believe the failure to protect hastened her death.

Summary

The purpose of the chapter on integument and injury addresses the physiology of the aging integument, wounds, and the potential for provider over- or underidentifying physical abuse of older persons. The diagnosis of physical abuse by licensed HCPs and knowledge about the existing comorbidities offer explanations for the seriousness of the actual or potential injury, creating complexities for the provider in the diagnosis of elder physical abuse. Self-neglect by an older person with competence and capacity is a protected constitutional liberty related to self-determination, even if others see the situation as a danger to health. Slow decline with disease states, such as seen in hydrocephalus or dementia, requires a full medical workup with the permission of the older person. Consequently, the authors recommend a full medical workup followed by a collaborative effort by coordinated community resource and response teams in analyzing the findings, sharing the report, and making recommendations that include the wishes of the older person whenever possible.

References

Berry, J., & Mancini, M. (2018). *Classification of burns.* Retrieved from https://www.urmc.rochester.edu/encyclopedia/content.aspx?ContentTypeID=90&ContentID=P09575.

Broughton, G., 2nd, Janis, J. E., & Attinger, C. E. (2006). The basic science of wound healing. *Plastic and Reconstructive Surgery, 117*(7 Suppl. l), 12s–34s. https://doi.org/10.1097/01.prs.0000225430.42531.c2.

Burgess, A. W., Commons, M. L., Safarik, M. E., Looper, R. R., & Ross, S. N. (2007). Sex offenders of the elderly: Classification by motive, typology, and predictors of severity of crime. *Aggression and Violent Behavior, 12*(5), 582–597.

Center for Disease Control and Prevention [CDC]. (2018a). *Elder abuse: Risk and protective factors.* Retrieved from https://www.cdc.gov/violenceprevention/elderabuse/riskprotectivefactors.html.

Center for Disease Control and Prevention [CDC]. (2018b). *Elder abuse: Definitions.* Retrieved from https://www.cdc.gov/violenceprevention/elderabuse/definitions.html.

Center for Disease Control and Prevention. (2019). *Burns.* Atlanta, GA: CDC. Found at https://www.cdc.gov/masstrauma/factsheets/public/burns.pdf.

Center for Substance Abuse Treatment. (2014). *Trauma-informed care in behavioral health services: Treatment improvement protocol (TIP) series, no. 57.* Retrieved from https://www.ncbi.nlm.nih.gov/books/NBK207209/.

Clarysse, K., Kivlahan, C., Beyer, I., & Gutermuth, J. (2018). Signs of physical abuse and neglect in the mature patient. *Clinics in Dermatology, 36*(2), 264–270. https://doi.org/10.1016/j.clindermatol.2017.10.018.

Dong, X. (2012). Advancing the field of elder abuse: Future directions and policy implications. *Journal of the American Geriatrics Society, 60*(11), 2151–2156. https://doi.org/10.1111/j.1532-5415.2012.04211.x.

Dong, X., Simon, M., Mendes de Leon, C., Fulmer, T., Beck, T., Hebert, L., … Evans, D. (2009). Elder self-neglect and abuse and mortality risk in a community-dwelling population. *Journal of the American Medical Association, 302*(5), 517–526. https://doi.org/10.1001/jama.2009.1109.

Earl-Royal, E., Shofer, F., Ruggieri, D., Frasso, R., & Holena, D. (2016). Variation of blunt traumatic injury with age in older adults: Statewide analysis 2011–14. *Western Journal of Emergency Medicine, 17*(6), 702–708. https://doi.org/10.5811/westjem.2016.9.31003.

Genes and Disease. (1998a). *Skin and connective tissue.* Retrieved from https://www.ncbi.nlm.nih.gov/books/NBK22247/.

Genes and Disease. (1998b). *Glands and hormones.* Retrieved from https://www.ncbi.nlm.nih.gov/books/NBK22231/.

Grey, J. E., Enoch, S., & Harding, K. G. (2006). Wound assessment. *British Medical Journal (Clinical Research Ed.), 332*(7536), 285–288. https://doi.org/10.1136/bmj.332.7536.285.

Grossman, M. D., Miller, D., Scaff, D. W., & Arcona, S. (2002). When is an elder old? Effect of preexisting conditions on mortality in geriatric trauma. *The Journal of Trauma, 52*(2), 242–246.

Horan, T. C., Andrus, M., & Dudeck, M. A. (2008). CDC/NHSN surveillance definition of health care–associated infection and criteria for specific types of infections in the acute care setting. *American Journal of Infection Control, 36*(5), 309–332. https://doi.org/10.1016/j.ajic.2008.03.002.

Informed Health Online. (2009). *How does skin work?*. Retrieved from https://www.ncbi.nlm.nih.gov/pubmedhealth/PMH0072439/.

Jacobs, D. G., Plaisier, B. R., Barie, P. S., Hammond, J. S., Holevar, M. R., Sinclair, K. E., ... Wahl, W. (2003). Practice management guidelines for geriatric trauma: The EAST practice management guidelines work group. *The Journal of Trauma, 54*(2), 391–416. https://doi.org/10.1097/01.Ta.0000042015.54022.Be.

Johnson, J. (2018, January 29). Serosanguineous drainage: Is it normal? *MedicalNewsToday*. Found at https://www.medicalnewstoday.com/articles/320765.php.

Lachs, M. S., & Pillemer, K. (1995). Abuse and neglect of elderly persons. *New England Journal of Medicine, 332*(7), 437–443. https://doi.org/10.1056/nejm199502163320706.

Lachs, M. S., Williams, C. S., O'Brien, S., Pillemer, K. A., & Charlson, M. E. (1998). The mortality of elder mistreatment. *Journal of the American Medical Association, 280*(5), 428–432.

Lane, P., Sorondo, B., & Kelly, J. J. (2003). Geriatric trauma patients-are they receiving trauma center care? *Academic Emergency Medicine, 10*(3), 244–250.

Larner, J., Matar, H., Goldman, V. S., & Chilcott, R. P. (2015). Development of a cumulative irritation model for incontinence-associated dermatitis. *Archives for Dermatological Research. Archiv für Dermatologische Forschung, 307*(1), 39–48. https://doi.org/10.1007/s00403-014-1526-y.

LeLievre, S. (2000). Skin care for older people with incontinence. *Elderly Care, 11*(10), 36–38.

Lofaso, V. M., & Rosen, T. (2014). Medical and laboratory indicators of elder abuse and neglect. *Clinics in Geriatric Medicine, 30*(4), 713–728. https://doi.org/10.1016/j.cger.2014.08.003.

MacKenzie, E. J., Rivara, F. P., Jurkovich, G. J., Nathens, A. B., Frey, K. P., Egleston, B. L., ... Scharfstein, D. O. (2006). A national evaluation of the effect of trauma-center care on mortality. *New England Journal of Medicine, 354*(4), 366–378. https://doi.org/10.1056/NEJMsa052049.

McGwin, G.,J., MacLennan, P. A., Fife, J. B., Davis, G. G., & Rue, L. W., 3rd (2004). Preexisting conditions and mortality in older trauma patients. *The Journal of Trauma, 56*(6), 1291–1296.

McQuown, C., Frey, J., Steer, S., Fletcher, G. E., Kinkopf, B., Fakler, M., & Prulhiere, V. (2016). Prevalence of strangulation in survivors of sexual assault and domestic violence. *American Journal of Emergency Medicine, 34*(7), 1281–1285. https://doi.org/10.1016/j.ajem.2016.04.029.

Morris, J. A., Jr., MacKenzie, E. J., & Edelstein, S. L. (1990). The effect of preexisting conditions on mortality in trauma patients. *Journal of the American Medical Association, 263*(14), 1942–1946.

National Council on Aging. (2018). *Elder abuse facts*. Retrieved from https://www.ncoa.org/public-policy-action/elder-justice/elder-abuse-facts/.

Navarro, A. E., Wysong, J., DeLiema, M., Schwartz, E. L., Nichol, M. B., & Wilber, K. H. (2016). Inside the black box: The case review process of an elder abuse forensic center. *The Gerontologist, 56*(4), 772–781. https://doi.org/10.1093/geront/gnv052.

Newgard, C. D., Holmes, J. F., Haukoos, J. S., Bulger, E. M., Staudenmayer, K., Wittwer, L., ... Renee, Y. (2016). Improving early identification of the high-risk elderly trauma patient by emergency medical services. *Injury, 47*(1), 19–25. https://doi.org/10.1016/j.injury.2015.09.010.

O'Malley, T. A., O'Malley, H. C., Everitt, D. E., & Sarson, D. (1984). Categories of family-mediated abuse and neglect of elderly persons. *Journal of the American Geriatrics Society, 32*(5), 362–369.

Ong, A. W., Omert, L. A., Vido, D., Goodman, B. M., Protetch, J., Rodriguez, A., & Jeremitsky, E. (2009). Characteristics and outcomes of trauma patients with ICU lengths of stay 30 days and greater: A seven-year retrospective study. *Critical Care, 13*(5), R154. https://doi.org/10.1186/cc8054.

OpenStax College. (2018). *Age related changes to the integumentary system [chapter 5]. AtD course.* Rice College. Retrieved from http://cnx.org/contents/14fb4ad7-39a1-4eee-ab6e-3ef2482e3e22@7.1@7.1.

Paranitharan, P., & Pollanen, M. S. (2008). The interaction of injury and disease in the elderly: A case report of fatal elder abuse. *Journal of Forensic and Legal Medicine, 16*(6), 346–349. https://doi.org/10.1016/j.jflm.2008.12.019.

Pavlik, V. N., Hyman, D. J., Festa, N. A., & Dyer, C. B. (2001). Quantifying the problem of abuse and neglect in adults—analysis of a statewide database. *Journal of the American Geriatrics Society, 49*(1), 45–48. https://doi.org/10.1046/j.1532-5415.2001.49008.x.

Pillemer, K., & Finkelhor, D. (1988). The prevalence of elder abuse: A random sample survey. *The Gerontologist, 28*(1), 51–57. https://doi.org/10.1093/geront/28.1.51.

Pritchard, A. J., Reckdenwald, A., & Nordham, C. (2017). Nonfatal strangulation as part of domestic violence: A review of research. *Trauma, Violence, and Abuse, 18*(4), 407–424. https://doi.org/10.1177/1524838015622439.

Sattin, R. W. (2002). Geriatric trauma: The continuing epidemic. *Journal of the American Geriatrics Society, 50*(2), 394–395.

Seifert, A. W., Monaghan, J. R., Voss, S. R., & Maden, M. (2012). Skin regeneration in adult axolotls: A blueprint for scar-free healing in vertebrates. *PLoS One, 7*(4), e32875. https://doi.org/10.1371/journal.pone.0032875.

Simon, P. E., Moutran, H. A., & Romo, T. (2018, May 24). *Skin wound healing.* Medscape. Retrieved from https://emedicine.medscape.com/article/884594-overview#a3.

Speck, P. M., Hartig, M. T., Likes, W., Bowdre, T., Carney, A. Y., Ekroos, R. A., ... Diana, K. (2014). Case series of sexual assault in older persons. *Clinics in Geriatric Medicine, 30*(4), 779–806. https://doi.org/10.1016/j.cger.2014.08.007.

Takeo, M., Lee, W., & Ito, M. (2015). Wound healing and skin regeneration. *Cold Spring Harbor Perspectives in Medicine, 5*(1), a023267. https://doi.org/10.1101/cshperspect.a023267.

Tan, C. P., Ng, A., & Civil, I. (2004). Co-morbidities in trauma patients: Common and significant. *New Zealand Medical Journal, 117*(1201), U1044.

Timms, L. (2011). Effect of nutrition on wound healing in older people: A case study. *British Journal of Nursing, 20*(11), S4–S10. https://doi.org/10.12968/bjon.2011.20.Sup6.s4.

US Legal Inc. (2016). *Washerwoman syndrome law and legal definition.* Retrieved from https://definitions.uslegal.com/w/washerwoman-syndrome/.

Wiglesworth, A., Austin, R., Corona, M., Schneider, D., Liao, S., Gibbs, L., & Mosqueda, L. (2009). Bruising as a marker of physical elder abuse. *Journal of the American Geriatrics Society, 57*(7), 1191–1196. https://doi.org/10.1111/j.1532-5415.2009.02330.x.

Wilkinson, H. N., & Hardman, M. J. (2017). The role of estrogen in cutaneous ageing and repair. *Maturitas, 103*, 60–64. https://doi.org/10.1016/j.maturitas.2017.06.026.

Young, L. M. (2014). Elder physical abuse. *Clinics in Geriatric Medicine, 30*(4), 761–768. https://doi.org/10.1016/j.cger.2014.08.005.

Zilkens, R. R., Phillips, M. A., Kelly, M. C., Mukhtar, S., Aqif, S., James, B., & Smith, D. A. (2016). Non-fatal strangulation in sexual assault: A study of clinical and assault characteristics highlighting the role of intimate partner violence. *Journal of Forensic and Legal Medicine, 43*, 1–7. https://doi.org/10.1016/j.jflm.2016.06.005.

Ziminski, C. E., Wiglesworth, A., Austin, R., Phillips, L. R., & Mosqueda, L. (2013). Injury patterns and causal mechanisms of bruising in physical elder abuse. *Journal of Forensic Nursing, 9*(2), 84–91. https://doi.org/10.1097/JFN.0b013e31827d51d0. Quiz E81-E82.

Zimmer-Gembeck, M. J., Southard, P. A., Hedges, J. R., Mullins, R. J., Rowland, D., Stone, J. V., & Trunkey, D. D. (1995). Triage in an established trauma system. *The Journal of Trauma, 39*(5), 922–928.

6

SEXUAL ASSAULT AND RAPE OF THE OLDER PERSON

Patricia M. Speck,[1] Diana K. Faugno[2]

[1]School of Nursing, Department of Family, Community & Health Systems, University of Alabama at Birmingham, Birmingham, AL, United States;
[2]Eisenhower Medical Center, Rancho Mirage, CA, United States

CHAPTER OUTLINE
Introduction   140
Definitions   141
Aging and the Genitalia   141
Case 1   142
   Discussion   143
Sexuality and the Older Person   143
Case 2   145
   Discussion   145
Offenders With Paraphilias That Include Older Persons   146
Case 3   148
   Discussion   148
Sexually Transmitted Diseases   149
Case 4   149
   Discussion   150
Sex, Rape, and Genital Injury   150
Sexual Assault, Sexuality, and Dementia   152
Case 5   152
   Discussion   153
Case 6   154
   Discussion   155
Overcoming Trauma   155
Case 7   156
   Discussion   156
Conclusion   157
References   158
Further Reading   162

Elder Abuse. https://doi.org/10.1016/B978-0-12-815779-4.00006-9

Introduction

All older persons are vulnerable to sexual maltreatment if there is a rapist in their midst. Effects of sexual assault and rape have lifelong consequences for the young victim who denies the person's quality of life and health in their older years. Thus, sexual assault and rape is a life-altering event, undermining an individual's confidence and perception of safety, regardless of the developmental age or stage of life. The acute traumatic reaction and allostatic load following a sexual assault or rape are the beginning of stress-related biological processes that promote an evolutionary response that results in a diminished physical and mental health, especially for the older person (McEwen, 1998; McEwen & Seeman, 1999; Schafran, 1996; Stein et al., 2004). Although morbidity and mortality increases in older victims following various forms of violence, including sexual assault, not all succumb to disability, frailty, or death, even with serious chronic stressors (Bright & Bowland, 2008; Brown, 2012; Fisher & Regan, 2006). Who will overcome the biological responses of trauma is predictable for populations of frail older persons without social support, but not for the individual elder. The need for research about the elder's response to violent crime is necessary to understand what is required to promote health and well-being following sexual assault because whether aware or not, the older person is at an increased risk of a sudden health decline and even possible death (Anda et al., 2009; Burgess, Brown, Bell, Ledray, & Poarch, 2005; Burgess, Dowdell, & Prentky, 2000; Juster, McEwen, & Lupien, 2010; B. McEwen, 2002; Selye, 1956; Selye, 1974).

Sexual assault and rape is a violent invasion that is intentional and harmful toward an individual or group of individuals, usually female. These are crimes perpetrated by individuals or groups with preferential paraphilias toward older people, but they are also variable with multiple modi operandi (Lasher, McGrath, & Cumming, 2014). The opportunity for rape occurs with community and institutional dwellers, those with full capacity, diminished capacity, and those with no capacity to consent (Speck et al., 2014). Health-care providers rarely have all information about an older person, including their early life experiences of war, rape, or significant loss, even if the older person dwells in a supervised institution. Therefore, in this chapter, a structured presentation of current information hopes to provide the reader with evidence-based knowledge and demonstrations of typical scenarios of sexual assault reports by raising suspicion and subsequent reporting of situations where there is risk for or actual elder sexual maltreatment.

Definitions

"Rape is a legal term … [referring] to any penetration of a body orifice (mouth, vagina, or anus) involving force or the threat of force or incapacity (i.e., associated with young or old age, cognitive or physical disability, or drug or alcohol intoxication) and non-consent" (Linden, 2011, p. 834). The Center for Disease Control and Prevention (CDC) is a leader in understanding sexual violence, including sexual assault and rape, and reporting the effectiveness of programs designed to prevent the crimes associated with sexual violence. The current understanding about sexual violence is divided into the following types:

- Completed or attempted forced penetration of a victim
- Completed or attempted alcohol/drug-facilitated penetration of a victim
- Completed or attempted forced acts in which a victim is made to penetrate a perpetrator or someone else
- Completed or attempted alcohol/drug-facilitated acts in which a victim is made to penetrate a perpetrator or someone else
- Nonphysically forced penetration which occurs after a person is pressured verbally or through intimidation or misuse of authority to consent or acquiesce
- Unwanted sexual contact
- Noncontact unwanted sexual experiences (Basile et al., 2016).

Aging and the Genitalia

There is atrophy of the older persons sex organs (e.g., penis, testes, clitoris, labia minora, and vagina) that is a direct result of diminished sex hormone levels.

Aging is a process determined by genetics, environment, and lifestyle. As women and men age, the integument loses elasticity, moisture, and circulation. This process is discussed in detail in Chapter 5: Wound Identification in Physical Abuse. The gradual loss of estrogen in women and testosterone in men diminishes the sexual response. Older persons, both male and female, have physiologic changes promoting the possibility of injury with coitus. Physical limitations can also create challenges in positioning due to normal physical limitations of aging, hence sexual activities primarily including touch without penetration are common (Lamonica & Pagiaro, 2006). The aging female has functional changes that include thinning tissue, friability, and loss of adipose and connective tissue support, as well as loss of pubic hair (Clark, Newman, & Speck, 2017; Faugno & Speck, 2011; Phanjoo, 2000). Female genitalia after menopause continue to lose form in structure and tissue, resulting in vulvar atrophy (Faugno & Speck, 2011; Muram, Miller, & Cutler, 1992; Phanjoo, 2000; Poulos & Sheridan, 2008). There is atrophy of the older persons' sex organs, such as of the penis, testes, clitoris, labia minora, and vagina. This is a direct result of diminished sex hormone levels. Not only are erections of poor quality, there is a reduced desire for coital sex, however not of intimacy or touch. Women may specifically experience thinning of vaginal mucosa and reduction in lubrication, which leads to dyspareunia pain during intercourse, painful orgasms, and they are susceptible to injury (Phanjoo, 2000; Poulos & Sheridan, 2008). Topical estrogens are often prescribed for the sexually active woman to promote a reduction in dyspareunia, provide incontinence control, and reduce frequent urinary tract infections (Raz, 2011). In the women who use topical estrogens, there is a cellular response of hypertrophy and hyperplasia from the vaginal epithelium with concurrent improved blood flow and turgor related to reestablishment of the integument matrix. There is some evidence that estrogen is protective in consensual coitus, but also in forced coitus as estrogen improves the healing process because the postmenopausal vaginal vault responds with lower pH, which in turn diminishes growing pathogens in basic vaginal environments (McCann, Miyamoto, Boyle, & Rogers, 2007; Raz, 2011; Speck, 2007). Regardless, in older women, the vagina shortens and narrows, but the older male penis also shortens, where phallus erections delay and are less hard. Even if older persons cannot complete the act of coitus due to aging changes, older persons need and seek physically intimate relationships throughout their lives up until they die.

Case 1

Jeannie was 70 years old and met a 65-year-old man. She wanted to have sex with him but anticipated that it would hurt. She had sex anyway. Her symptoms began the next day and included dysuria, with burning and hesitancy. She was also incontinent, more than usual. She went to her primary care provider and asked if she caught a sexually transmitted disease (STD or STI), but more importantly, was there was anything to help her have sex. She told the provider that before her husband died 20 years before, she had a cream that helped her have sex with her husband. Since then, she never met a man she wanted to have sex with, until this one. Jeannie's physical examination of the genitalia showed marked inflammation, edema, and tears that separated superior and posterior labial adhesions, as well as superficially transected posterior fourchette and fossa navicularis margins at the six o'clock position. The urethra was prolapsed with petechiae. The vulva and proximal vaginal areas were edematous and weeping a serosanguinous fluid. There was no distal vagina injury. The cervix was identified as a small slit and was without injury. When asked, Jeannie reported that "he couldn't get on a full hard-on," which explains the possibility of local vulva and proximal vaginal injury with lack of upper vaginal or cervical injury.

Discussion

Older persons are the fastest growing population with new STIs. While menopausal women do not worry about pregnancy, the thinning tissue makes them high risk for blood-borne pathogens, such as HIV, hepatitis B and C, human papillion virus (HPV), as well as local infections including chlamydia, gonorrhea, or *Escherichia coli*. The risk for infection is particularly high if there is injury during intercourse. In Jeannie's case, the urine was negative for pathogens, and the STI workup was negative. The provider prescribed estrogen cream intravaginally. Within 24 hours of topical application, Jeannie reported she was improving and no longer incontinent. On a return visit, Jeannie reports that the sex is improving for both partners, and she has no problems with penetration or during and after the act of sex.

Sexuality and the Older Person

The benefits of healthy sexuality, not lost with aging, create a sense of normalcy in older persons lives.

Loss is associated with aging and includes loss of health, loss of loved ones, loss of youthful appearance, and loss of mental agility, all which has been covered in other chapters. The fact is that aging has gains and includes experience and wisdom, and sometimes new partners. For many, aging also includes growing families and large networks of friends, gathered over a lifetime of experiences and interests, including sexual interests. One area not frequently covered by a society influenced by agism is sex and sexuality in the older person, and the agism attitudes transmit to those with disability and dementia (Connolly et al., 2012; Tsatali & Tsolaki, 2014).

Older persons today include the old-old (the Greatest Generation), the old (Silent Generation), and those entering old age (the Baby Boomer). The Greatest Generation did not talk about sex. The Silent Generation produced Master's and Johnson's landmark study about sex and sexuality, and the Baby Boomers experimented with sex, drugs, and rock 'n roll. Today, the Baby Boomers entering old age expect sex to be part of their lives and they expect to self-determine the type of sex they practice, a subject taboo to their parents. Responding to the consumer demand, medicine originally developed for blood pressure is used for its desired side effect of improving erection. Testosterone herbals developed to diminish body fat are also popular with aging males for this reason. Estrogen replacement remains a frequent request from menopausal women experiencing vaginal burning and pain with voluntary coitus. The Baby Boomers continue to have their appetite for sexual activity and intimacy long past their old age.

All older persons want to feel loved and seek out loving stimulation. The benefits of healthy sexuality creates a sense of normalcy in older persons lives, which is not replaced with friends or other social activities (DeLamater & Sill, 2005; Inelman, Gasparini, & Enzi, 2005; Lichtenberg, 2014; Lindau et al., 2007). Unfortunately, society suffering from agism continues to view older adults as asexual (Anderson & Sheridan, 2012). In fact, older adults are sexually responsive and enjoy a variety of sexual activities. Today, masturbation is accepted by most, and older couples frequent sex shops; older person enjoy a variety of sexual activities, each self-determined (Tarzia, Fetherstonhaugh, & Bauer, 2012). The benefit of frequency in a healthy sexual relationship promotes an intimate routine in the lives of older adults, which cannot be replaced with friendships or other social interaction (DeLamater & Sill, 2005; Inelman et al., 2005; Karraker, Delamater, & Schwartz, 2011; Lichtenberg, 2014; Lindau et al., 2007). However, nursing homes commonly restrict sexual activities among residents, whereas progressive homes expect and provide privacy for sexual activity among residents (Somes & Donatelli, 2012). As the older population grows to become one in five persons, the expectation is that institutions will change to accommodate the sexually active older person, even in dementia care, to meet the demand of the older persons' sexual autonomy. The puritanical days of "no sex for older persons" are fading rapidly.

Case 2

Bernie met his wife, Janice, at church. Both Bernie and Janice's spouses died a few years before. Bernie and Janice enjoyed church activities together, and as they fell in love, all children approved of their marriage. Five years after they met, they married and remained active in the church until Janice developed Alzheimer's disease 15 years later. After the diagnosis, Bernie tried to care for Janice at home, but he was getting too old to safely care for her, so he admitted Janice into the nursing home where she quickly deteriorated. However, Bernie visited every day. During his visits, he closed the door to Janice's room. Nursing home personnel heard grunting from the room and found what appeared to be semen on Janice's sheets and underwear. The physician told Bernie to stop the conjugal visits. Bernie argued that it was good for Janice who had no symptoms or genitalia injury and was always calm and settled after he left to go home in the evening. The nursing home supervisor told Janice's children about their suspicions, and one daughter filed a complaint with the police. Police arrested Bernie for sexual assault of a dependent adult, his wife.

Discussion

Children often do not tolerate sexual activities between their parent and another. In this case, Bernie was the husband and legal guardian to Janice, and under their state law, Bernie had conjugal rights. Bernie admitted he was rubbing against Janice because Janice liked to fondle him, even in her dementia, but he denied penetration. Janice's daughter filed for guardian status, removing Bernie and severing not only his conjugal rights as Janice's husband but his right to visit his wife. The daughter sought a "no contact" order from the judge, who complied. The sexual assault case moved forward. In the meanwhile, without the daily routine with Bernie, Janice quickly deteriorated. Within 3 weeks of Bernie's arrest and lack of contact, Janice died. The jury found Bernie not guilty, but not in time to tell his wife goodbye.

Often children make decisions that are not in the best interest of their parent, but rather, adult children's decisions are rooted on their beliefs about what the "golden" age should be like. Conjugal visits are controversial in most communities. If the nursing home has not addressed the issue, specifically limits of acceptable activity, miscommunication occurs. Bernie reported to the newspaper that had he known the nursing home would not allow conjugal visits, he would have kept Janice at home, and he mused, she probably would still be alive. Nursing homes that allow residents to develop relationships and act on the relationships in the privacy of their rooms, without supervision, do exist (Bauer, 1999; Lester, Kohen, Stefanacci, & Feuerman, 2016). The choice of the activity and relationship includes changing partners frequently. The progressive attitudes about older persons' autonomy in sexual relationships promises to prevent situations like Bernie and Janice for many in the future.

Offenders With Paraphilias That Include Older Persons

Latest reporting shows as many as 14% of residents in nursing home facilities are registered sex offenders.

Offenders plan their sexual crimes through fantasy and practice, using failed attempts to plan differently in future opportunities (Lasher et al., 2014; Mitchell, Angelone, Kohlberger, & Hirschman, 2009; Terry & Freilich, 2012). Common perpetrators of elder sexual abuse include friends, live-in nursing aids, nursing home assistants, family members, other relatives, quasi-relatives, and other types of care providers that are alone to care for the elderly individual (Speck et al., 2014), engaging in unusual or inappropriate actions that appear to be from a sex role relationship between the perpetrator of elder sexual abuse and the victim. The typical signs and indicators of sexual abuse against the elderly can be either behavioral or physical. They include the following:

- Sustaining a pelvic injury
- Having problems walking or sitting
- Developing a STD
- Torn, bloody, or stained underwear
- Bruises of the genitals or inner thigh
- Bleeding from the anus or genitals
- Irritation or pain of the anus or genitals

- Panic attacks
- Signs of posttraumatic stress disorder
- Symptoms of agitation
- Social or emotional withdrawal from others
- Engaging in inappropriate, unusual, or aggressive sexual activities
- Suicide attempts

Sex offenders that target older persons have paraphilias that support a proclivity toward elders called gerontophilia (Burgess, Commons, Safarik, Looper, & Ross, 2007). Older literature classified offenders by severity of and motivation for the crime (Burgess et al., 2007). The offender classification includes opportunistic and nonsadistic rapists, those who commit the lowest severity levels of crime, such as touching without penetration. Another classification includes offenders who are classified as pervasive anger and vindictive, those who commit the highest severity of crime scores, ranging from no penetration to multiple rapes and murders. Predicting factors by severity included expressed aggression, mood state with anger, victim restraint, and offense planning (Burgess et al., 2007). Recent literature describing convicted rapists of elder women reports that men who "offend against older women are generally younger, are more violent, and are more likely to use a weapon and cause injury and death..." (Browne, Hines, & Tully, 2018, p. 16). However, the selection bias in the Burgess or Brown study of men convicted reflects those in prison and not men who escape detection in the community through the development of relationships for financial or other gain. In these cases, grooming is the process by which an offender draws a victim into a sexual relationship and maintains that relationship in secrecy using their authority and possibly supervision, such as in an institution as caregiver, to delay and avoid deception (Terry & Freilich, 2012). These offenders comprise a class that goes undetected, committing unspeakable sex crimes against older persons.

Coupled with the propensity toward nondisclosure about sex, even if rape, the older person is trapped until or unless an accidental disclosure occurs. Sexual predators often choose environments to work or visit where they have access to victims who are vulnerable or unsupervised. As release of sexual offenders from prisons increases because of increasing medical needs of older incarcerated men, some are moving into nursing home. Latest reporting shows as many as 14% of residents in nursing home facilities are registered sex offenders (Government Accounting Office, 2006).

Case 3

Anna, a 65-year-old woman, was a resident of a skilled nursing home since her car crash 10 years ago. In a vegetative state, Anna receives scheduled tube feedings and medications. At 6:00 a.m., the staff nurse walked into her room to find a male maintenance worker in Anna's bed, spooning her from behind. The male coworker got out of the bed and left the room without speaking. The staff nurse implemented the emergency protocol for individual incidents and called an ambulance to transport Anna to the hospital. The health-care provider examined Anna and described a traumatic hemorrhoid with slight weeping of serosanguinous fluid and active bleeding from several anal fissures, along with feces stains. A kit collection occurred, and police took the kit and Anna's clothing to the forensic laboratory.

Discussion

Anna was dependent on the care of others in a nursing home. In this case, nursing homes that choose to provide 24/7 care year-round have a responsibility for maintaining safe environments. Nursing staff turnover is significant in nursing homes, particularly during austere times in governmental, not-for-profit, or commercial enterprises. In this case, the state investigatory agencies evaluated the personnel to patient ratios, as well as the policies and procedures for handling sexual assault cases. Regardless, there were strong recommendations for retraining personnel about mandatory reporting when there is suspicion of sexual assault or abuse.

In this case, there was an eyewitness, and the forensic laboratory evaluation discovered male DNA from the anal fold. The male worker matched the detected DNA. There was also an eyewitness to circumstantial elements of the assault, placing the worker with Anna at the time reported. Although the eyewitness could not see the actual assault, actions taken on discovery create strong correlations between the injury and DNA deposits. It would be difficult to determine cause and mechanism of injury had there not been a witness.

In similar cases with no witness, the untrained health-care provider might label the detected injury as related to vigorous wiping during perineal care, which could lead to no need for evaluation of the rectum. Vigorous wiping may also be a sign of assault, and many offenders have described sexual pleasure through vigorous rubbing of female genitalia, injuring tissue and creating pain in vulnerable older persons (Burgess, 2006).

There was no prosecution because there was no credible witness, which is a constitutional guarantee, as even the staff nurse witness did not see the actual injury of penetration. The opinion of the medical evaluator about injury due to penetration was conjecture. Therefore, the sheriff and prosecutor declined to consider that Anna's event met the criteria necessary for prosecution. The suspect did not return to work.

Sexually Transmitted Diseases

Older persons experiencing sexual assault have an increased risk of disease transmission due to the menopausal changes in the anogenital regions and other body systems, for example, the changes in integumentary. Injuries most commonly occur in the vulva and vagina, as well as the anus, when there is penetration. These common injuries are seen in the labia minora crural folds, the posterior fourchette, and the fossa navicularis. Other injuries include vaginal stretching, leaving horizontal streaks along the Langerhan lines. Anal injuries carry the same risk as assaults on younger persons due to the increased vasculature of the rectum. Hence, there are recommendations for treatment postsexual assault. The medical treatment recommendations include an empiric antimicrobial regimen for chlamydia, gonorrhea, and trichomonas and postexposure vaccine for Hepatitis B. HIV postexposure prophylaxis (PEP) recommendations are individualized according to risk. Emergency contraception and HPV vaccination are not recommended for obvious reasons. For more information, see CDC 2015 Sexually Transmitted Diseases Treatment Guidelines located at https://www.cdc.gov/std/tg2015/sexual-assault.htm.

Case 4

Althea is a 95-year-old community dweller who lives with her boyfriend of 20 years. Althea said she was having difficulty with her balance. She said, "I got out my cane" for walking. Then, Althea reported that she was home alone when a man came to the door and asked for a drink of water. She said to him, "wait on the porch, and I'll fetch some." When she went to the kitchen, he entered the home and raped Althea. Althea reported he was real nice, let her walk slowly back to the living room, and he put her on the couch before he raped her, but she couldn't get up to call for help. She said she thinks he robbed her too. But, she then said that she often misplaces things. The forensic nurse completed the medical forensic evaluation and shared her findings with Althea and discussed providing Althea medication to prevent disease. Althea was happy to take antibiotics but refused the PEP saying, "Young lady, I'll die before HIV can kill me!"

Discussion

Older persons have wisdom about life and losses. In this case, Althea refused medication that would make her ill, possibly more ill than contracting a disease. Additionally, older persons view death for their loved ones and themselves uniquely. Like other old-old, most are not worried about death per se, but rather are worried about being in pain while dying and the impact on those left behind (Chan & Pang, 2007; Fleming, Farquhar, Cambridge City over-75s Cohort study collaboration, Brayne, & Barclay, 2016). A consult with Althea's primary care provider resulted in an estrogen cream prescription to promote healing, and a guaranteed follow-up visit within 24 hours of the event. At the primary care provider's office, the evaluation and laboratory confirmed that Althea was under great stress, with electrolyte imbalances and an elongated ST segment on the electrocardiogram. As a result, she was hospitalized for management of the aberrations. The nurse advised the prosecutor about the need for judicial proceedings in Althea's case because there is the risk of death following rape of an older person. The hospital interventions were unsuccessful, and Althea died in her sleep 5 days after the rape. The rapist was caught, but the prosecutor declined to prosecute for manslaughter, believing Althea died from natural causes. Future research should focus on the association between rape trauma and hastened death in older persons.

Sex, Rape, and Genital Injury

Distinguishing between forced penetration and consensual coitus is difficult in older persons for the reasons discussed in previous sections and chapters. History is an important component of the health-care provider's decision-making process and, as such, is integral for the clinical diagnosis of cause and manner of injury. In addition, the history also provides guidance for additional laboratory tests and imaging. Unlike law enforcement, which has access to all aspects of an investigation, the health-care provider has limited access to information, specifically the information from the patient themselves or the patient's representative.

Older women are thought to have more locations of injury and more serious injury following rape. The evidence is lacking and the empirical assertions arise from knowledge of the genitalia following menopause. Regardless, scarring and injury patterns provide information about some elements of a penetration, including shape and size of tears, stage of healing, and location. Not uncommon are injuries in the vulva, fossa navicularis, posterior fourchette, and perineum. Diagnosing the cause of injury is complex, especially with the addition of a condition or disease. Coexisting conditions include incontinence, static moisture, and vulvar atrophy. The presence of neutral or basic fluids, for example, urine and feces, and hospital genitourinary procedures such as catheterization are also identified conditions that may be present. Individual scratching and poor diaper conditions can also cause complications. Coexisting disease includes local infection from fecal contamination, lichen sclerosus, or growths, including cancer. As a result, the tissue becomes friable and breaks down, and the injured tissue anastomoses, creating superior or anterior labial and/or vaginal adhesions. Frequently, tearing of the labial adhesions occurs with positioning on the toilet or during genital cleaning. With indwelling catheters, iatrogenic injury is visible on the vestibular tissue, and urinary tract infections are common. If fecal incontinence is present, then bowel organisms place the dependent incontinent elder at risk for fulminant urinary tract infections and integument breakdown. This can lead to infections with the risk of developing sepsis. There is also a phenomenon of pressure sores on either side of the labia minor from indwelling catheters. However, these injuries do not transect Langerhan lines, which is common in forced or consensual coitus from the stretching of the vaginal orifice. Tears from a penis stretching the vagina initially create fibrinogen and collagen ruptures in the dermal tissue, followed by bleeding of ruptured capillaries into the dermal spaces, much like a stretch mark. The "stretch marks" follow the vaginal tube to the depth of the penetration, which may include the cervix, and there is the possibility of rupture of the posterior fornix. When any tissue exceeds the capacity to stretch, the horizontal Langerhan lines tear vertically and often transect into the fossa navicularis and perineum. Occasionally, the transection extends into the vagina and to the posterior fornix, which is a medical emergency. The genital injury scale assists forensic nurses in the evaluation of sexual assault to quantify findings (Kelly, Larkin, & Paolinetti, 2017). In the very old-old patient, injuries that warrant surgical consult require frank conversations about the benefits and risks of anesthesia. Tears that occur in the cul-de-sac are dangerous in the older female, and a decision to proximate the injury surgically is necessary. All the injuries discussed do not typically occur when there is routine topical estrogen use before the rape. However, women experiencing surgical menopause, treatments for estrogen-dependent cancer, or long-term progesterone use have similar tearing patterns when the tissue is stretched beyond capacity.

Sexual Assault, Sexuality, and Dementia

Information involving sexual assault and dementia in the elder person can be supported through information found in other chapters. The discussion of dementia and intentional injury is covered in Chapter 3. The complexity of sexual assault across the life span becomes more complex during a persons' older years, particularly if the older person is experiencing some form of dementia, moving backward through life experiences. Chapter 4 helps the reader understand the different types of dementia and examples of maltreatment. This chapter section addresses the complaints of rape when memory is a factor. Additionally, the criminal justice response following sexual assault of an older person is covered in Chapter 12. A foundational principle for the criminal justice response is that the US Constitution guarantees an individual's liberty, that is, until a court removes their liberty and appoints a guardian. A factor in the decision to prosecute includes the guarantee that an accused has the right to face their accuser. When the older person has memory decline, regardless of the aging or disease process, the credibility of the witness is undermined. Unless the prosecution can secure court recorded testimony from the witness with the opportunity for defense to challenge the witness, prosecution is unlikely if the witness lives. If the witness dies, the task of the prosecutor is to tie the hastened death to the criminal event. Without an autopsy identifying the cause as autonomic stress reaction and the manner of death as homicide or manslaughter, prosecution is unlikely. A decision tree for the medical forensic health-care provider to understand likelihood of prosecution following sexual assault of an older person sometimes relies on the assessment of memory and the capacity to consent for treatment, outlined in Fig. 6.1.

Case 5

Mary is an 85-year-old female who is a community dweller. She has lived in her home for the last 50 years. Her husband died

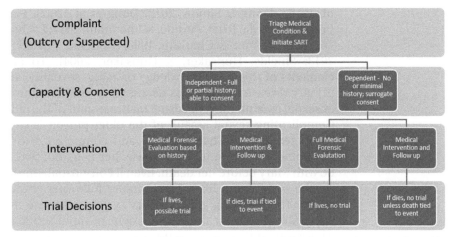

Figure 6.1 Algorithm to understand the likelihood of prosecution following sexual assault of an older person.

almost 25 years ago, and now her children checked on her daily. Mary's children became concerned because Mary was running out of money, asking for help to pay her utilities and food at the end of the month. Mary told her son that she was paying the neighbor to do some odd jobs around the house. The son confronted the neighbor, who said he, and Mary were a couple and he "loved" her. The son told the neighbor to stay away. A few days later the son went to go check on Mary, who had not been answering the son's phone calls. He found his mother deceased in the trunk of her care wearing her nightgown.

Discussion

The police opened an investigation. When questioned, the 50-year-old neighbor male told the police that he visited Mary frequently and said she hires him to "do odd jobs" around her house. He said Mary pays him $100 for each of his jobs. When questioned about the jobs, he admitted that some last only 15 minutes. He was quick to report that he "loves" Mary and he is very upset that she is deceased. He said they were drinking and dancing just the night before. He said he left her to go to bed. The neighbor's explanation was she was drunk and wandered to the garage and got in the trunk. The autopsy found genital lesions, and the forensic laboratory identified DNA belonging to the neighbor. The urinary bladder had alcohol in it, but the vitreous humor did not. The police charged the neighbor with murder. Sexual abuse or rape of the elderly is more common than previously thought, rarely recognized, and often the cause of death (Dong & Simon, 2013; Dong et al., 2009; Fisher, 2003; Friedman, Avila, Rizvi, Partida, & Friedman, 2017; Lachs, Williams, O'Brien, Pillemer, & Charlson, 1998; Schofield, Powers, & Loxton, 2013; Shields, Hunsaker, & Hunsaker, 2004). To analyze the elements of this case, knowledge of aging, sexuality, and genitourinary disease processes is necessary to evaluate the complaint of sexual assault, rape, or sexual maltreatment of the older person. Complicating sexual assault of the older person is capacity and competence. Mary had capacity and competence to remain in her home. However, in Mary's case, her neighbor was the last to be with Mary before her death. Even if consensual, the coital event can be painful and likely leaves injury following years of menopause. The resulting genitourinary system response may not be adequate to prevent the development of rapid septic symptoms caused by coitus, with confusion as a cardinal sign of sepsis. The alcohol found in the bladder is a by-product of the death process and the lack of alcohol in the vitreous humor belies the truth—alcohol consumed is concentrated in the vitreous humor when alive. In trial, the neighbor's defense was that he loved her, she frequently hired him for odd jobs for many years, and they were occasionally affectionate. The jury did not convict or acquit, so the judge declared a mistrial.

Case 6

Gertrude is an 85-year-old community dweller, living in her home of 50 years. The neighborhood declined, and her children encouraged her to move in with them, particularly since her development of cancer. Gertrude declined citing the memories were too important to her to give them up. She added, "maybe later, if I beat this cancer." One day she was working in her yard and was approached from behind by a tall male who grabbed her and put a knife to her neck. She said, "I did exactly what I was told to do"! He took me into my house and "raped me on my husband's bed! I can't go home now." Gertrude's son and daughter arrived at the clinic while Gertrude was undergoing a medical forensic evaluation. When the forensic nurse finished the medical forensic evaluation, the nurse summoned the daughter to join her mother. After the tearful reunion, the forensic nurse proceeded to offer medical prophylaxis. Gertrude declined the medication, citing that she wants to go to her oncologist before taking any more medication. The forensic nurse called the oncologist and provided a list of CDC recommended medications. The oncologist spoke to Gertrude about her frail condition due to the cancer treatments and the risks involved, so she declined the medications offered by the forensic nurse.

Discussion

Police found and arrested a suspect identified by Gertrude in a lineup. Unfortunately, Gertrude's declination of medication was fatal. She developed fulminant hepatitis B. However, before she died, the prosecutor had Gertrude testify before a grand jury, where she was cross-examined by the suspect's attorney. The grand jury charged the suspect with rape. The forensic nurse advised the prosecutor to test the suspect's blood for hepatitis B carrier status. A warrant and a visit by the prosecutor, the defense attorney, a law enforcement officer, and the forensic nurse, who drew the blood and handed it to law enforcement for transfer to the awaiting lab, resulted in a spontaneous statement from the suspect during the blood draw, "Well, I'm f*#;@d, the blood bank told me not to come back because I have the Hep thing all the time." While Gertrude died within 6 months of the rape, the grand jury testimony, along with the spontaneous admission of knowledge about the chronic hepatitis B, resulted in a charge of second degree murder. The accused pled guilty. Gertrude's case is an example of when a highly functioning community dwelling older person is able to cooperate and face the accused, where it is likely charges are filed; in this case, justice prevailed.

Overcoming Trauma

> Health-care providers do not want to talk about sex with their patients—partially due to embarrassment, a lack of knowledge, or awareness of sex.

In the early lives of the older person today, virginity had value as property. Civil courts award husbands loss of consortium in the event "his property" is damaged (Gartner, McCarthy, & Conley, 2014). This social construct that through millennia places value on virginity persists in the minds of older persons who experienced early formative years in a society valuing virginity. Even today talking about older person, sexuality remains taboo (Speck et al., 2014). In the United States, persons charged with sexual crimes publicly support their acts with justifications about the older victim behavior, particularly if sexualized in dementia. When alcohol and consent is used to justify the opportunity, for example, stating that"she did not say no," or when the opportunistic rapist lacks insight about the victim's view of the event or the extent of dementia, the rapist is likely to repeat the behavior (Abbey, 2011; Wegner, Abbey, Pierce, Pegram, & Woerner, 2015). When rapists are publicly charged with a crime, their marginal logic may blame the victim, say it was consensual, claim they were in a relationship, or the suspect may cry foul because there was no intent to harm because "I love them", which is a new defense for crimes. Understanding the victim reactions and the rapist's proclivity toward a specific victim, in this case an older or elderly person helps health-care communities plan evidence-based prevention programs, intervention, and mitigation strategies designed to prevent or improve a patient's predictable negative health outcomes (Speck et al., 2014).

Case 7

Althea, a 70-year-old female, was home asleep when a neighbor broke into her home, looking for money. He saw her asleep in the bed and crawled into Althea's bed. Holding her around her waist, he started humping her from behind. When he finished, Althea got up and grabbed his privates, holding very tight, threatening to pull off his "johnson" if he didn't walk with her to the phone. He followed her instructions screaming all the while—"let me go"! She then dialed the police and told the dispatcher what happened, with the neighbor screaming, "make her let me go"! When the police arrived, Althea released the neighbor's privates and the police bagged her hands. At that time, her children also arrived to the scene; some were yelling, while others were hitting the neighbor with their fists. The police intervened and took the suspect to jail. Althea, along with her sons and daughters, followed the Sex Crimes Detective to the hospital clinic for a medical forensic evaluation. The waiting room was full of family, with more arriving every moment, and the hospital resources were strained during their health-care response to the crime.

Discussion

Victims of crime who actively intervene in a successful outcome following trauma feel relief. If the outcome was poor, as in someone hurt, feelings are conflicted. In this case, Althea responded as she would to her children with sudden and stern action.

In turn, the neighbor, who was the same age as her children, responded in submission. Althea is a strong person with life experiences that provided skills necessary for a physical response to the neighbor. Reported by her as a typical response to aberrant behavior in her children today, she had no regret for her actions, not recognizing the potential for poor outcomes (Chan & Pang, 2007). Althea did, however, lament that the children now know about the rape, a humiliation, because she doesn't talk about sex. She showed concern for one daughter who was raped as a "youngster." She also expressed that her provider does not want to talk about sex because she was personally embarrassed. She also has a lack of knowledge and awareness of sex and the terms the provider needed to hear, and she feared of wasting their time (Gott & Hinchliff, 2003; Moreira, Glasser, Nicolosi, Duarte, & Gingell, 2008). Fortunately, the institution planned trauma informed care at all levels—micro, which involves the patient and family, mezzo, with the extended, church family, and community of supporters, and macro, which involves the overall hospital system (Center for Substance Abuse Treatment, 2014). Althea's use of these services promotes a quick recovery from the trauma, along with her ability to witness justice in the eyes of her community of supporters.

Conclusion

Sexual assault of older persons is "forced or unwanted sexual interaction of any kind with an older adult. This may include unwanted sexual contact or penetration or noncontact acts such as sexual harassment" (CDC Understanding Elder Abuse, 2016) There are a variety of reasons that older persons have difficulty speaking about sex, much less sexual assault, which makes reporting difficult. There are a variety of responses to sexual violence, some resulting in a rapid physiological demise, such as the trauma response when there are comorbid diagnoses, or others resulting in confirmation that the action taken was correct, protective, and empowering. Support structures from family and community seem to be protective for the older person but less so for the "old-old" person who laments about lifetime losses.

Many older persons want to protect their children from knowing about such events, partially fearing their children's insistence to move to a protected home such as an assisted living or nursing home or feeling self-blame for a behavior, for example, forgetting to lock the door. Others are reliving rapes from their past, as in progressive dementias.

Prosecution of rape of older persons is inconsistent. Successful prosecution is related to a witness with clear cognition and full memory of the event, becoming increasingly difficult as the older person ages through the seventh, eighth, and ninth decades. Prosecution is guaranteed if homicide is an outcome. In between, factors that influence prosecutorial decisions include the constitutional guarantee to face an accuser. Until circumstantial evidence, coupled with an understanding of medical complexities, is woven to create a nearly complete puzzle, older persons who have diminished memory or capacity to identify their assailants must rely on other evidence. This evidence, which includes DNA, the victim's property, or use of their credit cards, must suffice in the justice system. Ultimately, safety and justice for the older person is the goal.

References

Abbey, A. (2011). Alcohol's role in sexual violence perpetration: Theoretical explanations, existing evidence and future directions. *Drug And Alcohol Review, 30*(5), 481–489. https://doi.org/10.1111/j.1465-3362.2011.00296.x.

Anda, R. F., Dong, M., Brown, D. W., Felitti, V. J., Giles, W. H., Perry, B. D., ... Dube, S. R. (2009). The relationship of adverse childhood experiences to a history of premature death of family members. *BMC Public Health, 9*(106). https://doi.org/10.1186/1471-2458-9-106.

Anderson, J. C., & Sheridan, D. J. (2012). Female genital injury following consensual and nonconsensual sex: State of the science. *Journal of Emergency Nursing, 38*(6), 518–522. https://doi.org/10.1016/j.jen.2010.10.014.

Basile, K. C., DeGue, S., Jones, K., Freire, K., Dills, J., Smith, S. G., & Raiford, J. L. (2016). *Stop SV: A technical package to prevent sexual violence*. Atlanta, GA: Centers for Disease Control and Prevention, National Center for Injury Prevention and Control. Retrieved from https://www.cdc.gov/violenceprevention/sexualviolence/definitions.html.

Bauer, M. (1999). Their only privacy is between their sheets. Privacy and the sexuality of elderly nursing home residents. *Journal of Gerontological Nursing, 25*(8), 37–41.

Bright, C., & Bowland, S. (2008). Assessing interpersonal trauma in older adult women. *Journal of Loss And Trauma, 13*(4), 373–393. https://doi.org/10.1080/15325020701771523.

Brown, L. (2012). Assessing, intervening, and treating traumatized older adults. In *Paper presented at the biennial trauma conference: Addressing trauma across the lifespan, integration of family, community, and organizational approaches, Florida*.

Browne, K. D., Hines, M., & Tully, R. (2018). The differences between sex offenders who victimise older women and sex offenders who offend against children. *Aging And Mental Health, 22*(1), 11–18. https://doi.org/10.1080/13607863.2016.1202892.

Burgess, A. W. (2006). *Elderly victims of sexual abuse and their offenders*. Boston College, Boston, MA: U.S. Department of Justice. National Institutes of Justice Office of Justice Programs.

Burgess, A. W., Brown, K., Bell, K., Ledray, L. E., & Poarch, J. C. (2005). Sexual abuse of older adults. *American Journal of Nursing, 105*(10), 66–71.

Burgess, A. W., Commons, M. L., Safarik, M. E., Looper, R. R., & Ross, S. N. (2007). Sex offenders of the elderly: Classification by motive, typology, and predictors of severity of crime. *Aggression And Violent Behavior, 12*(5), 582–597.

Burgess, A. W., Dowdell, E. B., & Prentky, R. A. (2000). Sexual abuse of nursing home residents. *Journal of Psychosocial Nursing And Mental Health Services, 38*(6), 10–18.

Center for Disease Control [CDC]. (2016). *Understanding elder abuse fact sheet.* Retreieved from https://www.cdc.gov/violenceprevention/pdf/em-factsheet-a.pdf.

Center for Substance Abuse Treatment. (2014). *Trauma-informed care in behavioral health services: Treatment improvement protocol (TIP) series, No. 57.* Retrieved from https://www.ncbi.nlm.nih.gov/books/NBK207209/.

Chan, H. Y., & Pang, S. M. (2007). Quality of life concerns and end-of-life care preferences of aged persons in long-term care facilities. *Journal of Clinical Nursing, 16*(11), 2158–2166. https://doi.org/10.1111/j.1365-2702.2006.01891.x.

Clark, M., Newman, B. S., & Speck, P. M. (2017). Sexual assault among older adults. In A. P. Giardino, D. K. Faugno, M. J. Spencer, M. L. Weaver, & P. M. Speck (Eds.), Sexual assault victimization across the life span: Evaluation of children and adults (2nd ed.). *2*, 344. St. Louis, MO: STM Learning.

Connolly, M. T., Breckman, R., Callahan, J., Lachs, M., Ramsey-Klawsnik, H., & Solomon, J. (2012). The sexual revolution's last frontier: How silence about sex undermines health, well-being, and safety in old age. *Generations, 36*(3), 43–52.

DeLamater, J. D., & Sill, M. (2005). Sexual desire in later life. *The Journal of Sex Research, 42*(2), 138–149. https://doi.org/10.1080/00224490509552267.

Dong, X., & Simon, M. A. (2013). Association between elder self-neglect and hospice utilization in a community population. *Archives of Gerontology And Geriatrics, 56*(1), 192–198. https://doi.org/10.1016/j.archger.2012.06.008.

Dong, X., Simon, M., Mendes de Leon, C., Fulmer, T., Beck, T., Hebert, L., … Evans, D. (2009). Elder self-neglect and abuse and mortality risk in a community-dwelling population. *Journal of the American Medical Association, 302*(5), 517–526. https://doi.org/10.1001/jama.2009.1109.

Faugno, D. K., & Speck, P. M. (2011). Basic anogenital and oral anatomy. In L. Ledray, A. Burgess, & A. P. Giardino (Eds.), *Medical response to adult sexual assault.* St. Louis, MO: STM Medical Publishing.

Fisher, C. (2003). The invisible dimension: Abuse in palliative care families. *Journal of Palliative Medicine, 6*(2), 257–264.

Fisher, B. S., & Regan, S. L. (2006). The extent and frequency of abuse in the lives of older women and their relationship with health outcomes. *The Gerontologist, 46*(2), 200–209.

Fleming, J., Farquhar, M., Cambridge City over-75s Cohort study collaboration, Brayne, C., & Barclay, S. (2016). Death and the oldest old: Attitudes and preferences for end-of-life care - qualitative research within a population-based cohort study. *PLoS One, 11*(4), e0150686. https://doi.org/10.1371/journal.pone.0150686.

Friedman, L. S., Avila, S., Rizvi, T., Partida, R., & Friedman, D. (2017). Physical abuse of elderly adults: Victim characteristics and determinants of devictimization. *Journal of the American Geriatrics Society, 65*(7), 1420–1426. https://doi.org/10.1111/jgs.14794.

Gartner, R., McCarthy, B., & Conley, C. A. (2014). *Sexual violence in historical perspective.* Oxford University Press.

Gott, M., & Hinchliff, S. (2003). How important is sex in later life? The views of older people. *Social Science And Medicine, 56*(8), 1617–1628.

Government Accounting Office. (2006). *Long term care facilities: Information on residents who are registered sex offenders or are paroled for other crimes.* Retrieved from http://www.gpo.gov/fdsys/pkg/GAOREPORTS-GAO-06-326/pdf/GAOREPORTS-GAO-06-326.pdf.

Inelman, E. M., Gasparini, G., & Enzi, G. (2005). HIV/AIDS in older adults: A case report and literature review. *Geriatrics, 60*(9), 26–30.

Juster, R. P., McEwen, B. S., & Lupien, S. J. (2010). Allostatic load biomarkers of chronic stress and impact on health and cognition. *Neuroscience And Biobehavioral Reviews, 35*(1), 2–16. https://doi.org/10.1016/j.neubiorev.2009.10.002.

Karraker, A., Delamater, J., & Schwartz, C. R. (2011). Sexual frequency decline from midlife to later life. *Journals of Gerontology Series B: Psychological Sciences And Social Sciences, 66*(4), 502–512. https://doi.org/10.1093/geronb/gbr058.

Kelly, D. L., Larkin, H. J., & Paolinetti, L. A. (2017). Intra- and inter-rater agreement of the genital injury severity scale. *Journal of Forensic And Legal Medicine, 52,* 172–180. https://doi.org/10.1016/j.jflm.2017.09.011.

Lachs, M. S., Williams, C. S., O'Brien, S., Pillemer, K. A., & Charlson, M. E. (1998). The mortality of elder mistreatment. *Journal of the American Medical Association, 280*(5), 428–432.

Lamonica, P., & Pagiaro, E. M. (2006). Sexual assault intervention and the forensic examination. In R. M. Hammer, B. Moynihan, & E. M. Pagliaro (Eds.), *Forensic nursing: A handbook for practice* (pp. 547–578). Sudbury, MA: Jones and Bartlett Publishers.

Lasher, M. P., McGrath, R. J., & Cumming, G. F. (2014). Sex offender modus operandi stability and relationship with actuarial risk assessment. *Journal of Interpersonal Violence, 30*(6), 911–927. https://doi.org/10.1177/0886260514539757.

Lester, P. E., Kohen, I., Stefanacci, R. G., & Feuerman, M. (2016). Sex in nursing homes: A survey of nursing home policies governing resident sexual activity. *Journal of the American Medical Directors Association, 17*(1), 71–74. https://doi.org/10.1016/j.jamda.2015.08.013.

Lichtenberg, P. A. (2014). Sexuality and physical intimacy in long-term care. *Occupational Therapy in Health Care, 28*(1), 42–50. https://doi.org/10.3109/07380577.2013.865858.

Lindau, S. T., Schumm, L. P., Laumann, E. O., Levinson, W., O'Muircheartaigh, C. A., & Waite, L. J. (2007). A study of sexuality and health among older adults in the United States. *New England Journal of Medicine, 357*(8), 762–774. https://doi.org/10.1056/NEJMoa067423.

Linden, & Judith, A. (2011). Care of the adult patient after sexual assault. *New England Journal of Medicine, 365*(9), 834–841. https://doi.org/10.1056/NEJMcp1102869.

McCann, J., Miyamoto, S., Boyle, C., & Rogers, K. (2007). Healing of hymenal injuries in prepubertal and adolescent girls: A descriptive study. *Pediatrics, 119*(5), e1094–1106.

McEwen, B. (1998). Stress, adaptation, and disease: Allostasis and allostatic load. *Annals of the New York Academy of Sciences, 840,* 33–44. https://doi:10.111/j.1749-6632.1998.5b09546.x.

McEwen, B. (2002). Sex, stress and the hippocampus: Allostasis, allostatic load and the aging process. *Neurobiology of Aging, 23*(5), 921–939.

McEwen, B. S., & Seeman, T. (1999). Protective and damaging effects of mediators of stress. Elaborating and testing the concepts of allostasis and allostatic load. *Annals of the New York Academy of Sciences, 896*, 30–47.

Mitchell, D., Angelone, D. J., Kohlberger, B., & Hirschman, R. (2009). Effects of offender motivation, victim gender, and participant gender on perceptions of rape victims and offenders. *Journal of Interpersonal Violence, 24*(9), 1564–1578. https://doi.org/10.1177/0886260508323662.

Moreira, E. D., Glasser, D. B., Nicolosi, A., Duarte, F. G., & Gingell, C. (2008). Sexual problems and help-seeking behaviour in adults in the United Kingdom and continental Europe. *BJU International, 101*(8), 1005–1011. https://doi.org/10.1111/j.1464-410X.2008.07453.x.

Muram, D., Miller, K., & Cutler, A. (1992). Sexual assault of the elderly victim. *Journal of Interpersonal Violence, 7*(1), 70–76. https://doi.org/10.1177/088626092007001006.

Phanjoo, A. L. (2000). Sexual dysfunction in old age. *Advances in Psychiatric Treatment, 6*(4), 270–277. https://doi.org/10.1192/apt.6.4.270.

Poulos, C. A., & Sheridan, D. J. (2008). Genital injuries in postmenopausal women after sexual assault. *Journal of Elder Abuse and Neglect, 20*(4), 323–335. https://doi.org/10.1080/08946560802359243.

Raz, R. (2011). Urinary tract infection in postmenopausal women. *Korean Journal of Urology, 52*(12), 801–808. https://doi.org/10.4111/kju.2011.52.12.801.

Schafran, L. H. (1996). Topics for our times: Rape is a major public health issue. *American Journal of Public Health, 86*(1), 15–17.

Schofield, M. J., Powers, J. R., & Loxton, D. (2013). Mortality and disability outcomes of self-reported elder abuse: A 12-year prospective investigation. *Journal of the American Geriatrics Society, 61*(5), 679–685. https://doi.org/10.1111/jgs.12212.

Selye, H. (1956). *The stress of life.* New York: McGraw-Hill.

Selye, H. (1974). *Stress without distress.* Philadelphia, PA: Lippincott.

Shields, L. B., Hunsaker, D. M., & Hunsaker, J. C., 3rd (2004). Abuse and neglect: A ten-year review of mortality and morbidity in our elders in a large metropolitan area. *Journal of Forensic Sciences, 49*(1), 122–127.

Somes, J., & Donatelli, N. (2012). Sex and the alder adult. *JEN: Journal of Emergency Nursing, 38*(2), 168–170. https://doi.org/10.1016/j.jen.2011.11.007.

Speck, P. M. (2007). Hymen injury in elderly consensual partners. In *Paper presented at the American academy of forensic science, 60th annual scientific assembly, Washington, DC.*

Speck, P., Hartig, M., Likes, W., Bowdre, T., Carney, A., Ekroos, R., … Faugno, D. (2014). Case series of sexual assault in older persons. *Clinics in Geriatric Medicine, 30*(4), 779–806. https://doi.org/10.1016/j.cger.2014.08.007.

Stein, M. B., Lang, A. J., Laffaye, C., Satz, L. E., Lenox, R. J., & Dresselhaus, T. R. (2004). Relationship of sexual assault history to somatic symptoms and health anxiety in women. *General Hospital Psychiatry, 26*(3), 178–183. https://doi.org/10.1016/j.genhosppsych.2003.11.003.

Tarzia, L., Fetherstonhaugh, D., & Bauer, M. (2012). Dementia, sexuality and consent in residential aged care facilities. *Journal of Medical Ethics, 38*(10), 609–613. https://doi.org/10.1136/medethics-2011-100453.

Terry, K. J., & Freilich, J. D. (2012). Understanding child sexual abuse by catholic priests from a situational perspective. *Journal of Child Sexual Abuse, 21*(4), 437–455. https://doi.org/10.1080/10538712.2012.693579.

Tsatali, M., & Tsolaki, M. (2014). Sexual function in normal elders, MCI and patients with mild dementia. *Sexuality And Disability, 32*(2), 205–219. https://doi.org/10.1007/s11195-014-9353-9.

Wegner, R., Abbey, A., Pierce, J., Pegram, S. E., & Woerner, J. (2015). Sexual assault perpetrators' justifications for their actions: Relationships to rape supportive attitudes, incident characteristics, and future perpetration. *Violence Against Women, 21*(8), 1018–1037. https://doi.org/10.1177/1077801215589380.

Further Reading

Kalra, G., Subramanyam, A., & Pinto, C. (2011). Sexuality: Desire, activity and intimacy in the elderly. *Indian Journal of Psychiatry, 53*(4), 300–306. https://doi.org/10.4103/0019-5545.91902.

Traxler, C. (May 13, 2018). *Sexual abuse: Sexual abuse of the elderly.* Retrieved from https://www.nursinghomeabusecenter.com/elder-abuse/types/sexual-abuse/.

PSYCHOLOGICAL ABUSE

Russel Neuhart,[1] Amy Carney[2]

[1] *Human Development Department, California State University, San Marcos, CA, United States;* [2] *School of Nursing, California State University San Marcos, San Marcos, CA, United States*

CHAPTER OUTLINE
Psychological Abuse: Elder Harm Without Visible Injury **163**
The Need for Both Forensic and Medical Analysis of Psychological Abuse **164**
Understanding the Life Space of the Elder **165**
Psychological and Developmental Factors **166**
Impact and Consequences of Psychological Abuse **168**
Perpetrators of Psychological Elder Abuse **169**
    Family as Caregivers 170
    NonFamily Caregivers 170
Varieties of Psychological Abuse **171**
    Verbal Abuse: Aggression, Threats, and Intimidation 171
    Isolation and Social Abuse 172
Challenges in Documentation: Assessment and Evaluation Tools **173**
Abandonment: An Emerging Trend in Psychological Abuse **178**
Case Study **179**
References **180**

Psychological Abuse: Elder Harm Without Visible Injury

The existence of psychological abuse (PA) of the aging population worldwide has rapidly become a globally recognized concern (World Health Organization [WHO], 2017). Recent research estimates have suggested that one in six people in the worldwide aging population have suffered some form of abuse. In the United States, while overall prevalence data are lacking, the available data suggest 10% of US elders experience some form of abuse, with

Elder Abuse. https://doi.org/10.1016/B978-0-12-815779-4.00007-0

approximately one million persons in this population being abused annually. In 2017, a systematic review of the prevalence of abuse placed the estimates for PA of persons 60 years and older at approximately 11.6% worldwide (Yon, Mikton, Gassoumis, & Wilber, 2017). A national prevalence study, based on a sample of 5777 adults aged 60 years and older found a 1-year prevalence rate of 4.6% for emotional abuse (EA), higher than the rates for physical and sexual abuse combined (Acierno et al., 2010). The reported incidence and prevalence of PA is often affected by research methodology, theoretical perspectives, and definitions used to conceptualize PA. For example, in the literature, it has been referred to as EA, psychological elder abuse or PEA (Johannesen & LoGiudice, 2013), and PA of older adults (Conrad, Iris, Ridings, Langley, & Anetzberger, 2011) when referring to a category of abuse perpetrated on aging victims. The National Center on Elder Abuse (NCEA) defines emotional or PA as the infliction of anguish, pain, or distress through verbal or nonverbal acts. Emotional and PAs are terms often used synonymously, describing behavior including, but not limited to, verbal assaults, insults, threats, intimidation, humiliation, and harassment. In addition, treating an older person like an infant, isolating an older person from his or her family, friends, or regular activities, giving an older person the "silent treatment," and enforcing social isolation are examples of PA. Such treatment would typically occur in private and be difficult for third parties to detect. Signs and symptoms of emotional or PA range from a person being emotionally upset or agitated to unusual behavior often attributed to dementia, such as sucking, biting, or rocking (NCEA, 2003). PA in any form is associated with significant life stress and may have significant and long-lasting mental and physiological impacts, which result in reduced psychological well-being for the older adult (Conrad et al., 2011; Yon et al., 2017).

The Need for Both Forensic and Medical Analysis of Psychological Abuse

Both the impact of PA on the elder person and the resulting symptoms are complex due to the nature of the elder person's life, their often-complicated care needs, the persons providing the needed care, the living situation of the elder, the nature of social and familial relationships, and the ongoing psychological development of the elder themselves. When the care needs of the individual include the existence of psychiatric symptoms before the abuse, the determination of PA is compounded. Together these factors, experiences, and psychological and environmental contexts form the "life space" in which the elder victim exists. Understanding the array of symptoms that may occur and the impact PA may have on an elderly victim necessitates professionals to also understand their own life space, in conjunction with the elder's ongoing personal development. When the abuse is evaluated and assessed from this perspective, and includes the current personal, familial, and societal contexts which form the elder's life or in which the elder is living, this evaluation can be referred to as using a Contextual Theory of Abuse as advocated by Roberto and Teaster (2017) and other researchers. Using this model gives insight and understanding of the impact and exhibited symptomology and provides a framework for effective assessment.

In identified cases of criminal abuse, this assessment may be forensic and medical. The goal of the forensic exam is to determine the existence of the abuse, identify the perpetrator, and document evidence of the abuse; the nature of the threat and criminal intent must also be evaluated. This is particularly difficult in verbal abuse or EA, where there are no wounds to evaluate or injuries to assess. The impact of this assessment on the elder must be taken into account, along with an evaluation of their ongoing protective needs.

Understanding the Life Space of the Elder

It may be tempting for professionals to see the elder's life as less complex than that of younger victims of interpersonal violence. However, the complicated nature of the elder's world, their psychological and physical needs, and their web of relationships all combine to form an often diverse array of caretaking situations, social environments, and community experiences in which the PA may exist. In addition, life experiences, including the occurrence of PA, must be seen in the context of the elder's ongoing development, the social meaning of aging, social and familial relationships, and their caretaking situations. This approach is supported by the ecological, life course, and contextual theories of elder abuse. Sociocultural contexts and relational factors in elder abuse are also the premise proposed by the National Academies of Sciences (NAS) in their theoretical framework of elder abuse. The NAS theoretical model proposes elder abuse as a series of transactions between a person who has gained the older person's trust and then uses that trust relationship to exploit or abuse the elder. The abuser and the elder person are embedded in a social context where there exist both power exchanges and an inequality in the relationship status between the abuser and the elder (Bonnie & Wallace, 2003).

To understand and determine the existence of PA, professionals must understand the environmental contexts and the unique individual experiences that the elder person's daily life may comprise. Understanding this life space is crucial to determining not only where and how the PA occurred but by whom the abuse was perpetrated and the impact of the abuse on the elder's functioning. The elder person's life is embedded in a variety of systems that include medical, social, familial, caretaking, religious, government, and other community support, all which interact with and have an effect on each other, the etiology of the abused person, and the impact of PA on the elder and their life. For example, an elder who wants or needs to use public transportation to a senior center or medical appointment could experience PA from a number of sources. A paid caretaker or a family member who is attempting to control an elder victim may use intimidation or threats to limit outside public contact, when the elder wishes to use a public transportation system, rather than depending on the caretaker for transportation. Alternately, the driver of a public transport such as a "LIFT" service or a private transport such as Uber may also see the elder as a potential target for abuse; they may verbally discredit the elder's family for not providing their transportation and threaten to make an Adult Protected Services (APS) report, attempting to shame the elder or use other forms of coercion to intimidate them as a means to begin to establish control or dependency.

Psychological and Developmental Factors

The professionals who will interface with elder victims should be aware of the elder's connections in their multiple life space contexts. This is true whether the victim accesses care through a community setting such as a medical clinic, emergency department, home-based care, or long-term care setting (McGann & Moynihan, 2006, pp. 271–278). Therefore, assessment of the individual in one or perhaps several of these settings becomes a critical component in determining the existence of PA. There is also a need to determine how the PA effects the mental health of the victim, and if the ongoing healthy development of the elder has been compromised. An elder victim may experience shame, guilt, a loss of self-esteem, a compromised sense of their own self-worth, and a distrust in their own ability to function in the world around them; this in turn can lead to physical decline.

The feelings of shame and guilt that the elder have concerning their inability to deal with the abuse may also be accompanied by previous feelings of loss in relation to one's overall efficacy, which often occurs as a person ages and likely existed before the abuse occurred. The occurrence of PA will often escalate these feeling in the elder victim due to the previously mentioned distrust in their functional ability and a similar distrust in their ability to determine the danger that other people in their life space may pose.

Another potential loss experience for the abused elder that may arise when conducting the assessment is the victim's loss of attachment to the perpetrator, who may be a family member, a caregiver, or both. Although this may seem at first confusing for the professional, who may think that the elder would naturally want to detach themselves from the abuser, it is important to understand that the abuser was once part of a trusted relationship, an important psychological support for the elder, and formed a significant part of the ecological environment in which the elder lives. Attachment theory describes how an emotional bond forms between individuals, such as a mother and child, and supports the child's ongoing growth and development. As a person grows and ages, this attachment may form with other individuals beyond a parent. In the last few decades, attachment theory has been studied in life events from childhood into late middle age, and more recently into old age (Cicirelli, 2010). The purpose of the attachment system is to protect an individual from danger; when a human of any age is exposed to a threat, either real or symbolic, the attachment system is activated. The person may then feel a need to seek closeness with an attachment figure to experience security. In the elderly, this may take place as a form of role reversal; the parent was the attachment figure for their child when they were young, but the grown children may become attachment figures for their elder parent as they age (Milberg & Friedrichsen, 2017). Caring for an elderly family member can be very stressful and challenging: stressful for the elder in needing to receive care, and for the family member who is witnessing the decline of someone who has been a primary source of love and support, and whose loss they are facing (Karantzas & Simpson, 2015). In elder abuse, the loss of attachment is particularly acute, when the elder realizes they are being abused by someone they love and trust.

When the perpetrator is in the category of a previously trusted relationship, an older adult may be reluctant or even refuse to report instances of PA to protect themselves from a loss of attachment with this person, especially in situations where the perpetrator is a family member. Mixed with these feelings of attachment loss, there may also be feelings of guilt for reporting the perpetrator, concerns that there may be an increase in the mistreatment for reporting the abuse, or a desire on the part of the elder to avoid unwanted attention, stigmatization, and even loss of other freedoms, if the elder is seen as unable to care for themselves. The elder victim's fears of stigmatization and loss of additional freedom is particularly relevant when the elder victim is already feeling shame for their own perceived inability to have prevented the abuse or their lack of efficacy in handling the situation.

Impact and Consequences of Psychological Abuse

The occurrence of PA to an elderly victim results in a variety of symptoms that correspond to the form, intensity, duration, and the perpetrator of the abuse. These symptoms can include depressed mood, withdrawal from activities of daily life, self-imposed alienation from other people, lowered self-esteem, and suicidal ideation or behavior. PA perpetrated on elders include threatening of bodily harm or assault, intimidation, humiliation of the elder individual, demeaning of one's skills and abilities, and isolation from friends or family. These commonly perpetrated abusive behaviors can result in not only the previously mentioned symptoms but also feelings of despair, a sense of worthlessness, and a loss of hope by the elder individual. This overall dysthymic mental state and any accompanying mental illness may also lead to a lack of self-care displayed by the victim. This lack of self-care may be one of the important indicators of the existence of PA, and sometimes the only visible indicator, especially if the elder's self-care was appropriate before existence of PA.

The distress resulting from PA is associated with reduced psychological well-being and increases in morbidity and mortality in older adults (Dong, Chen, Chang, & Simon, 2013). Therefore, psychological distress and well-being become critical components in the overall health and aging process. The typical aging process brings increased vulnerability and risk factors of loneliness, losses associated with reduced social contact, anxiety about one's future, and often depression. When PA interrupts and interferes with healthy aging, not only does the elder victim experience increased emotional distress, loneliness, and isolation but also the potential for a sustained and chronic reduction in psychological well-being is significantly increased. These factors interact and multiply

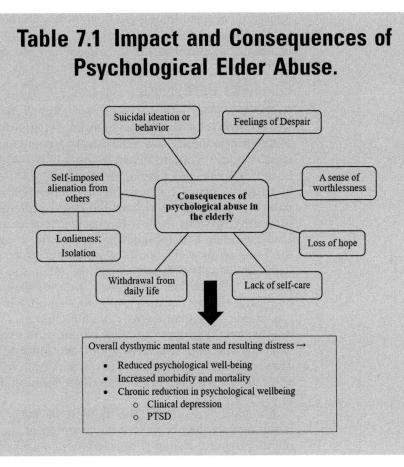

Table 7.1 Impact and Consequences of Psychological Elder Abuse.

the elder victim's experiences resulting in clinical depression, post-traumatic stress disorder, and other negative psychological health outcomes (Eisikovits & Band-Winterstein, 2015) (Table 7.1).

Perpetrators of Psychological Elder Abuse

It has been reported by the US Preventive Services Task Force (2013) that 1 in 10 older adults experience some form of abuse by a person who is trusted by the victim, and as previously discussed, the prevalence of abuse placed the estimates for PA of persons 60 years and older at approximately 11.6% worldwide (WHO, 2017). Because it is within the context of relationships that elder abuse occurs, therefore as is suggested by many theoretical perspectives of abuse, the relationship contexts of the abused elder need to be examined. Although these relationships are dynamic, variable over time, and not formulaic, they should be seen as a central part of the assessment process.

Family as Caregivers

Unless the older adult is forthright about how they are being treated, it may be significantly harder to determine who in their social context the abusive individual is. A common social situation is older adults who are reliant on an adult child for care. Just as healthy growth and development can be seen as described in attachment theory, the stressful interdependent and intertwined nature of caregivers and later life care recipients can foster an unhealthy dynamic leading to an abusive relationship situation. Understanding and recognizing family care dynamics that form the basis of these relationships is vital for professionals working with families. The family caregiver, often the daughter, may perceive the situation as obligatory but less than ideal; they may be raising children of their own, working outside the home, and also caring for aging parents. An adult child may feel the need to also financially support an older parent, who may be living on a fixed income and unable to afford care outside of their home. These stressors can lead to loss of patience, verbal arguments, and raised voices and must be evaluated during the investigation of elder abuse.

Caregiver stress, and the burden of living with an elder requiring care, has been well documented in the literature. The number of hours required for activities of daily living, the physical burden of caring for a dependent elder, and anxiety on the part of the caregiver all have serious health effects, particularly if the caregiver is an elderly spouse (Amankwaa, 2017). When maltreatment is found in the context of the family dynamic, the professional working with the elder must be able to provide resources not only to the victim of abuse but also to those caring for them. Respite care for caregiver, such as time spent by the elder in activities at a senior center, may help alleviate some of the burden and decrease the stress in the relationship.

NonFamily Caregivers

Family members, friends, and neighbors may be reluctant to envision nonfamily caregivers as alleged perpetrators, preferring instead to perceive them as the older adult's primary source of support. When paid caregivers are living with the elder, there may be no family members nearby who can evaluate the situation and watch for abuse. There may be no one else to witness instances of verbal abuse inside the home, and only the elder would be able report this. Friends and neighbors may notice changes in the elders' behavior and should be encouraged to report to family or law enforcement if abuse is suspected.

Care may take place in a variety of settings outside the victim's home, and the elder may feel helpless to advocate on their own behalf. As with abuse in the home, maltreatment that occurs in a care facility or group home may be difficult to assess. Instances of yelling and belittling might further frighten a confused elder, and sources of assistance might not be known. Clues may be apparent in evaluating the emotional well-being of an abused senior, such as changes in weight, appearance, or affect. These clues may indicate the need for intervention in the caretaker–elder relationship.

Varieties of Psychological Abuse

PA presents in many forms, all of which inflict mental stress on the victim. It can occur as actions of intended violence, threats that cause fear, isolation and social abuse, deprivation, shaming, and verbal abuse or intimidation, such as bullying. The type and frequency of abuse and violence result in varying levels of psychological distress with verbal abuse being a significant predictor of elder victim's psychological distress (Pico-Alfonso et al., 2006).

Verbal Abuse: Aggression, Threats, and Intimidation

Verbal abuse occurs in a variety of forms, but it can be capsulized as the use of language and other forms of verbal communication to inflict mental stress. Verbal aggression is the communication-based version of throwing a punch at the elder victim, with the intent to induce a desired emotional response. Verbal abuse can also take the form of bullying, which is emotional intimidation perpetrated by a person who is stronger than or in a position of power over the victim. Although bullying is most commonly associated with children or youth, the power differential between the elderly and their caretakers leaves them open to this common form of victimization, with accompanying mental stress (Countouris, 2018). This mental stress can cause an emotional response of fear, psychological discomfort, or psychological pain in the elder victim. Verbal aggression can be the use of cursing, swearing and vulgar language, or other emotionally charged communication targeted at the elder. This verbal abuse may be intended to make the elder more compliant or deferential, less combative, or to establish a power disparity between the victim and the perpetrator. Verbalizations of intended violence can be used to reinforce their fear, leaving the victim feeling weak and helpless. Threats and verbal intimidation are often perpetrated in conjunction with other forms of elder abuse such as financial maltreatment, where threats are used to gain access to an older adult's assets, property, or funds (Acierno et al., 2018).

Other actions may also lead to an elder feeling powerless or shamed. Verbal insults and attempts to humiliate an elder, threatening to harm a family member, and emotional or economic blackmail further isolate the victim and decrease their feelings of control (Pico-Alfonso et al., 2006). This can lead to an increase in the elder's despair, depression and anguish, and further impact their mental health.

Isolation and Social Abuse

Social isolation or withdrawal is the loss of contact with other people and social circles of support. Social isolation has been linked with increased mortality and poor health outcomes. More than one in four adults aged 65 and older are living alone; for women aged 75 and older, almost half live alone (Wilber, 2018). Isolation may also be a response to abuse. However, it is not only the self-imposed removal of social contact due to the experience of PA by an elder victim but also a type of abuse perpetrated on the elder. This form of abuse is characterized by the intentional separation of the older adult from family, friends, and other community connections. The intent may be as a punishment, or as a method to make the older adult more susceptible to coercion by a caretaker or family member, and to establish control over the elder by limitation of outside influences and contact.

Social isolation can contribute to situations in which abuse occurs. Vulnerability and dependency play a role in social isolation, which in turn is linked to loneliness and psychological dependency. Isolation can also lead to increased abuse, as the elder victim may be alone with their abuser most of the time (Mysuk, Westendorp, & Lindenberg, 2016). This deepens the loss of the feeling of connectedness and increases feelings of desolation and hopelessness.

Social abuse may also take the form of preventing an elder from spending time with pets, hobbies, or activities outside of the home environment. Having a pet has especially shown benefits for seniors: animals can be a source of companionship and friendship; caring for a pet can provide a sense of purpose and structure and provide comfort and support in a time of bereavement. Those who walk dogs engage in more physical activity, and pet owners often describe a decreased sense of loneliness (While, 2017). Depriving an elder of these experiences can lead to a decline in mental health.

Challenges in Documentation: Assessment and Evaluation Tools

Research efforts have mostly focused on developing elder PA screening tools as precursors to further inquiry, rather than useable brief assessments for abuse substantiation decisions that will generate reliable information. The screening tools developed thus far have been designed primarily for use in clinical or health-care settings leaving alternative investigations such as in the context of APS or police abuse investigations lacking tools.

The complexity in an elder's life space, the existence of multiple personal relationships from which a perpetrator may come, the fear or existence of loss in personal or family relationships, the person's reduced self-esteem or feelings of incompetence related to the abuse, along with the potential concern by the victim that there may be further consequences of reporting abuse will all contribute to the challenges in correctly and thoroughly conducting a forensic assessment. The occurrence of PA is complex to assess within an elder's report of being verbally or emotionally mistreated, an important component when the elder can verbally express this and is willing to disclose the abuse. However, in many circumstances, the resulting symptoms of PA often become the most significant warning signs that abuse is occurring. Therefore, the assessment being conducted must be sensitive to the existence of potentially compounding factors, presenting symptomology and the ongoing needs of the elder victim.

A Mental Status Exam that adopts a biopsychosocial approach and includes a substance abuse, social isolation, and suicide risk assessments is a good first step when suspected abuse is encountered. This approach is supported by the ecological and life course perspective theories of elder abuse (Roberto & Teaster, 2017). The elder person's life is embedded in a variety of systems which interact with each other, the abused individual, the impact of the PA, and even the etiology of it. In addition, the elder's life and experiences, including PA, must be seen in the context of their ongoing development, the social meaning of aging, their social and familial relationships, etc. A biopsychosocial and global approach to assessment can help to uncover the more subtle and perhaps overlooked symptoms such as alcohol abuse, medication noncompliance, and self-neglect behavior, which often accompany the elder's feelings of hopelessness, loss of self-esteem, or depression.

The global assessment of an individual must not only respect the elders' concerns for privacy and confidentiality but must also be guided by the victim's potential feelings of powerlessness or humiliation. The professional completing the assessment must also be aware of the potential for the elder to have fears of retribution. These fears may be of retribution from not only the perpetrator but also family members, who may be both unaware of the abuse and embarrassed about the elder's disclosure to a professional. As stated previously, the abused elder may also have feelings of shame for their own reduced efficacy in dealing with the abuse and the abuser. These feelings of shame and guilt about the inability to deal with the abuse may also be accompanied by feelings of loss in relation to the elder victim's overall efficacy as they age. These feelings of lost efficacy in dealing with one's life that existed before the abuse can escalate in circumstances of abuse and overwhelm the coping ability of elder victims.

In 2008, the World Health Organization, citing elder abuse as a global public health issue, noted that several tools had been developed for screening at the primary health-care level, but almost all were from North America. In two of the tools, the elders themselves are the respondent: the Hwalek–Sengstock Elder Abuse Screening Test (H–S/EAST) and the Elder Abuse Suspicion Index (EASI) (Perel-Levin, 2008).

As noted in Chapter 2, the H–S/EAST was the earliest developed tool and was noted to be one of the few validated instruments. It addressed elder abuse in three areas: violation of personal rights or direct abuse; characteristics of vulnerability; and potentially abusive situations. With just 15 items, it was noted to be useful in identifying situations likely to be, or become, abusive or neglectful (Perel-Levin, 2008). The H–S/EAST was brief, is useful in multiple environments, and is seen as the precursor for the development of other instruments (Gallione et al., 2017).

The EASI, developed in Canada, was designed for use in clinical settings to help physicians identify patients who might be experiencing abuse. It was tested only on cognitively intact elders, those who had scored at least 24 on the Mini Mental Status Exam (MMSE). The EASI has just six items, five of them being yes or no questions for the patient. The sixth item is answered by the physician noting any change in behavior or appearance that may indicate abuse. The EASI was then correlated with the Social Work Evaluation given to the same population. Overall, sensitivity and specificity were 0.47 and 0.75, respectively; the two most common responses were in the areas of reliance and dependency and verbal or PA. It was found that the EASI required a short administration time and provided direct information from the elder but was only tested in cognitively intact elders who spoke English or French (Gallione et al., 2017).

Several other tools were developed that did not have the elder as the respondent. The Brief Abuse Screen for the Elderly (BASE) is a simple five-item screen to be used by a trained practitioner. Used to assess the likelihood of abuse, the practitioner answers the five questions on the BASE after assessing the elderly patient. CASE, the Caregiver Abuse Screen, uses eight questions asked of the caregiver to identify abuse in cognitively impaired adults. It does not address the patient directly but may identify potentially abusive caregivers. Two instruments, the Indicators of Abuse Screen, used to identify abuse in health and social services clients, and the Elder Assessment Instrument, used to identify victims who need referral for further assessment, can only be used by trained professionals (Perel-Levin, 2008).

The Vulnerability Abuse Screening Scale (VASS) was specifically tested on women, with one of the three cohorts aged 70–75. The VASS is an adaption of the H–S/EAST and could be administered quickly, exploring four areas: dependence, dejection, vulnerability, and coercion. It utilizes 12 yes and no questions, 10 of which are from the H–S/EAST and two additional questions: "Has anyone close to you called you names or put you down or made you feel bad recently"? and "Are you afraid of anyone in your family"?' The VASS may be able to predict decline in both mental and physical health over a 3-year period (Gallione et al., 2017).

Most assessments of elder abuse have considered multiple abuse forms, sometimes including PA, but without specific focus on conceptualizing and assessing PA. Of the assessment tools specifically oriented at PA, very few have been validated as reliable and fewer are culturally transferable. Three assessment instruments that address PA are the Elder Psychological Abuse Scale (EPAS), Caregiver Psychological Elder Abuse Behavior Scale (CPEABS), and the Older Adult Psychological Abuse Measure (OAPAM). EPAS studied the phenomenon of elders institutional-ized in Taiwan. It used a combination of 32 items to detect abuse which focused on discussion, active observation, and an inter-view with the caregiver. The CPEABS focused on identifying abusive behavior by the caregiver. This assessment used a 1–4

Likert scale with 20 items and found that although PA was the most widespread form of mistreatment, it was also the least intercepted. Although both of these tools have a brief administration time, it was observed they had low cultural transferability and had been tested on small to medium samples. Additionally, they needed to be paired with a general screening tool to capture other types of abuse (Gallione et al., 2017).

The presence of PA was also evaluated by Conrad et al. in developing the OAPAM, which was one self-report scale of the Older Adult Mistreatment Assessment. OAPAM evaluated 226 cases reported to social services in Chicago, Illinois, each of which had at least a 17 on the MMSE and had already suffered one episode of violence. Thirty-one items evaluated multiple areas of client-reported PA including disrespect, insensitivity, shaming, isolation, threats, blaming, and intimidation. The researchers concluded that the OAPAM could be widely used in elder abuse research and practice, noting that the elder's self-report of internal mental states is an essential indicator of abuse (Conrad et al., 2011; Gallione, 2017).

As discussed in Chapter 2, another useful assessment tool is the Conflict Tactic Scale (CTS), which is one of the most widely used to measure several types of elder abuse, including PA. Versions of the CTS, such as the modified Conflict Tactics Scale (m-CTS), have been used globally in research on maltreatment. The m-CTS consists of a 10-item scale with five indicators of psychological maltreatment: screaming and yelling, threat of physical force, threat of abandonment, name calling, and swearing, along with five items of physical maltreatment. It is interesting that one of the physical maltreatment items is creating fear in the victim that the caretaker may hit or try to hurt the care recipient. Using the Japanese version of the m-CTS, Kishimoto et al. (2013) studied the prevalence of abusive behavior toward older persons with clinically mild cognitive impairment by family caregivers. The average age of the care recipient was 75.4 years. In their results, the authors note family caregivers reported that in the previous month they had screamed or yelled at a care recipient, used a harsh tone of voice, threatened to stop taking care of or abandon the care recipient, and that the carer was afraid they might hit or hurt the care recipient. Factors affecting the caregiver's behaviors included being a male caregiver, presence of neuropsychiatric symptoms, the care burden, and the cognitive impairment of the care recipient. Citing Kishimoto's study, Toda et al. (2018) utilized the m-CTS to evaluate predictors of potentially harmful behavior (PHB) by family members in patients with dementia in Japan. PHB was defined as behavior that is detrimental to the psychological and physical well-being of the care recipient, but not necessarily severely abusive. They studied 133 pairs of dementia patients and their family caregivers and found that 48.9% of the caregivers showed PHB. Screaming and yelling at the care recipient was the most common behavior. As per Kishimoto et al. (2013), high caregiver burden was a predictor of PHB. Family caregivers were also the focus of a study done in Ireland assessing PHBs. A cross-sectional survey was mailed to 4000 family caregivers of older people across the country; 2311 responses were received. The average age of the care recipient was 80 years. Using the m-CTS, over one-third of the respondents reported PHBs, with most reporting using a harsh tone of voice, insulting or swearing at the older person, and screaming or yelling at the older person. The authors noted the importance of detecting PHB early to introduce preventive interventions that will keep situations with caregivers from escalating into serious cases of elder abuse (Lafferty, Fealy, Downes, & Drennan, 2016). Also using the m-CTS, a South Korean study of prevalence and risk factors for psychologically abusive behaviors (PsAB) and physically abusive behaviors (PhAB) was done, and the prevalence of abusive behaviors was compared between Asian and Western countries. More than half of the caregivers reported PsAB in the previous 3 months. Using a meta-analysis of 12 studies, the researchers found that PhAB and PsAB were as prevalent in family caring for people with dementia in Asian countries as in Western countries. Consistent with other studies, caregiver burden was strongly associated with an increase in PsAB and PhAB (Kim et al., 2018).

The Elder Abuse Decision Support System (EADSS) was designed for use in APS investigations. Beach et al. (2017) noted that APS support services and budgets have been drastically cut across the United States, while reports of abuse have increased by as much as 24%. It was found that the EADSS was effective in helping to substantiate abuse, but in its long form was time consuming to administer, given increased caseloads. The authors developed four EADSS short forms that offered effective and concise measures of emotional, financial, and physical abuse and neglect. It was estimated that all four short forms would take about 10−15 minutes to administer. APS workers recorded yes or no to each question on the short forms, and if a "yes" was recorded additional questions from the long form EADSS could be used to collect further evidence. Beach et al. stated that the need for improved elder abuse screening and detection tools remains unmet, but the EADSS short form provides for comprehensive data collection with low respondent burden and can be administered in diverse settings.

Abandonment: An Emerging Trend in Psychological Abuse

A feeling of safety and security is necessary for psychological well-being. Whether they are being cared for in their own house, in a family member's residence, or in a care facility, the elderly must feel they have a home where they are sheltered and protected. Abandonment removes that shelter and leaves the elder without care. The NCEA defines abandonment as the desertion of an elder by an individual who has assumed responsibility for them or who has physical custody of them. This often means the individual is left alone in a public place, such as an emergency department at a hospital. Caregiver stress has been noted previously as a contributor to PA and has also been found to contribute to abandonment. Feelings of being overwhelmed by the burden of care, stress, and chronic fatigue may lead a caregiver to feel they have no other choice than to leave the elder for someone else to care for. Substance abuse by the caregiver, psychological disorders, and financial burdens may also lead to the older person being abandoned. Abandonment can take various forms: a caregiver may give false contact information when an ill elder is admitted to a hospital, leaving no way for them to be contacted regarding medical or health issues or how to get the elderly patient home; they may be left at a care facility with a note pinned to their clothing asking for help, with no identification; or they may simply be left in a park or shopping center. If the patient suffers from dementia they may not know who they are or where they have come from. Abandonment differs from elder neglect in that neglect is withholding care, whereas abandonment is completely deserting the elder in an attempt by the caregiver to rid themselves of an elderly dependent person (Rzeszut, 2017).

When an elder has been moved into a care facility, it takes time to become used to the new surroundings and to trust they will be cared for. Over time, this new place becomes home, and the elder is presented with a new routine for daily living. There may be times when the elder needs to leave the facility for a period of time, such as for an emergency room visit. In this instance, the older patient has a reasonable expectation they will be returned to their care facility home after treatment. However, in the last few years many instances of an elderly patient not having a place to return have occurred. "Dumping" of nursing home residents is becoming more widely reported in the news. In 2017, National Public Radio (NPR) noted that eviction is the leading complaint against nursing homes nationwide. NPR noted that in California alone there had been a 73% increase in complaints regarding involuntary discharge from nursing homes since 2011. While nursing home residents have rights at both the state and federal levels, these laws are often not enforced. A resident is supposed to be given 30 days notice before being moved involuntarily, and the facility has to hold their bed for 7 days if they are admitted to a hospital, but if this is not done, the elder is often left waiting to be accepted by another facility (Jaffe, 2017). Facilities who engage in these practices have cited many reasons why an elder may be moved involuntarily, without notice to the patient or family: the patient may need care the facility is unable to provide, the elder may pose a safety risk to other patients or to staff, or the patient may no longer have the funding the facility requires. If the elder is the ward of the state and has no family, the guardian is supposed to be notified, but often this does not occur (Curtin, 2016).

When evaluating the victim of abandonment, professionals must understand the fear and sense of loss the elder may be feeling. They may not understand the sudden change in their surroundings or the new "home" environment when they get one. Loss of attachment or finding they no longer have personal items, such as family photos, may cause depression or distress that this can happen to them again. These anxieties may compound existing conditions, such as insomnia or eating disorders. Specialists working with these victims need to know the resources available to the elderly, such as legal and aging advocates who can intervene on behalf of the victim of abandonment, as well as appropriate avenues of documentation and reporting to law enforcement. As with other forms of PA, abandonment may only be one form of maltreatment the elder is experiencing, but may have the most deleterious and lasting effect.

Case Study

Law enforcement was called to the home of a 78-year-old widower when neighbors heard loud voices and the sound of glass breaking. Inside, they found the man with his adult son, who reported himself as his father's caretaker. The son told the officers that his father had "become lost inside his own house" and had broken some dishes in the kitchen. The father and son were separated and then interviewed individually.

The son reported that he took good care of his elderly father, making sure he had enough food and that he always got his medicine. He admitted that he sometimes became frustrated with his father, but had never harmed him. The officers noted that besides the broken dishes in the kitchen, the home was clean and well-cared for; they saw there was food in the kitchen and pill bottles on the counter.

When the widower was interviewed, he first said that everything in the home was fine but soon became tearful. He told the officers that while it was true his son never physically hurt him, the son was mean and often yelled at him, calling him names and threatening to leave him alone in the home to care for himself. When he broke something or left a mess for his son to clean up, the son would tell him he was "worthless" and would take his Social Security money and "leave him with nothing." The elderly man told them he loved his son but was often afraid of his temper and the things he said. He was afraid he would say or do something that would make his son leave. After speaking with both father and son, the officers were able to obtain names of family members who could take the father for counseling and provide resources for respite care for the son. They also contacted APS to have them open and follow the case for the widower's safety.

This case study demonstrates the need to be able to identify instances of PEA as well as the need to interview the family members separately. This allows law enforcement to be able to evaluate if a crime has been committed and to be able to provide resources for all those involved before the abuse escalates into physical harm. Although PA may leave no physical marks, it can leave lasting trauma and poor health outcomes for the elderly.

References

Acierno, R., Hernandez, M., Amstadter, A., Resnick, H., Steve, K., Muzzy, W., & Kilpatrick, D. (2010). Prevalence and correlates of emotional, physical, sexual, and financial abuse and potential neglect in the United States: The national elder mistreatment study. *American Journal of Public Health, 100*(2), 292–297.

Acierno, R., Watkins, J., Hernandez-Tejada, M., Muzzy, W., Frook, G., Steedley, M., & Anetzberger, G. (2018). Mental health correlates of financial mistreatment in the national elder mistreatment study wave II. *Journal of Aging and Health.* https://doi.org/10.1177/0898264318767037.

Amankwaa, B. (2017). Informal caregiver stress. *The ABNF Journal, 28*(4), 92–95.

Beach, S., Liu, P.-J., DeLiema, M., Iris, M., Howe, M., & Conrad, K. (2017). Development of short-form measures to assess four types of elder mistreatment: Findings from an evidence- based study of APS elder abuse substantiation decisions. *Journal of Elder Abuse and Neglect, 29*(4), 229–253. http://doi.org/10.1080/08946566.2017.1338171.

Bonnie, R., & Wallace, R. (2003). *Elder mistreatment: Abuse, neglect, and exploitation in an aging America.* Washington, D.C.: National Academies Press.

Cicirelli, V. (2010). Attachment relationships in old age. *Journal of Social and Personal Relationships, 27*(2), 191–199.

Conrad, K., Iris, M., Ridings, J., Langley, K., & Anetzberger, G. J. (2011). Self-report measure of psychological abuse of older adults. *The Gerontologist, 51*(3), 354–366.

Countouris, P. (2018). Bullying: It doesn't end on the childhood playground. *Aging Today*, 3. September-October.

Curtin, L. (2016). Dumped: When nursing homes abandon patients to the hospital. *American Nurse Today, 11*(10), 2, 1.

Dong, X., Chen, R., Chang, E., & Simon, M. (2013). Elder abuse and psychological well- being: A systematic review and implications for research and policy-a mini review. *Gerontology, 59*, 132–142.

Eisikovits, Z., & Band-Winterstein, T. (2015). Dimensions of suffering among old and young battered women. *Journal of Family Violence, 30*, 49–62.

Gallione, C., Molin, A., Cristina, F., Ferns, H., Mattioli, M., & Suardi, B. (2017). Screening tools for identification of elder abuse: A systematic review. *Journal of Clinical Nursing, 26*, 2154–2176.

Jaffe, I. (2017). *AARP foundation sues nursing home to stoop illegal evictions.* Retrieved Ffrom https://www.npr.org/sections/health-shots/2017/11/13/563710785/aarp-foundation-sues-nursing-home-to-stop-illegal-evictions.

Johannesen, M., & LoGiudice, D. (2013). Elder abuse: A systematic review of risk factors in community-dwelling elders. *Age and Aging, 42*, 292–298.

Karantzas, G., & Simpson, J. (2015). Attachment and aged care. In J. Simpson, & W. Rholes (Eds.), *Attachment theory and research: New directions and emerging themes* (pp. 319–345). New York: The Guilford Press.

Kim, T., Jeong, H., Han, J. W., Kwak, K. P., Kim, B., Kim, S., … Kim, K. (2018). Prevalence and risk factors of abusive behaviors in the caregivers of people with dementia in Korea. *Psychiatry Investigation, 15*(7), 677–686.

Kishimoto, Y., Terada, S., Takeda, N., Oshima, E., Hajime, H., Yoshida, H., … Uchitomi, Y. (2013). Abuse of people with cognitive impairment by family caregivers in Japan (a cross-sectional study). *Psychiatry Research, 209*, 699–704.

Lafferty, A., Fealy, G., Downes, C., & Drennan, J. (2016). The prevalence of potentially abusive behaviors in family caregiving: Findings from a national survey of family carers of older people. *Age and Aging, 45*, 703–707.

McGann, E., & Moynihan, B. (2006). Elder abuse. In V. Lynch (Ed.), *Forensic nursing*. St. Louis: Mosby.

Milberg, A., & Friedrichsen, M. (2017). Attachment figures when death is approaching: A study applying attachment theory to adult patients' and family members' experiences during palliative home care. *Supportive Care in Cancer, 25*, 2267–2274.

Mysuk, Y., Westendorp, R., & Lindenberg, J. (2016). Perspectives on the etiology of violence in later life. *Journal of Interpersonal Violence, 31*(18), 3039–3062.

National Center on Elder Abuse. (2003). *The basics: Major types of abuse.* Retrieved from http://www.elderabusecenter.org.

Perel-Levin, S. (2008). *Discussing Screening for elder abuse at primary health care level.* Geneva, Switzerland: World Health Organization.

Pico-Alfonso, M., Garcia-Linares, M., Celda-Navarro, N., Blasco-Ros, C., Echeburua, E., & Martinez, M. (2006). The impact of physical, psychological, and sexual intimate male partner violence on women's mental health: Depressive symptoms, posttraumatic stress disorder, state anxiety, and suicide. *Journal of Women's Health, 15*(5), 599–611.

Roberto, K., & Teaster, P. (2017). Theorizing elder abuse. In X. Dong (Ed.), *Elder abuse research practice and policy* (pp. 21–41). Cham, Switzerland: Springer.

Rzeszut, S. (2017). The need for a stronger definition: Recognizing abandonment as form of elder abuse across the United States. *Family Court Review, 55*(3), 444–457.

Toda, D., Tsukasaki, K., Itatani, T., Kyota, K., Hino, S., & Kitamura, T. (2018). Predictors of potentially harmful behavior by family caregivers towards patients treated for behavioral and psychological symptoms of dementia in Japan. *Psychogeriatrics, 18*, 357–364.

U.S. Preventive Services Task Force. (2013). *Final recommendation statement intimate partner violence and abuse of elderly and vulnerable adults: Screening*. Retrieved from https://www.uspreventiveservicestaskforce.org/Page/Document/RecommendationStatementFinal/intimate-partner-violence-and-abuse-of-elderly-and-vulnerable-adults-screening.

While, A. (2017). Pet dogs as promoters of wellbeing. *British Journal of Community Nursing, 22*(7), 332–336.

Wilber, K. (2018). Top of the aging advocacy agenda: Family caregiving, elder abuse, and isolation. *Aging Today, 39*(3), 1–12.

World Health Organization. (2017). *Abuse of older people-1 in 6 affected*. Retrieved from http://www.who.int/mediacentre/news/releases/2017/abuse-older-people/en.

Yon, Y., Mikton, C., Gassoumis, Z., & Wilber, K. (2017). Elder abuse prevalence in community settings: Asystematic review and meta-analysis. *The Lancet, 5*, 147–156.

8

MULTIDISCIPLINARY COLLABORATION

Jennifer Lynn Johnson[1,2]

[1]*Emergency Department FACT Program, AdventHealth Shawnee, Merriam, Kansas, United States;* [2]*Johnson Legal Nurse Consulting, LLC, Shawnee Mission, KS, United States*

CHAPTER OUTLINE
Introduction   183
The Multidisciplinary Team   184
Law Enforcement   185
    Responding Officer   185
    Crime Scene Investigator   187
    Law Enforcement Investigator   187
Medical Response   188
    Medical Provider and Physician   188
    Forensic Nurse Examiner   190
The Justice System   192
    Adult Protective Services   192
    Prosecuting Attorney   193
    District Attorneys Office: Victim Assistance Advocate   194
Bringing the Collaboration Together   194
Case Example   195
References   197

Introduction

Elder abuse is a multifaceted issue that knows no ethnic boundary and sociodemographic strata and preys on those that have increased vulnerabilities (Marshall & Hale, 2018; Twomey & Weber, 2014; Vognar & Gibbs, 2014). Abuse can increase the mortality and morbidity of the individual, as well as the development of consequences that can cause poor quality of life, loss of life, loss

Elder Abuse. https://doi.org/10.1016/B978-0-12-815779-4.00008-2

of security, and significant psychological stress (Jogerst et al., 2003; Mysyuk, Westendorp, & Lindenberg, 2013).

In one study, it was noted that in 97% of elder abuse cases, the referring agency found the team helpful in assessing and identifying potential abuse and documenting any cognitive deficits the individual may possess, including discussions of the medical findings. These observations also included their implications regarding abuse and forming the type of action that is required by law enforcement to provide an immediate response (Mosqueda, Burnight, Liao, & Kemp, 2004). Therefore, there is a need for a multidisciplinary collaboration approach to provide comprehensive medical forensic examinations, advocacy, and adult protective and criminal justice services for victims of elder abuse in a compassionate, culturally sensitive manner with the goal to hold the offender accountable (Dong, 2012; Nancarrow et al., 2013; Navarro et al., 2016; Twomey & Weber, 2014).

This chapter will focus on the necessity for a multidisciplinary approach for the identification, assessment, and investigation of elder maltreatment. The multidisciplinary team will be formed with professionals from the legal system, forensic nursing, medicine, social services, adult protective services (APS), and law enforcement.

The Multidisciplinary Team

The multidisciplinary team exists to collectively work together to provide a combined approach for treating, evaluating, investigating, and prosecuting cases of elder abuse. The team may share past experiences from previous cases for lessons learned and the identification of best practices for the jurisdiction in which they are working. Providing knowledge and expertise in each perspective section that handles elder abuse and calling on that expertise is important to facilitate a successful investigation. Using this collaborative approach, the team members collectively communicate with each other to resolve issues and identify any difficulties with current elder abuse cases or concerns that may arise with other individuals on the team. This communication is facilitated through respect and being receptive to each other's opinions. Additionally, each team member values others and their roles to advance knowledge and provide specific training and further resources to facilitate additional collaboration opportunities (Nancarrow et al., 2013). To fully understand the significance and benefit of the multidisciplinary team, it is crucial to understand each team member's specific role and responsibilities in assessing elder abuse.

Law Enforcement

Law enforcement may be the initial contact for individuals that are in an abusive relationship. This may occur in a residence, nursing home, group home, an environment in which the elder is residing under the care of a family member. In this situation, the elder or someone in the community notifies law enforcement of concern for abuse. As a result, an officer will respond to the location of the elder to begin the initial response and take a report of the abuse that is occurring. This notification initiates a chain reaction that may result in further investigation by a detective and the crime scene investigator (CSI).

Responding Officer

The responding officer answers the notification that elder abuse is suspected or that safety is endangered or a crime has been committed; this may be from a concerned neighbor, friend, or medical facility (Twomey & Weber, 2014). On arrival, the officer assesses the medical needs of the individual and interviews the victim to determine jurisdiction and whether a crime has been committed. If the individual requires medical intervention, the officer will notify emergency personnel who will provide an initial assessment and transport the individual for further examination, either to the closest medical center or at a medical center of the victim's choice (Rosen, Hargarten, Flomenbaum, & Platts-Mills, 2016; Twomey & Weber, 2014).

The officer evaluates the scene and considers contacting the investigation division or crime scene unit to further assist in processing the scene for potential evidence related to the crime. The officer provides information to the investigator or the prosecuting attorney's office concerning legal access to the site. An officer may also collect evidence, document the scene, and submit a written report regarding the conditions at the crime scene to the case investigator. The officer provides an accurate and thorough assessment of the crime to aid in the reconstruction of what happened. The goal is to have a full understanding of the incident, with supporting evidence, to resolve the case promptly.

The officer provides services with the objective of obtaining information and collecting evidence to construct a thorough report. The officer must also provide a referral in an environment that is nonjudgmental and maintains respect for the dignity of the victim. If the individual does not speak English, the officer will use an interpreter to assist the victim during the interview phase as needed to promote communication and ensure that the information gathered is accurate. Law enforcement respects the human dignity and uniqueness of the victim, unrestricted by considerations of gender, ethnicity, age, social status, economic status, personal attributes, the nature of health problems, or the nature of the abuse (Vognar & Gibbs, 2014).

Assessment of the individual by emergency medical personnel for any possible immediate medical needs to render treatment of any injuries that may have been sustained, as well as provide psychological analysis as appropriate for ongoing safety and care. It may inappropriate or unsafe to return the victim to their current living situation. An explanation of the examination is necessary for evidence collection and should include that evidence could be lost, which may lead to a delay in apprehending and prosecuting the offender, adversely affecting the case (National Forensic Science Technology Center [NFSTC], 2013).

Law enforcement ensures legal access to the crime scene or related sites so that evidence is collected legally, which guarantees its admissibility in courtroom proceedings. The responding officer gathers pertinent information for the initial police report which includes documentation of witnesses and information regarding the crime scene to the investigator. The officer may request additional resources to investigate the crime, such as request assistance from the crime lab or evidence technicians.

Identification and collection of crime scene evidence is determined by the victim's history of the assault, if the victim is able to articulate the events that transpired. The officer may have to initiate steps to obtain consent for a medical forensic exam if the victim is otherwise unable to consent. The officer may arrange transportation to a medical facility after obtaining the victim's agreement. They may also communicate with the medical provider regarding the case and offer other information to guide the medical forensic examination, if one is provided by the medical facility.

Once the collection of evidence is completed, the officer ensures it is safely secured. The evidence is transported to the agency's property room by following the chain of custody per departmental policy and standards for evidence management. During this process, the officer will maintain appropriate confidentiality of both the individual and any witnesses who provided information about the incident. In conclusion, the officer will complete a thorough and accurate written report of the scene, using information collected or obtained from contact with the victim, to testify in court as needed.

Crime Scene Investigator

The CSI processes crime scenes to identify evidence, reconstruct events, and help bridge the investigative and forensic aspects of an elder abuse case. The CSI gathers evidence that may be inherently informative or which may be analyzed by forensic scientists to give additional value to the evidence. Providing complete identification and proper collection of potential evidence is important so that the details of a crime align with the facts to assure a complete view of the events that transpired.

The CSI maintains an objective approach to the investigation in determining the processing required for on-scene identification and collection of evidence. The CSI is knowledgeable on the use of camera equipment sufficient to capture a clear and accurate record of the crime scene to aid in the reconstruction of events. If potential evidence related to the case is identified, it is collected and packaged to sufficiently protect the evidence once it leaves the crime scene (National Institute of Standards and Technology [NIST], 2013.)

Once the crime scene is processed, the CSI maintains the chain of custody and submits items to the criminalistics laboratory for further forensic analysis. The CSI will provide access to a written report to the case investigator's agency and to the prosecuting attorney's office of any information gleaned from the evaluation and collection of scene evidence. The CSI also communicates directly with the case investigator or the prosecutor to attain additional information or to request evidence standards "known" for any suspect(s) or other identified individuals pertinent to the case.

Once the evidence is analyzed, the CSI may provide feedback regarding processing, lab analysis, and collection of evidence to the investigators, the forensic nurse or medical provider, and the prosecuting attorney, as needed. Ultimately, the CSI will testify in court to the collection of evidence, maintenance of the chain of custody, submission to the lab, and other pertinent information gathered from the investigation.

Law Enforcement Investigator

The investigator for law enforcement gathers evidence to conduct a fair, impartial, sensitive, and professional investigation. Providing a clear and complete synopsis of the evidence and facts of the case facilitates the judgment by the prosecutor to issue the case and proceed through the judicial process (Nancarrow et al., 2013; Navarro et al., 2016). The investigator provides evidence to the prosecutor, which assists in resolving the investigation, with the overriding goal of successfully prosecuting offenders.

One focus of the investigation is for the investigator to maintain an objective approach. When possible, the investigator provides the victim or their family with time to process the information by taking into consideration the trauma experienced. The victim can also be provided with updates on the status of the investigation until the case is turned over to the prosecuting attorney's office and any questions can be answered that may become evident through the investigation. The law enforcement investigator ensures that the victim and their family is aware of the services provided by advocacy, social services, and other community providers that could benefit the victim and family.

The investigator will conduct necessary interviews with any individuals present or anyone who may have information relative to the case. The investigator may utilize forensic interviewing specialists if available for those that exhibit cognitive deficiencies.

If a medical examination is completed, the investigator requests the report from the forensic nurse examiner (FNE) or medical provider regarding the medical forensic examination, the findings identified from the examination, and their relation to the act of the crime committed. If there is additional evidence identified following an interview, the investigator collects and preserves this (NFSTC, 2013). Once the information pertinent to the case is known, the investigator prepares an investigative report, submits evidence to criminalistics laboratory for analysis, and ultimately presents the case to the prosecuting attorney if requested.

Medical Response

Medical Provider and Physician

Emergency departments have been recognized as an important location for the identification of abuse, especially elder abuse and neglect (Evans, Hunold, Rosen, & Platts-Mills, 2017). As the individual ages, metabolic abnormalities, infections, immunological diseases, and other medical conditions may predispose the elder to situations that increase the risk of abuse or neglect. This requires emergency room providers to be both knowledgeable and intuitive about potential abuse and comorbid medical conditions in the elderly.

The medical provider completes an evaluation and provides any treatment required. The provider will also assess if the victim requires further services, such as hospital admission for any injuries sustained as a result of the physical abuse or neglect. If the victim presents with concerning injuries that cannot be explained by the history that was provided, consultation with other professionals may be necessary, including social services, law enforcement, and FNEs to adequately and appropriately respond to the victim's immediate needs. This includes action planning for the next steps to provide for ongoing safety (Evans et al., 2017).

The aging patient presents to the emergency department for evaluation and treatment for many varying reasons. On arrival, the elder is assessed for their current and past medical history, medications, allergies to medications, and their chief complaint or reason for their visit. During this assessment, the individual may have injuries or the suspicion of injuries that may be due to abuse or neglect. If suspected, the provider will consult with a FNE if available. If one is not available, the medical provider will complete the interview with the elder, without others in the room, to provide a safe, comfortable, and trusted environment for the elder to disclose the situation.

The provider communicates with the elder about the examination, and if the victim agrees, the provider may initiate a law enforcement response to further assist with legal issues identified. Informed consent is the process by which an individual is provided the opportunity to agree to or refuse the medical examination. Informed consent is paramount for the medical evaluation and assessment of an individual. Any nonconsensual touching, including contact required for a medical examination, is considered battery under civil law (Brendel, Wei, Schouten, & Edersheim, 2010). It is important to mention that informed consent is not based on the written consent provided by an individual but the plenary conversation of what to expect and identification of the outcomes, risks, and benefits to completing the examination. During informed consent, the medical provider may become aware that the elder is not able to consent because of lack of capacity. In this case, the provider should consult behavioral health to further assess the individual's ability to understand and formulate their decision-making process (Brendel et al., 2010).

While communicating with the patient, the provider develops a plan for treatment, which can include laboratory analysis and radiological studies to further characterize whether there is a need for additional concern for the elder's safety and well-being. The laboratory analysis may provide insight into other issues that are present due to the abuse or neglect, which require additional intervention. If injuries are present, or concern for underlying injuries is identified, it is prudent that the medical provider facilitates the use of radiological studies to detect underlying injuries that may not be able to be diagnosed otherwise. These radiological studies can provide a wealth of information regarding new injuries, including injuries that occurred recently and are in the process of healing, or injuries that may be a result of accidental trauma (Rosen, Hargarten, Flomenbaum, & Platts-Mills, 2016; Twomey & Weber, 2014).

Using the information provided by the elder and the laboratory, radiological and physical examination will aid the provider in determining if abuse or neglect has occurred. Using this information, the medical provider will determine if the individual can be discharged to their residence, be admitted for further treatment or assistance in placement, or should be moved to another facility for safety or further care (Twomey & Weber, 2014; Vognar & Gibbs, 2014). If admission is required for treatment or for safe placement in an alternative residence, the medical provider consults with social services to provide further assessment of the elders needs before discharge. Together, they may facilitate further outreach to community partners and additional medical providers for safe disposition in an environment to further protect the elder from abuse or neglect.

On completion of the assessment, treatment, and disposition of the elder when abuse has been suspected or identified, the medical provider documents the findings from the assessment in the medical record. Additionally, a completed mandatory report to APS or other appropriate agency provides information specific to the abuse identified in the examination.

Forensic Nurse Examiner

An FNE is a registered professional nurse or nurse practitioner licensed in the state in which the medical forensic examination will be completed. The nurse examiner has completed specific training and education regarding abuse, sexual assault, injury presentation, and mechanism of injuries.

The FNE performs a medical forensic examination for any individual that has sustained injuries, disclosed abuse, or injuries that are suggestive of abuse. In elder abuse cases, this may be challenging if the victim has a cognitive deficit or is unable to verbalize the events that have occurred (Aequitas, 2017). The FNE provides an accurate, comprehensive, culturally sensitive medical assessment while determining the further needs of the elder abuse victim. This will include obtaining forensic photography, the collection of perishable biological and trace evidence for further laboratory analysis, activation of law enforcement, consultation with other medical providers, completing a mandatory report of abuse to APS, and ultimately testifying in court to the findings of the examination.

The forensic nurse may be the first person to engage the victim of elder abuse when seeking medical care for any injuries that may have been sustained or when neglect has occurred. The forensic nurse documents the medical history of the victim while considering the potential for comorbidities in their existing health history and the type of abuse that is occurring. The FNE explains the medical forensic examination to the individual and obtains written consent to proceed with the examination, either from the victim or their durable power of attorney. The FNE discusses the issues of abuse with the individual in a compassionate, nonjudgmental, nonbiased, and nonblaming manner by using open-ended questions while gathering information for the case and provides an opportunity to utilize resources and collaborate with other disciplines as appropriate (Vognar & Gibbs, 2014). The examiner uses the information provided during the initial assessment to determine if laboratory analysis or radiological studies are indicated. The FNE should also determine if a mental health assessment should be requested.

During the verbal exchange it may become evident that the elder is not able to consent to the examination. If this is identified, the nurse examiner will initiate further steps to obtain authority for a medical forensic exam by either the individual's durable power of attorney or from law enforcement, to document injuries, with a court order signed by a judge. This may occur on a case-by-case basis, depending on the jurisdiction. In some situations, the victim may not desire to initiate a police response at that time. However, if law enforcement presented with the victim or the victim chooses to report to law enforcement with the assistance of the forensic nurse, the FNE will often communicate with law enforcement before and after the exam to identify further information that may provide additional insight to the incident, including types of injuries that may be present. The FNE obtains an incident or case number from law enforcement at that time and assures that this information is provided in both the medical record and the medical forensic report. If in the community there are advocates that can respond to the facility to support the victim and family, the forensic nurse will initiate this referral to assure an ongoing supportive measure for both the victim and the family.

The FNE provides information about the process of an examination to allow the victim to make a knowledgeable, informed decision about consenting to the medical forensic examination. Once consent is obtained, the FNE conducts the medical forensic examination and the collection of any perishable biological evidence. The examiner documents the exam findings by use of a written report and photographs (Vognar & Gibbs, 2014). The written report will focus on the disclosure provided by the elder, the presence of injuries and how those injuries were sustained, and the type of injury including the description in written form. If forensic photography is completed, the FNE will complete a body map diagram depicting the specific location on the body and type of injury. Once the examination is completed, the FNE will release all evidence collected, including forensic photography, to the responding officer or detective assigned to the elder abuse case.

One of the other functions that the FNE provides are referrals for follow-up care, written discharge instructions, community resources, and facilitation of a safe place postdischarge. As noted previously, this occurs if the victim is not admitted for further evaluation and treatment of injuries or if the return to the residence or facility is unsafe for the victim. The FNE maintains confidentiality of the records, photographs, and communication concerning the medical examination per the Health Insurance Portability and Accountability Act (HIPAA) guidelines set forth by federal regulation to protect the victim from further potential harm and to protect the information that was shared with the examiner (Brendel et al., 2010).

The FNE determines a forensic conclusion related to the interview and objective and subjective physical examination findings. Ultimately, the forensic nurse will provide consultation and testimony about the findings from the medical forensic examination and any evidence collected by the examiner.

The Justice System

Adult Protective Services

APS provides services to adult individuals based on four ethical principles as cited by Vognar and Gibbs (2014): the right to safety, the right to retain civil and constitutional rights, the right to decisions that may not be recognized by others as normal but do not cause harm to self or others, and the right to refuse all services. Most APS caseworkers are social workers that respond to alleged and suspected abuse, neglect, exploitation, and issues with self-neglect. They ensure the safety and well-being of individuals where a concern may be present and provide appropriate resources and assistance (Twomey & Weber, 2014; Vognar & Gibbs, 2014). The APS investigation may be concurrent to the criminal investigation; these two investigations can yield a wealth of information, but it is unlikely that an APS investigation would provide all the information required for adjudication (Aequitas, 2017).

After receiving the report from a concerned individual or mandatory reporter that a suspected abuse, neglect, exploitation, or issue with self-neglect exists, the APS caseworker will provide a response to the individual to initiate a report and begin investigation of the circumstances and issues that may be present. During this response, they are charged with investigating the allegations of the abuse, providing assistance in locating a safe environment for residing, and any other assistance that may be needed or identified from the APS investigation. The initial response typically occurs where the individual is residing to provide a personal face-to-face interview to identify concerns and to begin formulating next steps that may be needed and to determine if the individual needs or desires additional services. If the victim voluntarily welcomes protective services, the caseworker will continue to provide ongoing monitoring and evaluation of the situation to continue to assure that the elder is in the safest environment. This is paramount for prevention of further potential abuse and neglect either by another individual or through self-neglect. Also, the APS caseworker can arrange for a myriad of other services that the elder may require, such as medical intervention, housing arrangements, activation of law enforcement, and economic and social assistance (Twomey & Weber, 2014).

Prosecuting Attorney

The legal system functions to prosecute the perpetrator and holds the offenders accountable for the crime. It also protects society and assists in restoring a sense of safety and security for the victim. Justice is served by an appropriate resolution of the case.

The prosecution evaluates cases submitted by law enforcement and determines if sufficient credible evidence exists to support prosecution. The prosecuting attorney's office will include the victim whenever possible in decisions concerning the filing of the case, the reduction of charges, plea offers, dismissal, or other possible case dispositions. Other responsibilities include informing the victim of the status of the case, explaining the reasons for continuances, and seeking a mutually agreeable date for hearings that are rescheduled when appropriate. They will advise the victim of their option to have a support person and advocate present during interviews and in court. They will provide arrangement for interpretation services for victims and witnesses when necessary, if their identified language is not English. Many prosecution offices have advocates that can assist the victim with updates and communication of information between the courts, prosecutor, and the victim. If a decision to prosecute is made and a trial is imminent, the prosecuting attorney must coordinate with law enforcement and the CSI, investigator, medical provider, FNE, social services, APS, and any witnesses will be prepared for upcoming testimony (Aequitas, 2017).

District Attorneys Office: Victim Assistance Advocate

The victim assistance advocate helps victims and witnesses of all types of crime through the criminal court system. Victim assistance advocates strive to lessen the impact of victimization for persons who have suffered from crime by providing support and information about services to meet the needs experienced by crime victims and witnesses. This assistance is provided whether or not a suspect is apprehended and prosecuted. Victims and witnesses will have an understanding of the criminal court system and their role in the process.

The victim assistance advocate will provide information about the criminal justice system and the victim's role. The advocate will provide notice of court hearings and provide court support by attending interviews, hearings, or trials with the victim. The advocate will notify the victim of any change in the case status and the final disposition of the case, providing information to victims about their legal right to make a statement about how the crime impacted their life and also about crisis intervention, counseling services, crime victim compensation, and any other services identified that the victim may require.

Bringing the Collaboration Together

Knowledge and understanding of the roles and responsibilities of the multidisciplinary team members provides a better understanding of how this multifaceted team works together as a cohesive entity to investigate, facilitate coordination of care, provide for safety, ensure additional prevention from abuse, and ultimately hold the perpetrator accountable. A way this can be accomplished is through case review and consultation as the case is present initially and throughout the investigative process. This provides an opportunity for explanation of thoughts, ideas, opinions, and outcome potentials for the individual regarding safety and ongoing needs. It may also identify areas that have been overlooked or not considered identified by the member in their specific role within the multidisciplinary team.

Information sharing across the team can provide an avenue of enlightenment in other potential areas for concern and fine-tuning the investigation. It is imperative for the team members to effectively communicate their portion of the evaluation and assessment of the elder abuse case, in an aim to build on previous information and understanding of the complexity of the case. Ultimately, this information exchange may significantly impact the case, making the case more tenacious and concise. Case reviews can also provide an opportunity for brainstorming for additional referrals and resources that the elder and their family may require or the identification in changes that are required because of new information becoming available.

Case Example

A 70-year-old African-American female residing in an apartment with her daughter hears a knock on the apartment door. She is unable to answer the door because of an inability to stand. Her daughter answers the door, and on answering the door, she is greeted by emergency medical services (EMS) and law enforcement. She is informed that there has been a phone call concerning the elderly female residing in the home. The daughter replies that there are no issues that she is aware of. The police officer requests if he may enter the residence to check the welfare of her 70-year-old mother.

During this verbal exchange, the EMS providers and the officer notice a pungent odor coming from the residence. The daughter allows entrance into the apartment. The apartment is clean and well kept; on entering the furthest bedroom, they find an elderly woman sitting on the floor with food wrappers strewn across the floor, a mattress and box springs on the floor, and the 70-year-old female propped against the wall wearing minimal clothing and moaning.

On attempting to communicate with her, EMS identifies that she is not able to communicate and identifies that the elderly female needs medical attention. EMS readies the female for transport to a nearby medical facility that has a forensic nursing program within the emergency department. During preparation for transport, EMS provides the woman with coverage of her exposed body and visualization concerning wounds present to the buttocks, heels, lower extremities, and upper body.

Meanwhile, the responding officer is calling the police department to notify them of investigations of a possible elder abuse case. EMS transports the 70-year-old female to the emergency department for further evaluation. On arrival, she is placed in a room, and EMS alerts staff on the concern of elder abuse. During the information exchange between medical personnel, the EMS team provides information about the status of the residence previously mentioned and that the police are still at the residence.

Back at the residence, the investigator has arrived at the apartment and is engaging in a conversation with the daughter. He questions her about the smell of the apartment, and the daughter replies that she is unaware. When questioned about the condition of her mother, she reports to the investigator that she has been deteriorating over the last day or so, but she seemed fine.

During the medical evaluation in the emergency department, the FNE presents to the facility to consult on a suspected elder abuse case. On arrival, EMS discloses the information about the status of the apartment, the room the female was in, the presence of the police officer and investigator on the scene and that they were going to close out of the case, and return to service. The FNE enters the room to identify an elderly woman who has no ability to verbally communicate, comprehend questions, or engage in general conversation. Seeping wounds are identified on multiple areas of her body. Moments later, the investigator presents to the facility and engages in an information exchange with the FNE. The investigator discloses that the daughter will not be arriving at the facility and that they will be initiating a criminal investigation for abuse. The investigator requests a medical forensic examination with forensic photography to be completed.

The FNE completes a head-to-toe assessment, identifying the presence of multiple wounds located in multiple areas of the body. Body maps, injury identification, and documentation including the size, appearance, and type of injury are documented in the medical forensic report including forensic photography. Concurrently, the woman is being evaluated by the emergency room provider who formulates a plan of care that involves admission to the facility for further treatment of her metabolic issues, nutritional deficiencies, pressure ulcers, and gaping wound noted under her breast. The FNE and the physician exchange information about the case information that has become available on arrival of the investigator and on the wounds present with the implications of their presence. It is identified through the visual examination that the woman has been neglected and has significant wounds that will require extensive treatment. On admission, the FNE completes the mandatory report of abuse to APS. On receipt, the caseworker contacts the nurse examiner to ask additional questions pertinent to the APS investigation. Additional information is continued to be relayed to the caseworker as new pertinent changes appear in her condition, status, and the advancement to discharge planning.

The FNE communicates with the investigator that the woman is going to be admitted for further treatment. The FNE gathers case information from the investigator and documents the information in the medical record. Ongoing communication with the investigator is important throughout the woman's course of treatment to provide updates on the status of the woman. The investigator is informed that the woman will require surgery for undiagnosed breast cancer evident by the gaping wound beneath her left breast and debridement of the pressure ulcers on bilateral heels and left buttocks. Ultimately the patient improves, and discharge planning is initiated with the assistance of social services and APS to locate a safe and appropriate facility for the woman to further convalesce.

Once the female is discharged, further conversations between investigations, APS, and the prosecuting attorney office ensue to provide further management of the elder abuse case. In this case scenario, it was found prudent to gather the multidisciplinary team together to formulate the next steps in the prosecutorial process for continued exchange of information to aid in holding the daughter accountable for negligence, preventing seeking medical treatment, and causing great bodily harm. This collaboration of the multidisciplinary team is one example of the effectiveness of the team and providing an avenue for the open exchange of information through collaborative communication.

References

Aequitas. (2017). *The prosecutor's resource: Elder abuse.* Retrieved from http://www.aequitasresource.org/Prosecutors-Resource-on-Elder-Abuse.pdf.

Brendel, R., Wei, M., Schouten, R., & Edersheim, J. (2010). An approach to selected legal issues: Confidentiality, mandatory reporting, abuse and neglect, informed consent, capacity decisions boundary issues and malpractice claims. *Medical Clinics of North America,* 1229–1240.

Dong, X. (2012). Advancing the field of elder abuse: Further directions and policy implications. *Journal of the American Geriatrics Society, 60*(11), 2151–2156.

Evans, C., Hunold, K., Rosen, T., & Platts-Mills, T. (2017). Diagnosis of elder abuse in US emergency departments. *Journal of the American Geriatrics Society, 65*(1), 91–97.

Jogerst, G., Daly, J., Brinig, M., Dawson, J., Schmuch, G., & Ingram, J. (2003). Domestic elder abuse and the law. *American Journal of Public Health, 93*(12), 2131–2136.

Marshall, K., & Hale, D. (2018). Elder abuse. *Home Healthcare Nurse,* 51–52.

Mosqueda, L., Burnight, K., Liao, S., & Kemp, B. (2004). Advancing the field of elder mistreatment: A new model for integration of social and medical services. *The Gerontologist, 44*(5), 703–708.

Mysyuk, Y., Westendorp, R., & Lindenberg, J. (2013). Added value of elder abuse definitions. *Ageing Research Reviews, 12,* 50, 27.

Nancarrow, S., Booth, A., Ariss, S., Smith, T., Enderby, P., & Roots, A. (2013). Ten principles of good interdisciplinary team work. *Human Resources for Health, 11*(19), 1–11.

National Forensic Science Technology Center (NFSTC). (2013). *Crime scene investigation: A guide for law enforcement.* Retrieved from https://www.nist.gov/sites/default/files/documents/forensics/Crime-Scene-Investigation.pdf.

National Institute of Standards and Technology (NIST). (2013). *The biological evidence preservation handbook: Best practices for evidence handlers.* Retrieved from https://www.nist.gov/sites/default/files/documents/forensics/NIST-IR-7928.pdf.

Navarro, A., Wysong, J., DeLiema, M., Schwartz, E., Nichol, M., & Wilber, K. (2016). Inside the black box: The case review process of an elder abuse forensic center. *The Gerontologist, 56*(4), 772–781.

Rosen, T., Hargarten, S., Flomenbaum, N., & Platts-Mills, T. (2016). Identifying elder abuse in the emergency department: Toward a multidisciplinary team-based approach. *Annals of Emergency Medicine, 68*(3), 378–382.

Twomey, M., & Weber, C. (2014). Health professionals' roles and relationships with other agencies. *Clinical Geriatric Medicine,* 881–895.

Vognar, L., & Gibbs, L. (2014). Care of the victim. *Clinical Geriatric Medicine,* (30), 869–880.

9

DEATH INVESTIGATION

Stacey Mitchell,[1] Stacy A. Drake[2]

[1]College of Nursing, Texas A&M University Health Science Center, Bryan, TX, United States; [2]The University of Texas Health Science Center at Houston, Houston, TX, United States

CHAPTER OUTLINE
Introduction   199
The Medicolegal Death Investigation   200
    Death Investigation Systems   200
    Who Investigates Death?   200
    Components of a Death Investigation   202
The Elder Death Investigation   203
    Elder Deaths Occurring in a Health-Care Facility   204
    Elder Deaths Occurring in the Community   206
    Case Example   208
    Discussion   209
Conclusion   210
References   210

Introduction

Deaths involving older adults are often complicated, especially if the older adult is frail and in poor health. Initial assumptions of an older person's death may be incorrect (Drake, Pickens, Wolf, & Thimsen, 2018). Those who are charged with investigating the death consider many possibilities, with maltreatment being one of them. The loss of capacity due to various forms of dementia often contributes to the subsequent right of autonomy. Additionally, the risk for trauma and/or intentional injury is high in this population (Gioffre-Florio, Murabito, Visalli, Pergolizzi, & Fama, 2018). Comorbidities, medications, and the aging process increase the risk of serious injury that in turn may influence death

Elder Abuse. https://doi.org/10.1016/B978-0-12-815779-4.00009-4

investigation outcomes by masking the presence of elder abuse and neglect (Reske-Nielsen & Medzon, 2016). Consequently, intentional injury or neglect may be overlooked.

With the risk of intentional injury comes a high rate of poor health outcomes to include mortality (Ayalon, Lev, Green, & Nevo, 2016; Carney, 2015; Rosen et al., 2016). Knowing this, the medicolegal death investigator (MLDI) conducts a thorough investigation that involves medical records review, history from the family or caregivers, and if warranted, a scene examination which includes an examination of the decedent (American Board of Medicolegal Investigators [ABMDI], 2018). The purpose of this chapter is to describe the death investigation process and to present explanations about the complexities of this type of investigation.

The Medicolegal Death Investigation

Death Investigation Systems

Death investigation systems vary from state to state. The types of death investigation systems in the United States include medical examiner, coroner, or mixed, which is a combination of the two (CDC, 2016). Each state has laws mandating investigation of types of deaths or circumstances in which the death occurred, mainly sudden and unexpected. The laws vary from state to state. Therefore, those reporting a death to either the medical examiner or coroner should be well-versed and have knowledge of which circumstances require a death report. Basically, deaths that are sudden and often unexpected fall under the jurisdiction of the medical examiner or coroner. Table 9.1 below provides examples of reportable deaths.

Who Investigates Death?

The medical examiner is a forensic pathologist who is appointed or hired by the jurisdiction to investigate sudden unexpected deaths for purposes of determining cause and manner of death. The coroner has the same responsibilities but is often elected to the position. Requirements to fulfill the position vary from state to state. Some coroners are nurses, physicians, or forensic pathologists, whereas others do not have medical backgrounds. There are a number of states containing a mix of medical examiner and coroner systems.

In many jurisdictions, the medical examiner or coroner employs those who assist with the death investigation. The eyes

Table 9.1 Types of Reportable Deaths.

Examples of Types of Deaths Reportable to the Medical Examiner of Coroner

- Deaths occurring within 24 hours of admission to a health-care facility
- Deaths resulting from an accident, suicide, homicide, or an undetermined cause
- Deaths occurring in an emergency room, operating room, during or shortly after a medical procedure
- Deaths resulting from therapeutic procedures or shortly after the procedure
- Deaths due to unexplained causes or suspicious circumstances (poisonings, suffocation, smothering)
- Sudden death of a person in good health
- Death in which a trauma may be associated with the death (e.g., hip fracture, head trauma, lightning, radiation)
- All deaths while in the custody of law enforcement or while incarcerated in a public institution
- Deaths resulting from a disease that may be hazardous, contagious, or which may constitute a threat to public health and safety
- Death where there is no apparent cause or a found body
- Death due to injury of any type
- Death of a premature or stillborn infant
- Deaths due to occupational injuries
- Deaths resulting from a criminal act

Retrieved from: City and County of Denver. (2018). Reportable deaths. Retrieved from https://www.denvergov.org/content/denvergov/en/environmental-health/our-divisions/office-of-the-medical-examiner/reportable-deaths.html; Fulton County Government. (2011). Types of deaths reported to the medical examiner. Retrieved from http://www.fultoncountyga.gov/fcme-information-for-families/fcme-information-for-me-professionals/1941-types-of-deaths-to-be-reported-to-the-medical-examiner.

and ears of the medical examiner and coroner is the MLDI. The MLDI possesses knowledge regarding local, state, and federal laws concerning the death, medical issues, and investigative procedures (ABMDI, 2018). The death investigator applies his or her knowledge to the process of gathering and documenting information regarding a death. Educational requirements for the MLDI vary. Degrees in Forensic Science, Forensic Nursing, or other related fields build the foundation for conducting a medico-legal death investigation (ABMDI, 2018).

In some jurisdictions, forensic nurses fill the role of MLDI. A forensic nurse death investigator (FNDI) is a registered nurse with specialized education and clinical preparation who performs the death investigation (International Association of Forensic Nurses [IAFN], 2013). FNDIs apply the nursing process to the death investigation, interactions with family or survivors, and to the community as they address issues that impact the health and safety of populations (IAFN, 2013). Their knowledge of physical examination, physiology, pathophysiology, pharmacology, and other health-related topics is invaluable to the death investigation. Specifically, FNDIs have knowledge and experience to discern between expected natural and unexpected natural as well as causes and circumstances regarding nonnatural deaths. This ability is especially important when abuse and neglect are initial concerns or when the investigation raises suspicions.

Components of a Death Investigation

The death investigation of unexpected elderly deaths is often complex (Drake et al., 2018). Obtaining significant information from prior medical records or interviews of family needs to be compiled and correlated before rendering a conclusion about the cause and manner of death. First, the MLDI is notified that a reportable death occurred. Then, the MLDI must determine if medical examiner or coroner jurisdiction is warranted.

When deaths occur at a health-care facility, the MLDI obtains information from the provider regarding the circumstances and the care provided. Information necessary to determine if the decedent is released to the family or if the medical examiner or coroner retains jurisdiction includes demographics, medical and social history, medications, date and time of arrival to the hospital, date and time of death, primary care physician, and care provided during the hospitalization (Dudley, 2013). Importantly, information regarding the circumstances in which care was sought is obtained. Additional data can be obtained from the first responders who transported the person to the hospital. Their observations of the scene, family interactions, and the patient's responses also yield important data regarding circumstances of death.

If the MLDI determines the death needs further investigation, then the decedent is transported to the medical examiner or coroner's office. In most jurisdictions, records related to the hospitalization are sent with the decedent. After review, the MLDI may request additional medical records from primary and specialty care physicians. Other reports such as accident reports and any history of Adult Protective Services (APS) provide useful information about the circumstances of death.

There are instances where a scene investigation is warranted (Drake et al., 2018). Law enforcement secures the scene, documents the surroundings through photography and sketches, and collects any physical evidence. The MLDI approaches the scene to conduct a "walk-thru" to document the scene, making note of the general area, any change in scene conditions from law enforcement documentation, and locate the decedent (Maloney, 2018). Prescription medications found at the scene are recovered, inventoried, and secured. The MLDI is then responsible for documenting the scene, the initial physical examination, and documentation of additional interviews with family or providers. Furthermore, the decedent is examined and injuries are described in the MLDI report. Once the scene investigation is complete, preparations are made for transporting the decedent to the morgue.

At the morgue, the forensic pathologist may conduct an autopsy examination which consists of both external and internal examinations. Injuries and other physical findings are photographed, along with organ dissection. Biological samples such as blood, vitreous, bile, stomach contents, and other samples are often collected and submitted. Other items of physical or DNA evidence may be gathered during this examination.

Once the medical examiner, coroner, or forensic pathologist receives all information compiled from the death investigation, autopsy examination and any laboratory studies, the cause, and manner of death are determined. Cause of death is the injury or disease process that starts the chain of events that leads to death (Maloney, 2018). Examples include gunshot wounds, cancer, hip fractures, and cardiovascular disease. The manner of death describes the circumstances that result in death such as natural, homicide, suicide, accident, and undetermined (Maloney, 2018). The medical examiner or coroner completes the death certificate with this information, and it is placed on file with the state and is available to the family and the funeral home.

The Elder Death Investigation

The relationship between elder abuse and neglect and mortality is not forthright (Yunis, Hairi, & Yuen, 2017). Research demonstrates that the links between abuse, injury, and death vary depending on mental health status such as depression, suicidal thoughts, etc., social networks, overall health, and substance use and abuse (Yunis et al., 2017). The recognition of abuse and neglect is complex and frequently dismissed due to the presence of chronic disease, medications, dementia, and the aging process. Death is an expected outcome for old age and often for the elderly experiencing admission to a hospital. For this reason, those responsible for reporting and for investigating an elder death should consider the possibility that abuse and neglect may be a factor in the death (Homeier, 2014) and look for possible indications (Drake et al., 2018).

Elder Deaths Occurring in a Health-Care Facility

The Centers for Disease Control and Prevention (CDC) (2013) released a report indicating that emergency department (ED) visits by nursing home residents, arrivals by ambulance, and hospital admissions increased with age. The ED is a major avenue for hospital admissions. Although accreditation agencies mandate screening for abuse and neglect (The Joint Commission, 2015), the screen may not yield enough detail that warrants suspicion. Research shows that elders are hesitant to report abuse and maltreatment if the perpetrator has a relationship with the victim such as family, friend, or acquaintance (Acierno et al., 2018). Although a nondisclosure of abuse by offenders who are related is not surprising, it does make it difficult to correlate examination findings with abuse and neglect. Medical records and prehospital information become key components of the death investigation.

First responders such as emergency medical technicians (EMTs) and paramedics prepare reports that become part of the medical record. Often the first on the scene, the EMTs and paramedics elicit truthful information about the circumstances of an injury or medical emergency. Excited utterances from the elder or caregivers are often documented in the report. EMTs also make note of the conditions of the environment. Sights and smells are relayed by EMTs to health-care providers on arrival to the ED. The information assists in creating a picture of the elder person's living environment. The MLDI pays close attention to the information as the transferred information lays a foundation for the death investigation process.

In addressing elder deaths occurring in a hospital, the fundamentals of elder abuse and neglect are taught to recognize signs that may be present and to complete proper documentation. The medical record is an important tool in the death investigation. The MLDI reviews the medical record, starting with the death admission, including nursing notes, which may yield important information. Documentation of observations provides insight into interactions between the elder and their visitors. For example, if an elder suddenly becomes silent, with poor eye contact when a certain family member enters the room, the provider notes the situation, who is present, and the behaviors in a critical observation to note. Statements the elder patients make provide insight into the elder's home life, such as "They are mean to me" or "I don't like that place." The information leads the MLDI to initiate further investigation and notify other agencies as required by state mandatory reporting laws concerning possible elder abuse. Additionally, reviewing medical records for changes in trends of accessing care may prove to be important when considerations of neglect are raised.

The review of laboratory studies during hospitalization, health-care visits, and postmortem values should be reviewed. Malnutrition, hydration status, and vitamin deficiencies may be mistakenly related to aging, when conversely could be the result of neglectful behavior (Miller, 2017). For example, hypernatremia or elevated sodium levels, elevated blood urea nitrogen levels, elevated hemoglobin, and hematocrit levels suggest malnutrition (DeLiema, Homeier, Anglin, Li, & Wilber, 2016). Comparison between laboratory studies at death and those with previous admissions or office visits are helpful in developing a picture of the overall health of the older person.

The MLDI is continually aware of concerns for abuse and/or neglect through the evaluation of the physical assessments documented by all providers involved in the care of the elder. The skin assessments performed by nursing staff in the ED, especially on admission to the nursing units, are particularly useful in showing the elder's condition and functioning on arrival. The presence or absence of pressure ulcers may be indicative of the care provided to the elder outside of the hospital system. While pressure ulcers occur, even with good care, their presence may be suggestive of neglect (Miller, 2017). The MLDI reviews documentation of the care provided at home or nursing home in cases of elder deaths. Important questions to answer include

1. Does the staff have the knowledge and skills about wound care?
2. Has the family been adequately taught to care for the wounds at home?

Frailty, disease processes, functional ability, and hygiene disguise and cause difficulty in discerning abuse (DeLiema et al., 2016; Miller, 2017; Drake et al.2018).

The aging process affects the absorption, distribution, and elimination of medications (Ruscin & Linnebur, 2018). Toxicity occurs more quickly in the older population. Laboratory testing becomes more important when the possibility of maltreatment exists. Lower blood levels of medications also impact the health of the elderly. Therefore, the MLDI inventories medications and correlates the retrieved medication with current and previous prescriptions. Medications may be intentionally withheld or given in excess quantities in cases of elder maltreatment. Discrepancies in medication quantities deserve exploration by the

MLDI. Social Work or Case Management may have records to assist in building the evidence used in the determination of cause and manner of death.

The risk of trauma increases with age. The natural aging process produces changes in visual acuity, depth perception, and deterioration of reflexes amplifying the possibility of injury. Comorbidities and medication therapies along with various environmental concerns add to the risk as well (Gioffre-Florio et al., 2018). Any injury identified on an elder requires thorough investigation, whether the elder survives the injury or dies as a result thereof. Determining if the injury was intentional or unintentional requires additional investigation. Unintentional injuries can occur with frail elders. However, bruises that are pattern injuries, meaning they replicate objects such as belts or other objects, raise suspicion for abuse (Miller, 2017). Injuries to the lateral, or outside, areas of the arms may indicate being grabbed in that location (Ziminski, Wiglesworth, Austin, Phillips, & Mosqueda, 2013). Additionally, any injury under clothes, on genitals, or on multiple planes of the body should be evaluated for intentional injury.

Osteoporosis causes a number of fractures due to the loss of skeletal mass, resulting in high mortality rates (Gioffre-Florio et al., 2018). Perpetrators may use the aging process to conceal intentional lethal injuries. Repeated falls and other types of blunt injuries give rise to suspicion and should be investigated. Radiographs and CT scans assist the forensic pathologist during the autopsy, especially when the fracture was surgically repaired or healed, which yields information about the direction of force, pattern, and extent of the blunt force injury.

Hospital staff members have a responsibility and a unique opportunity in the documentation of care provided to the elder patient. Observations of interactions between the elder and family, laboratory and radiographic studies, and assessments yield much information useful to the death investigation.

Elder Deaths Occurring in the Community

Not all elders die in a health-care facility. Deaths often occur in the community. Elders may die at home or in another public location. In these cases, the MLDI responds directly to the scene to document the circumstances of death and the body. A death may initially appear to be due to natural causes, but through a thorough investigation, information may be revealed that the death was due to other means (Drake at al., 2018).

When an elderly person is found dead outside of a health-care facility, law enforcement receives the first call and responds to the scene. The patrol officer conducts a preliminary investigation to determine if a crime has been committed. Unfortunately, elder deaths are often first thought of as being an expected natural deaths, when in some cases, they are not. A trained MLDI with knowledge of the aging process, disease, medications, and factors of abuse and neglect is able to develop a complete picture of the elder person's life and death (Drake et al.2018).

If a person is found dead at home due to natural causes and a physician is available to sign the death certificate stating such, after the MLDI determines the death occurred due to expected natural causes, then the decedent is released directly to the funeral home (Texas Code of Criminal Procedure, Chapter 49.25). When a physician is unable to certify the cause of death, the medical examiner or coroner claims jurisdiction. The completion of a death certificate then becomes the responsibility of the medical examiner or coroner. Deaths occurring in other locations outside of the home, such as in a health-care facility, require a thorough investigation to rule out criminal activity and foul play.

The MLDI receives the initial notification from the police and asks questions to establish that a scene investigation is warranted. Death scenes are complex and examination is performed systematically (Drake et al., 2018). The MLDI identifies the primary and secondary scene. The primary scene consists of the body and the area directly surrounding the body, whereas the secondary scene, for example, includes other rooms in the dwelling (Maloney, 2018). Each jurisdiction has specific policies and procedures regarding how to process scenes. Generally, MLDI uses accepted techniques to systematically photograph the location and the decedent.

Presence of trauma and injury is included in the documentation. Broken furniture, blood stains, and the overall appearance of the scene are examples of information recorded by the MLDI. In the kitchen, photographs of refrigerator(s) and cabinet(s) may show the amount and the type of food the elder was eating. Diagrams and photographs of the location where the deceased is found may be beneficial to the examining forensic pathologist to know the exact location of the body.

The MLDI conducts a physical examination on the decedent. Body temperature is recorded. Signs of rigor mortis (stiffening of the body after death) and livor mortis (settling of the blood in the blood vessels, creating a purplish discoloration) are identified (Maloney, 2018). Any injuries are described in the report and photographed. The condition of the decedent's clothing is noted along with the temperature of the environment. Issues of hyper- or hypothermia may affect the ability to establish cause and manner of death.

At the scene, the MLDI searches area such as the kitchen, bathroom, and nightstand for medications, herbal supplements, and devices such as glucometers. An inventory of the above items contains the name of the patient, name of the pharmacy that filled the medication, prescribing physician, name of the medication, dosage, amount prescribed, prescribing date, or amount left in the bottle. Medications are reconciled with the medical records (Dudley, 2013). The scene examination also includes seeking primary care physician contact information, medical insurance documents, and disease-related information (Maloney, 2018).

Family members and caregivers present at the scene should be interviewed about the elder's medical, surgical, and social histories. They may also be able to provide details about the elder, creating a picture of the last day or days. Family members supply an abundance of information regarding the elder, hospitalizations, medications, social contacts, and deterioration of mental and/or physical status.

Other individuals who may be able to offer knowledge of the elder are primary care providers, specialty practitioners, neighbors, social workers, case managers, and power of attorney, if applicable. APS workers supply information regarding previous or open reports of abuse and neglect along with any interventions.

Case Example

An elder death is reported to the medicolegal death investigation agency when the patient presented to the ED after experiencing a fall 4 months prior. The caregiver brought the patient to the ED because the decedent had "confusion." Death occurred 72 hours later after a diagnosis of hip fracture and subsequent development of pneumonia and urinary tract infection. Radiological imaging of the head reveals no significant findings. Because of the presence of trauma, medicolegal jurisdiction is retained.

The following day at autopsy, the pathologist identifies stage IV pressure ulcers on the sacral region, emaciation, and associated low body mass index. Subsequently, a local detective is contacted to conduct an interview with the primary caregiver and document the scene in which the decedent had lived. Medical records are also requested. The caregiver is articulate; aware of person, place, and time; clean; and appropriately attired. The detective and the caregiver interact well, with the caregiver providing information about the fall, the care provided, the patient's medical history, and changes in status that led to the hospital admission. Review of the decedent's room, however, found it to be in deplorable and in malodorous condition, including insect infestation and fecal material on the bed. The remainder of the house, particularly the part of the house occupied by the caregiver, is clean and noncluttered. Additional review of the decedent's medical records reveals impairment of functional and cognitive status with a diagnosis of end-stage dementia. The death is classified as a homicide as a consequence of caregiver neglect. Case study adapted from Drake et al. (2018).

Discussion

In this case example, neglect is determined to be present because of observations made by the detective which include (1) delay in seeking treatment after a fall and (2) the condition of the elder's room in relation to the rest of the dwelling. The patient's diagnosis includes end-stage dementia and is bedridden. Pressure ulcers may be the result of immobility and other factors. However, the caregiver's ability to discuss events leading up to the hospital admission and the patient's change in status may show the caregiver's understanding of the patient's condition. The disorder of the patient's room is in contrast to the rest of the dwelling, thus highlighting the neglect on the part of the caregiver. Because the caregiver's neglect directly impacted the patient's outcome, the death could only be classified as a homicide. In some jurisdictions, the MLDI may accompany the detective to the scene. There are jurisdictions where the MLDI would not accompany the detective and instead would request a copy of the police report for the pathologist.

In the event the patient died at home, a MLDI would be dispatched to the scene to examine the decedent, document the scene, and talk with the caregiver. The scene documentation would have shown the differences in the cleanliness of the decedent's room in comparison to the rest of the home.

The critical pieces in this case that lend support to neglect are the condition of the home and the interaction between the detective and the caregiver. By having investigating, personnel trained in aspects of elder maltreatment will ensure that cases are thoroughly investigated for a proper determination of cause and manner of death. In addition, educated health-care providers will be able to identify possible abuse and neglect and alert authorities more quickly, thus prompting a more timely investigation.

Conclusion

The death investigation involving older persons has many complex activities, including extensive medical record reviews, interviews with family and caretakers, physical assessment of the decedent, and scene investigations. Even with this enormous amount of information, it may be difficult for the medical examiner or coroner to determine if the death was due natural or unnatural causes. Confounding factors such as the aging process, effects of medications, disease processes, and often deteriorating cognition mask the signs of abuse and neglect. In addition to the autopsy, the medical examiner and coroner rely on documentation in the medical record along with the death scene in determining the cause and manner of death. The importance of the health-care provider's observations during the patient encounter cannot be underscored when caring for the older person who is at or near death. Documentation of observations provides important information as the MLDI paints the picture of the life and death of the older person. Injuries, disease processes, and medications play a pivotal role in a death investigation. The death investigation is a multidisciplinary effort and without it, justice for those whose deaths are due to abuse and neglect is not served.

References

Acierno, R., Steedley, M., Hernandez-Tejada, M., Frook, G., Watkins, J., & Muzzy, W. (2018). Relevance of perpetrator identity to reporting elder financial and emotional mistreatment. *Journal of Applied Gerontology*, 1–11. https://doi.org/10.1177/0733464818771208.

American Board of Medicolegal Investigators [ABMDI]. (2018). *FAQ*. Retrieved from http://www.abmdi.org/faq.

Ayalon, L., Lev, S., Green, O., & Nevo, U. (2016). A systematic review and meta-analysis of interventions designed to prevent or stop elder maltreatment. *Age and Ageing, 45*(2), 216–227.

Carney, A. (2015). Indicators of abuse in the elderly ICU patient. *Critical Care Nursing Quarterly, 38*(3), 293–297.

Centers for Disease Control and Prevention. (2013). *Emergency department visits by persons aged 65 and over: United States, 2009-2010*. Retrieved from https://www.cdc.gov/nchs/products/databriefs/db130.htm.

Centers for Disease Control and Prevention. (2016). *Death investigation systems*. Retrieved from https://www.cdc.gov/phlp/publications/coroner/death.html.

City and County of Denver. (2018). *Reportable deaths*. Retrieved from https://www.denvergov.org/content/denvergov/en/environmental-health/our-divisions/office-of-the-medical-examiner/reportable-deaths.html.

DeLiema, M., Homeier, D. C., Anglin, D., Li, D., & Wilber, K. H. (2016). The forensic lens: Bringing elder neglect into focus in the emergency department. *Annals of Emergency Medicine, 68*(3), 371–377. http://doi.org/10.1016/j.annemergmed.2016.02.008.

Drake, S. A., Pickens, S., Wolf, D. A., & Thimsen, K. (2018). Improving medicolegal death investigation gaps of fatal elder abuse. *Journal of Elder Abuse and Neglect.* https://doi.org/10.1080/08946566.2018.1537017.

Dudley, M. (2013). *Death and accident investigation protocols.* Boca Raton, FL: CRC Press.

Fulton County Government. (2011). *Types of deaths reported to the medical examiner.* Retrieved from http://www.fultoncountyga.gov/fcme-information-for-families/fcme-information-for-me-professionals/1941-types-of-deaths-to-be-reported-to-the-medical-examiner.

Gioffre-Florio, M., Murabito, L., Visalli, C., Pergolizzi, F., & Fama, F. (2018). Trauma in elderly patients: A study of prevalence, comorbidities and gender differences. *Il Giornale Di Chirurgia, 39*(1), 35—40. http://doi.org/10.11138/gchir/2018.39.1.035.

Homeier, D. (2014). Aging: Physiology, disease, and abuse. *Clinical Geriatric Medicine, 30,* 671—686.

International Association of Forensic Nurses [IAFN]. (2013). *Forensic nurse death investigator education guidelines.* Elkridge, MD: IAFN. Retrieved from https://www.forensicnurses.org/page/EducationGuidelines.

Maloney, M. S. (2018). *Death scene investigation procedural guide* (2nd ed.). Boca Raton, FL: Taylor and Francis Group.

Miller, C. A. (2017). *Elder abuse and nursing: What nurses need to know and can do about it.* New York, NY: Springer Publishing Company.

Rosen, T., Clark, S., Bloemen, E. M., Mulcare, M. R., Stern, M. E., Hall, J. E., … Eachempati, S. R. (2016). Geriatric assault victims treated at U.S. trauma centers: Five-year analysis of the national trauma data bank. *Injury, 47*(12), 2671—2678. http://doi.org/10.1016/j.injury.2016.09.001.

Ruscin, J. M., & Linnebur, S. A. (2018). Pharmacokinetics in the elderly. Retrieved from https://www.merckmanuals.com/professional/geriatrics/drug-therapy-in-the-elderly/pharmacokinetics-in-the-elderly.

Texas Code of Criminal Procedure. Title 1 Ch. 49.25. Retrieved from https://statutes.capitol.texas.gov/Docs/CR/htm/CR.49.htm.

The Joint Commission. (2015). *Revisions to deemed program requirements for hospitals.* Retrieved from https://www.jointcommission.org/assets/1/6/HAP_Burden_Reduction2_July2015_emb.pdf.

Yunis, R. M., Hairi, N. N., & Yuen, C. W. (2017). Consequences of elder abuse and neglect: A systematic review of observational studies. *Trauma, Violence, and Abuse, 20*(2), 197—213, 1524838017692798.

Ziminski, C. E., Wiglesworth, A., Austin, R., Phillips, L. R., & Mosqueda, L. (2013). Injury patterns and causal mechanisms of bruising in physical elder abuse. *Journal of Forensic Nursing, 9*(2), 84—91. https://doi.org/10.1097/JFN.0b013e31827d51d0.

10

MEDICATION AND SUBSTANCE USE AND MISUSE IN THE ELDERLY

Amy Carney, Kimberly Liang

School of Nursing, California State University San Marcos, San Marcos, CA, United States

CHAPTER OUTLINE

Substance Use Disorder, Self-Neglect, and Comorbid
Conditions in the Elderly   213
Alcohol Use and Polysubstance Use Disorder   216
Benzodiazepine Use Disorder   217
Opioid Use Disorder   218
Over-the-Counter Medications   221
Medication Diversion: The Elderly as a Drug Source   223
Chemical Restraint   224
Conclusion and Implications   225
Case Study   227
References   227
Further Reading   229

Substance Use Disorder, Self-Neglect, and Comorbid Conditions in the Elderly

Misuse of substances has increased globally in the last few decades. Health-care professionals, caregivers, and researchers have especially seen misuse increase in the elderly. Ethyl alcohol (ETOH), prescription medications, and over-the-counter (OTC) preparations have been implicated in misuse. Polypharmacy, the use of multiple prescribed medications at the same time, contributes to adverse drug reactions and increased hospital admissions (Martin-Plank, 2019). In the United States, the opioid

Elder Abuse. https://doi.org/10.1016/B978-0-12-815779-4.00010-0

epidemic shed new light on the problem of addiction and the rise in the use of heroin when opioids were not available. Part of this trend has been recognized in the growth of the baby boomer population; 20.2% of the population will be 65 years of age or older by 2020. It has been noted that this demographic has had more experience with drugs and alcohol from an earlier age, which has been shown to be a risk factor for misuse in later years. Women comprise a larger portion of the aging population, but their patterns of substance misuse differ from men: The rate for alcohol dependence is lower, as is binge drinking and the past-year use of illicit drugs. However, although the incidence of substance misuse has risen for the entire elderly population, it often remains undetected and poorly treated. As with other areas of abuse and neglect, stigma keeps older people from seeking care and prevents the true extent of the problem from being known. Comorbidities commonly increase with age, and medical providers may confuse substance use with symptoms of age-related changes or other life stressors. Substance misuse compounds the dangers of underlying conditions, leading to sleep problems, falls, bone fractures, problems with memory, and increased risk of motor vehicle accidents (Chhatre, Cook, Mallik, & Jayadevappa, 2017; Kettaneh, 2015).

Substance misuse is one of many psychosocial factors that contribute to elder abuse. Loneliness, depression, isolation, cognitive decline, and lack of social support can all contribute to maltreatment in later life. Substance mistreatment can increase the risk of abuse in several ways: Cognitive impairment may compound the infirmity of older adults and make them less aware of abuse; elders with substance abuse issues may be more likely to self-neglect; elders with substance misuse problems tend to have poorer relationships with their caregivers, and this may lead to reduced motivation by the caregiver to provide for the elder, leading to risk of neglect (Chen & Dong, 2017).

In the fifth edition of the *Diagnostic and Statistical Manual of Mental Disorders*, the terms substance abuse and dependence are no longer used. It now refers to substance use disorders, defined as mild, moderate, or severe. The severity level is determined by the number of diagnostic criteria met by the individual. The Substance Abuse and Mental Health Services Administration has stated that there were several reasons the distinction between abuse and dependence disorders was eliminated. The main reason was the distinction provided little guidance for treatment and created a group of "diagnostic orphans" comprising individuals who expressed two dependence symptoms but no abuse symptoms and so did not meet any diagnostic criteria (The Opioid Crisis, 2018) (Table 10.1).

Table 10.1 DSM-5 Diagnostics.

Alcohol-related disorders (490)	Alcohol use disorder
	305.00 (F10.10) mild
	303.90 (F10.20) moderate
	303.90 (F10.20) severe
	Alcohol intoxication (497)
	Alcohol withdrawal (499)
	Unspecified alcohol-related disorder (503)
Opioid-related disorders (540)	Opioid use disorder (541)
	305.50 (Fl1.10) mild
	304.00 (Fl1.20) moderate
	304.00 (Fl1.20) severe
	Opioid intoxication (546)
	Opioid withdrawal (547)
	Other opioid-induced disorder (549)
	Unspecified opioid-related disorder (550)
Sedative-, hypnotic-, or anxiolytic-related disorders (550)	Sedative, hypnotic, or anxiolytic use disorders
	305.40 (Fl3.10) mild
	304.10 (Fl3.20) moderate
	304.10 (F13.20) severe
	Sedative, hypnotic, or anxiolytic intoxication (556)
	Sedative, hypnotic, or anxiolytic withdrawal (557)

DSM-5 criteria for substance use disorders:

1. Substance is often taken in large amounts or over a longer period of time than was intended
2. Persistent desire or unsuccessful efforts to cut down or control substance use
3. Great deal of time spent in activities to obtain the substance, use the substance, or recover from its effects[a]
4. Craving or strong desire to use the substance
5. Recurrent use resulting in failure to fulfill major role obligations at work, school, or home
6. Continued substance use despite persistent or recurrent social or interpersonal problems
7. Important social, occupational, or recreational activities are given up or reduced because of substance use
8. Recurrent substance use in situations in which it is physically hazardous
9. Substance use is continued despite knowledge of having a persistent physical or psychological problem that is likely to have been caused or exacerbated by the substance
10. Tolerance, as defined by either of following: (a) a need for markedly increased amount of achieved desired effect or (b) a markedly diminished effect with continued use of the same amount
11. Withdrawal, as manifested by either of the following: (a) characteristic withdrawal syndrome for the substance or (b) use of the substance or closely related substance is taken to relieve or avoid withdrawal symptoms

Selected DSM-5 Diagnosis for Substance-Related Disorders and Misuse.
Alcohol, Opioid, and Benzodiazepine Use Disorders.
[a]Presence of 2–3 symptoms indicates mild, 4–5 moderate, and 6 or more severe disorder.
American Psychiatric Association. (2013). Diagnostic and statistical manual of mental disorders (fifth ed.). Washington, DC: Author.

Alcohol Use and Polysubstance Use Disorder

Numerous terms are used across the literature to describe alcohol use and overuse. The words hazardous, heavy, high-risk, unhealthy, immoderate, and problematic have been used in relation to alcohol consumption. Similarly, what comprises the amount of alcohol a person drinks has to do with what beverage is being consumed: One 5-ounce glass of wine, one 12-ounce beer, or 1.5 ounces of distilled spirits as a "shot," all typically comprise a drink of 12g of absolute alcohol. Various organizations and agencies also differ on what is a safe limit of consumption and what constitutes a problematic number of drinks, which often varies with gender. Although consumption tends to decrease with age, any intake could pose health problems for the elderly due to metabolic changes, medications, and underlying medical conditions that make them more sensitive to alcohol (Arndt & Schultz, 2015).

Binge drinking alcohol has been reported as a significant public health concern. Binge drinking, or heavy episodic drinking, has been described as four to five drinks on a single occasion depending on gender and tends to be more prevalent in older men than older women. Serious health consequences such as stroke, liver damage, peripheral neuropathy, and dementia have been linked to binge drinking. Worsening of depression and increase in suicide attempts occur in the elderly who engage in heavy episodic drinking (Parikh, Junquera, Canaan, & Oms, 2015). Professionals working with this group might not be suspicious of substance use disorder if elders present at a time when they are not binge drinking, appearing to be well-nourished and groomed, and not to be under the influence of alcohol.

When ETOH is unavailable, unrecorded alcohol or surrogate alcohol might be sought in its place. These products are usually produced and consumed outside of government control and generally fall into four categories: Homemade alcohol for consumption by those that make them and those around them; informally produced for sale without government involvement, such as taxation; alcohol brought across a border; and surrogate alcohols not intended for human consumption. Some homemade beverages have been shown to contain toxic agents, such as battery acid or methanol. These products tend to be cheaper than regulated and taxed alcohol and are often more available in rural or socioeconomically disadvantaged areas (Probst, Manthey, Merey, Rylett, & Rehm, 2018). Seniors on low or fixed incomes without access to recorded ETOH may turn to unrecorded alcohol or other substances such as mouthwash. This can be deceptive when the elder is asked about alcohol use, as they may not consider the substance to be mainstream alcohol and deny intake. The desperation to consume these products is often the result of the withdrawal symptoms. This may be especially true in those elders who consider themselves "functional alcoholics," when symptoms such as shaking become noticeable to elders.

Alcohol use is often complicated by the concurrent use of other substances. Marijuana, illegal opioids, cocaine, and methamphetamine use have also been reported in older adults. Polysubstance use can make diagnosis of other disorders difficult, such as mental illness. Alcohol enhances the sedative effects of barbiturates, benzodiazepines, and muscle relaxers, which can lead to accidents and even death (Haighton et al., 2018; Kettaneh, 2015; Searby, Maude, & McGrath, 2015). These and other substances should be considered by the professional intervening in elder abuse or neglect by directly addressing the use not just of alcohol but all substances the older person is using.

Benzodiazepine Use Disorder

Benzodiazepines, a subset of the sedative-hypnotic-anxiolytic class, have been in use since the late 1950's with the introduction of chlordiazepoxide, also known as Librium. Up to that time, barbiturates were one of the few pharmacologic tools used to treat anxiety but were found to have disadvantages which included dependence and death due to overdose, commonly found in suicide. Meprobamate, marketed under the brand name Miltown, was approved by the Food and Drug Administration in the United States in 1955 and marketed as an anxiolytic without the detrimental properties of barbiturates. However, it was subsequently found not to be an anxiolytic and was removed from the North American Market in the mid-1960's due to problems with abuse, lethal overdoses, tolerance, and dependence, similar to the problems seen with barbiturates. The new family of drugs, which came to be known as benzodiazepines, was found to have qualities that included acting as a central muscle relaxant, some sedating properties, and having a calming effect on the patient without significant adverse effects. Diazepam, under the brand name Valium, was made available commercially in December 1963 (Lopez-Munoz, Alamo, & Garcia-Garcia, 2011).

Short-acting benzodiazepines, such as oxazepam and lorazepam, and long-acting ones, including diazepam and clorazepate, are often prescribed to elderly patients. In a study done by Maust and colleagues, the researchers found that benzodiazepine prescriptions, both new and continuation, were used by patients well into their 80's. They found that this prescribing pattern continues despite safety concerns, other available effective treatments, and existing alternative treatments for weaning chronic users. Although anxiety and insomnia were the two most common diagnoses for a benzodiazepine prescription, some prescriptions were given for reasons other than clearly defined mental disorders. This study, analyzing visits with office-based nonpsychiatrist physicians, noted that few patients were referred to psychotherapy or alternative safer medications (Maust, Kales, Wiechers, Blow, & Olfson, 2016). Withdrawal effects can also lead to misuse. These effects can range from diarrhea to panic attacks. Tapering off these medications should be done as soon as possible, as they are meant only for short-term use. Patients who have remained on short-acting benzodiazepines for years may be tapered off using long-acting formulations monitored by the provider (Brett & Murnion, 2015).

When investigating abuse and neglect, all professionals need to know the effect benzodiazepines have on the elderly and why the elder is taking them. Older adults may have a paradoxical reaction to these medications, causing them to develop insomnia, agitation, and excitement. Questions should include if they received a prescription or were given medication by someone else in an attempt to make them quiet or sleepy. It should also be noted if the medication was meant to be short term, such as during an episode of grief, or longer for a mental health diagnosis. Assessment should also include any cognitive deficits that may add to a patient's confusion or make them more vulnerable to maltreatment. Benzodiazepines can make an interview more difficult, and law enforcement or health-care professionals may need to wait until the effects lessen to speak with the elder (Table 10.2).

Opioid Use Disorder

The terms "opioid" and "opiate" are often used interchangeably. Opioids are derived from opium, which comes from poppy plants. Opiates generally refer to either natural or slightly modified components of opium such as morphine, heroin, or codeine. "Opioids" were originally intended to identify synthetic opiates

Table 10.2 ICD-10-CM Codes.

ICD-10 Category	Description
Substance abuse	Dysfunction habit of drug-taking, which may include damage to social functioning, physical well-being, or mental health. No physical dependence.
	DSM-5 Diagnosis: Substance use disorder, mild
Substance dependence	Chronic mental and physical condition related to the patients habitual drug use that is characterized by both physiological and behavioral response, including
	• strong desire to take the drug for its effects or to avoid the discomfort of sobriety
	• inability to stop the substance use
	• Physical dependence, such as tolerance and withdrawal
	DSM-5 Diagnosis: Substance use disorder, moderate or severe

ICD-10 codes	
Alcohol	(F10.10) alcohol abuse, uncomplicated
	(F10.121) alcohol abuse with intoxication delirium
	(F10.20) alcohol dependence, uncomplicated
Opioids	(F11.10) opioid abuse, uncomplicated
	(F11.221) opioid dependence with intoxication delirium
	(F11.23) opioid dependence with withdrawal
	(F11.920) opioid use, unspecified, uncomplicated
Sedatives, hypnotics, or anxiolytics	(F13.120) sedative, hypnotic, or anxiolytic abuse, uncomplicated
	(F13.221) sedative, hypnotic, or anxiolytic dependence with intoxication delirium
	(F13.939) sedative, hypnotic, or anxiolytic use, unspecified with withdrawal unspecified

Selected ICD-10 Codes for Substance Use, Abuse, and Dependence.
Alcohol, Opioid, and Benzodiazepine Abuse and Dependence.
WellCare. (2018). ICD-10-CM documentation and coding best practices Substances Use Disorders and DSM-5.

such as Fentanyl or OxyContin but now refer to the entire class of drugs. Narcotics is an older name that referred to any mind-altering compound with sleep-inducing properties. Opioids can give patients a sense of euphoria and well-being, and even when used legitimately for pain can produce tolerance and dependence. The opioid epidemic, which began in the 1990's, saw overprescription of potent pain medications. They quickly became the most prescribed class of medications in the United States, passing cardiac medications and antibiotics. Although pharmaceutical companies assured the medical community that addiction to opioids was rare, anywhere from 20 to 30% of patients misused them. Today, many people who use heroin first misused prescription opioids (Addictions and Recovery, 2018a, 2018b).

While opioid use disorder is more commonly seen in younger patients, misuse among the elderly is growing and poses special risks in an older population. Narcotic medications have been widely prescribed for conditions such as arthritis, back pain, peripheral neuropathies, and many other complaints seen in the elderly. Opioids are used for both acute and chronic pain, when the benefits are generally seen to outweigh the risks in cases such as palliative care or end-stage cancer treatment. Controversy exists over which medications should be prescribed in nonmalignant chronic pain and how long they should continue to be prescribed to patients. Management of pain in long-term care facilities also poses a challenge: The American Geriatric Society estimates that while up to 80% of older patients in residential care experience pain, about 25% receive no treatment. Drug–drug interactions are widespread in the elderly, as this group is often treated for multiple conditions, and adverse reactions are common (Suryadevara, Holbert, & Averbuch, 2018). Many chronic pain patients receive benzodiazepines and other muscle relaxants from more than one provider. These elders may have developing but not yet diagnosed respiratory issues, such as chronic obstructive pulmonary disease (COPD) or sleep apnea, which can place them at a greater risk for respiratory depression from these medications (Lee-Iannotti & Parish, 2014). However, some patients, such as those given short-term opiates postsurgically, seek to continue their use and may turn to illegally obtaining them. This can include "doctor shopping," feigning symptoms, and purchasing narcotics from someone for whom they were legally prescribed. Dependence can occur in as little as 2 weeks' time, withdrawal effects can be frightening for the elder and their family or caretaker, and may be the reason for the drug-seeking behavior. Withdrawal effects can range from mild tachycardia to signification muscle agitation and anxiety. A tapering off plan put in place proactively by the provider can anticipate the expectations of the patient about their pain and assist in minimizing withdrawal.

Assessing for opioid misuse in the elderly is often complicated by underlying conditions. Symptoms such as agitation and insomnia, common in elderly conditions, may be signs of withdrawal but may mimic other disorders. In evaluating medication use, all of the patient's medication containers should be assessed to verify that the name on the container matches the patient who is being assessed, to ascertain legitimate versus recreational use (Table 10.3).

Table 10.3 Selected Opioids.

Codeine	As one of the most commonly abused drugs, codeine is especially prevalent among individuals who need a cheap and convenient way to get high or drunk. It is usually incorporated into alcoholic or carbonated drinks to be consumed.
Hydrocodone (Vicodin, Hycodan)	Used independently or as an ingredient in other drugs, hydrocodone is indicated for pain relief and cough suppression. This drug can be chewed, snorted, injected, or smoked. It has a low potential for abuse.
Oxycodone (OxyContin, Percocet)	Available in pill, injectable, enema, or inhaled forms, oxycodone is a medication usually prescribed to patients to manage pain. With a similar chemical structure to morphine and its ability to produce a euphoric feeling, these drugs often have a psychoactive effect when misused.
Hydromorphone (Dilaudid)	Believed to be multiple times more powerful than morphine, hydromorphone has a quick onset and is often abused for its fast effects. This drug is available in tablet, liquid, and injection form.
Fentanyl (Duragesic)	With the potential to be 100 times more potent than morphine, fentanyl carries one of the highest chance of abuse out of all opioids. The possibility of overdose is extremely high.
Sufentanil (Dsuvia)	Recently approved by the US Food and Drug administration, this drug will be available in 2019. It has the ability to provide rapid relief when administered sublingually. Its use can be foreseen in urgent critical situations.

Description of Opioids From Least to Most Potent.
AddictionandRecovery.org and AmericanAddictionCenters.org (2018a, 2018b, 2018c, 2018d).

Over-the-Counter Medications

OTC medications are those that can be purchased directly, without a prescription. OTC medications are used to treat a wide range of symptoms and illnesses, including acne, cough, pain, diarrhea, and many others. Some of these medications contain ingredients with a potential for misuse when used in a way that is not indicated for the medication or at dosages that are higher than recommended. This can include mixing a variety of medications together to achieve a desired effect or taking them in a manner or at a higher dose than indicated on the package. It is estimated that there are over 300,000 OTC products available in the United States, with the elderly as their largest consumers. Older adults take an average of four OTC medications and about as many prescription medications, routinely, resulting in about 25% of elder patients on a combination of 10 or more prescription and OTC medications (Chui, Stone, Martin, Croes, & Thorpe, 2014).

Similar to prescription medications, OTC preparations can cause adverse events, including death.

Diphenhydramine and doxylamine are used in preparations for sleep. Diphenhydramine is also used in many other medications for allergies, as well as cough and colds. These medications are known to cause dizziness and increase the potential for falls. Pseudoephedrine, a decongestant commonly found in cold medication, can be used to make methamphetamine and is now kept "behind the counter" but may be purchased without a prescription. Two of the most abused OTC drugs are dextromethorphan (DXM or DM) and loperamide. DXM is found in many medications and is used as a cough suppressant. Often labeled "extra strength", it can be found as syrup, gel capsules, and tablets. Medications containing DXM often also contain antihistamines or decongestants. While it can be swallowed in its original form, often after being mixed with soda for flavor, it can also be injected. In large doses, DXM can act as a depressant and sometimes has a hallucinogenic effect, comparable to ketamine or phencyclidine (PCP). Short-term effects can range from mild stimulation to intoxication and at high doses can cause hallucinations, hyper excitability, panic, aggression, and respiratory depression. Patients who ingest large quantities of DXM may have a false positive PCP result on a urine drug screen. Loperamide is an opioid deliberately designed not to enter the brain and is usually swallowed. When loperamide is taken in large amounts and combined with other substances, it can act similarly to other opiates. The effects of loperamide include euphoria but can also cause fainting, vision changes, loss of consciousness, and irregular heartbeat. Patients may use this drug as a way to alleviate withdrawal side effects from opioids. Cardiotoxic effects can lead to death. Elderly patients with existing cardiac conditions are at higher risk for mortality (Borron et al., 2017). Misuse of either DXM or loperamide can lead to addiction (National Institute on Drug Abuse, 2017).

There are several clues to OTC misuse in the elderly population for family members, providers, and investigators. Suspicious purchasing, such as frequently buying larger amounts than would normally be needed, can be an indication of misuse. Older patients who usually do not have dizziness or cognitive difficulties may show signs of these symptoms intermittently while using these medications. A sudden addition of one of these medications, without a clinical indication, can also be a sign of misuse.

Medication Diversion: The Elderly as a Drug Source

Medication diversion is a serious problem for a patient of any age but particularly for the elderly. Diversion has been defined as the intentional removal of a medication from legitimate distribution and dispensing channels (Smith et al., 2013). Diversion can occur with any controlled substance, including those used for treatment of substance use disorders such as methadone and buprenorphine. Diversion has a negative impact not only on an individual through poor adherence to a recommended treatment but also to the community, with its effects on crime and public health. Demand for narcotics increases theft from pharmacies and homeowners and puts pressure on medical systems through increased cost for treatment of overdoses and associated illnesses, such as blood-borne virus transmission (Wright et al., 2015).

In many cases, the elder is unaware of the diversion but may notice having to fill prescriptions sooner than expected. An older person taking medication for pain may notice less relief or that the appearance of a tablet or capsule looks different, when something else has been substituted for the prescribed treatment. Once they are aware, elders may feel the need to protect the person stealing medication from them, fearing they will lose a caretaker if the diversion comes to the attention of the police and courts. In some cases, the elder may feel they are aiding a family member or friend by allowing them access to their medication. There are also instances of the elderly selling their medication to support their income.

Understanding the reason behind diversion can help to reduce its occurrence. In the case of opportunistic theft, an older person should be reminded to keep medications in a secure place, away from persons who might be tempted to take them. Prescribing in smaller amounts may reduce theft and help an elder better keep track of the amount of medication they have. Across the United States various entities have published guidelines for responsible prescribing of controlled substances that include written patient agreements, the use of urine drug screens, and restrictions on early refills (Downey, Pan, Harrison, Poza-Juncal, & Tanabe, 2017). Enlisting the help of family members or a trusted friend can also help reduce diversion in the vulnerable elderly population.

Chemical Restraint

When a patient is agitated, there are mechanisms that can be employed to manage their behavior. These include verbal management of the behavior, physical restraint, the use of medication, or a combination of these. Chemical restraint is used with agitated patients for their safety and for the safety of those around them. Chemical restraint is defined as any pharmaceutical that is administered by health-care professionals specifically for the purpose of controlling or limiting a patient's movement or behavior. There are multiple causes for agitation including hypoxia, head injury, illness, and drug or alcohol intoxications. In the elderly, the aging brain and underlying mental illness can also cause agitation (Augustine, 2015).

The purpose of chemical restraint is to safely and rapidly sedate a patient to control their symptoms and allow them to be safely managed, without posing a threat to themselves or to staff. Many factors must be considered when using a pharmacologic intervention to restrain a patient, such as medical history, body size, and previous response to sedatives. Agents that are commonly used include benzodiazepines, such as midazolam and lorazepam, and antipsychotics, such as haloperidol, chlorpromazine, olanzapine, and risperidone. Ketamine has also been used when a rapid-acting chemical restraint is needed (Macdonald & Albulushi, 2017).

Chemical restraint has also been inappropriately used to quiet or subdue elderly patients. In a highly publicized legal case in California in 2013, the director of a skilled nursing facility, Gwen Hughes, was sentenced to 3 years in prison for ordering the use of psychotropic medications on patients she found disruptive. In the course of its investigation, the state Department of Public Health found that at least 22 patients in the facility were overmedicated and three died. The medications caused the patients to suffer severe lethargy, preventing them from eating and drinking. Some lost weight or became incoherent. The physician who signed off on the orders after the drugs were given was also convicted and sentenced to 3 years felony probation. This case is believed to be the first in which nurses and doctors were held criminally liable for improperly administering psychotropic medications (Kotowski, 2013). In 2018, the news network CNN published a report on the findings of the Human Rights Watch on overmedication of patients. The document, titled "They Want Docile: How Nursing Homes Overmedicate People with Dementia,"estimated that every week more than 159,000 patients living in nursing homes in the United States are given psychotropic medications, without a psychiatric diagnosis. Most are elderly and have dementia; the report states the patients are given the medications as a chemical restraint to suppress behaviors and ease the burden on an overwhelmed staff. The researchers found that many times family members were unaware of the side effects of medications, and some felt they had no choice but to agree to the use of the drugs for fear their loved one would be evicted (Ravitz, 2018).

It is important for both family members and elder abuse investigators to be aware of the medications that are being used and the indication for them. An evaluation of the medical record may reveal no diagnosis to support the use of certain classifications of drugs, such as psychotropics and benzodiazepines. Clues such as changes in demeanor or behavior of an elder can raise suspicion that a medication regimen has been changed and that a medication review is warranted.

Conclusion and Implications

Screening and treatment for substance use and misuse is important in ensuring quality of life in the elderly population. As this population grows, so will the need for a range of services, including the need for treatment of substance use. It has been estimated that the number of older adults requiring treatment will grow to 4.4 million by the year 2020 (Chhatre et al., 2017). As mentioned in other chapters in this book, multiple screening tools have been developed to assess many aspects of abuse in older persons. The Screening, Brief Intervention, and Referral to Treatment model addresses alcohol and prescription misuse in both health-related and social services settings. Screening helps the provider to identify the severity of substance use and the suitable level of intervention. Brief intervention focuses on insight regarding the substance abuse and motivation for change. Referral for treatment provides access to further assessment and care as needed. Assessing for substance use may be limited to one question, such as "Do you drink wine, beer, or other alcoholic beverages"? or "Do you use prescription drugs differently than how they are prescribed"? with follow-up questions as indicated. Several tools have also been developed for this purpose. The Michigan Alcoholism Screening Instrument–Geriatric Version (MAST-G) was the first tool to be developed specifically for alcoholism in older adults. It consists of a 24-item scale, while the shorter version, the SMAST-G, has 10 items. The Alcohol Use Disorders Identification Test (AUDIT), a 10-item scale, is used to screen for excessive drinking. The National Institute on Drug Abuse (NIDA) developed the eight-question NIDA-Modified ASSIST screen to assess for type of drugs used, frequency of use, and symptoms suggestive of abuse or dependence (Blow & Barry, 2014; Siddiqui & Fleming, 2015). The Comorbidity Alcohol Risk Evaluation Tool (CARET) is the successor to the short Alcohol-Related Problems Survey and is used to identify at-risk drinking in older adults. This tool is self-administered and takes about 2–5 minutes to complete. It evaluates amount of alcohol use, comorbidities, symptoms, and medications to assess drinking risks (Moore et al., 2010). Many other short, and longer, assessment tools appear in elder screening research. The comprehensive geriatric assessment has been evaluated in multiple venues, offering various types of elder care. It is a multidimensional and multidisciplinary process that focuses on assessing an elder's medical, psychological, and functional capabilities. This assessment is then used to develop a coordinated and integrated plan of treatment and long-term care, focused on the individual elder's needs. A care plan is then created based on the comprehensive assessment. This must state the goals for the elder's care, who is responsible for achieving them, and establish a timeline to review progress (Palmer & Onder, 2018). However, it's been noted that there is a lack of standardization in the assessment and can be time consuming to administer.

Regardless of the length or the perceived value of the tool, there are challenges in assessing substance use and misuse in the elder population. The person must partake in the assessment freely, without coercion from family members, medical providers, or evaluators. When using a self-administered questionnaire, the older person must be able to read and understand it and be willing to be truthful about their substance use. If the evaluation is going to be lengthy, the elder should be advised of this and be allowed to take rest breaks. If treatment is offered or advised, and the patient is mentally competent and not a danger to self or others, evaluators must understand the patient has the right to refuse.

As the population ages, more medical, mental health, and forensic personnel will be needed to work with this group. Education will be needed in identification of substance use diagnoses with the aged, and more in-patient and out-patient treatment centers will be required. This will involve not only increased funding for infrastructure but also enhanced interprofessional and multidisciplinary collaboration to ensure treatment and follow-up with this at-risk population.

Case Study

Late one evening, an elderly cancer patient is brought to the emergency department by her adult daughter. The daughter is concerned about her mother's pain level, and in spite of giving her mother Percocet during the day as directed, her pain has gotten worse. She is unable to reach her mother's oncologist and was advised to bring her mother in. The daughter states that until today the medication had been working and that she brought it with her. On examination, the emergency room nurse and doctor realized the pills aren't Percocet and asks the daughter if anyone in the home could have stolen and replaced them with something else. The daughter replies that the only other person in the home is her teenage son, who helps care for her mother in the afternoons. Law enforcement is called and a report is filed; law enforcement advises the daughter they will be coming to the house to speak with her son and not to leave him alone with his grandmother's medication.

Medication diversion can occur even with trusted family members. The first indication that this has taken place may be a lesser degree of a medication's effect, such as an unexpected reaction. In this case, the pills that were given to the patient did not lessen her pain, as they had done previously. In an effort to decrease overprescribing, many medical offices will not give an early refill of pain medication without documentation that it was stolen, such as a police report. Controlled substances, even those perceived to have little potential for misuse, should be in a secure location and accessible only to the patient and a trusted caretaker.

References

Addictions and Recovery. (2018a). *Opioids: Addiction, withdrawal and recovery.* Retrieved from www.addictionsandrecovery.org/opioid-opiaterecovery.htm.

Addictions and Recovery. (2018b). *Oxycodone addiction: Symptoms and signs of abuse.* Retrieved from https://americanaddictioncenters.org/oxycodone/signs-of-abuse/.

American Addiction Center. (2018a). *Cough syrup with codeine abuse, also known as lean and purple drank.* Retrieved from https://americanaddictioncenters.org/codeine-addiction/cough-syrup/.

American Addiction Center. (2018b). *Fentanyl addiction: Symptoms and signs of abuse.* Retrieved from https://americanaddictioncenters.org/fentanyl-treatment/signs-of-abuse/.

American Addiction Center. (2018c). *How long does dilaudid withdrawal last?.* Retrieved from Chemical Restraint https://americanaddictioncenters.org/dilaudid-abuse/how-long-is-withdrawal/.

American Addiction Center. (2018d). *Hydrocodone addiction: Symptoms and signs of abuse*. Retrieved from https://americanaddictioncenters.org/hydrocodone-treatment/signs-of- abuse/.

Arndt, S., & Schultz, S. (2015). Epidemiology and demography of alcohol and the older person. In I. Crome, L. Wu, R. Rao, & P. Crome (Eds.), *Substance use and older people* (pp. 75–90). Chichester, West Sussex, UK: John Wiley & Sons.

Augustine, J. (2015). Restraint of an agitated patient. *EMS World, 44*(11), 14–18.

Blow, F., & Barry, K. (2014). Substance misuse and abuse in older adults: What do we need to know to help? *Generations-Journal of the American Society on Aging, 38*(3), 53–67.

Borron, S. W., Watts, S. H., Tull, J., Baeza, S., Diebold, S., & Barrow, A. (2017). International misuse and abuse of loperamide: A new look at a drug with "low abuse potential". *Journal of Emergency Medicine, 53*(1), 73–84.

Brett, J., & Murnion, B. (2015). Management of benzodiazepine misuse and dependence. *Australian Prescriber, 38*(5), 152–155.

Chen, R., & Dong, X. (2017). Risk factors of elder abuse. In X. Dong (Ed.), *Elder abuse research practice and policy* (pp. 93–107). Cham, Switzerland: Springer.

Chhatre, S., Cook, R., Mallik, E., & Jayadevappa, R. (2017). Trends in substance use admissions among older adults. *BMC Health Services Research, 17*, 1–8.

Chui, M., Stone, J., Martin, B., Croes, K., & Thorpe, J. (2014). Safeguarding older adults from inappropriate over-the-counter medications: The role of the community pharmacists. *The Gerontologist, 54*(6), 989–1000.

Downey, E., Pan, W., Harrison, J., Poza-Juncal, E., & Tanabe, P. (2017). Implementation of a schedule II patient agreement for opioids and stimulants in an adult primary care practice. *Journal of Family Medicine and Primary Care, 6*, 52–57.

Haighton, C., Kidd, J., O'Donnell, A., Wilson, G., McCabe, K., & Ling, J. (2018). I take my tablets with the whiskey: A qualitative study of alcohol and medication use in later life. *PLoS One, 13*(10). e0205956 https://doi.org/10.1371/journal.pone.0205956.

Kettaneh, A. (2015). Substance abuse among the elderly population: Overview and management. *Journal of Applied Rehabilitation Counseling, 46*(4), 11–17.

Kotowski, J. (2013). *Former nursing director sentenced to 3 years for inappropriately medicating patients*. Retrieved from https://www.bakersfield.com/news/former-nursing- director-sentenced-to-years-for-inapprpriately-medicating-patients/article_ ce583533- 5757-5f4c-8c0b-36db29cca62b.html.

Lee-Iannotti, J., & Parish, J. (2014). The epidemic of opioid use: Implications for the sleep physician. *Journal of Clinical Sleep Medicine, 10*(6), 645–646.

Lopez-Munoz, F., Alamo, C., & Garcia-Garcia, P. (2011). The discovery of chlordiazepoxide and the clinical introduction of benzodiazepines: Half a century of anxiolytic drugs. *Journal of Anxiety Disorders, 25*, 554–562.

MacDonald, R., & Albulushi, S. (May-June 2017). Articles that may change your practice: Chemical restraint of agitated patients. *Air Medical Journal, 36*(3), 101–104.

Martin-Plank, L. (2019). Polypharmacy. In L. Kennedy-Malone, L. Martin-Plank, & E. Duffy (Eds.), *Advanced practice nursing in the care of older adults* (2nd ed., pp. 470–473). Philadelphia: F.A. Davis Company.

Maust, D., Kales, H., Wiechers, I., Blow, F., & Olfson, M. (2016). No end in sight: Benzodiazepine use in older adults in the United States. *Journal of the American Geriatrics Society, 64*, 2546–2553.

Moore, A., Blow, F., Hoffing, M., Welgreen, S.,M., Davis, J., Lin, J., ... Barry, K. (2010). Primary care-based intervention to reduce at-risk drinking in older adults: A randomized controlled trial. *Addiction, 106*, 111–120.

National Institute on Drug Abuse. (2017). *Over the counter medicines.* National Institutes of Health, U.S Department of Health and Human Services. Retrieved from https://www.drugabuse.gov/publications/drugfacts/over-counter-medicines.

The opioid crisis. (2018). Understand the epidemic, report ICD-10-CM codes for opioid abuse. *Briefings on APCs, 19*(9), 8–11.

Palmer, K., & Onder, G. (2018). Comprehensive geriatric assessment: Benefits and limitations. *European Journal of Internal Medicine, 54*, e8–e9.

Parikh, R., Junquera, P., Canaan, Y., & Oms, J. (2015). Predictors of binge drinking in elderly Americans. *American Journal on Addictions, 24*(7), 621–627. Retrieved from https://onlinelibrary.wiley.com/doi/full/10.1111/ajad.12275.

Probst, C., Manthey, J., Merey, A., & Rylett, M. (2018). Unrecorded alcohol use: A global modelling study based on nominal group assessments and survey data. *Addiction, 113*, 1231–1241.

Ravitz, J. (2018). *Nursing homes sedate residents with dementia by misusing antipsychotic drugs, report finds.* Retrieved from https://www.cnn.com/2018/02/05/health/nursing- homes-dementia-antipsychotic-drugs/index.html.

Searby, A., Maude, P., & McGrath, I. (2015). Growing old with ice. A review of the potential consequences of methamphetamine abuse in Australian older adults. *Journal of Addictions Nursing, 26*(2), 93–98.

Siddiqui, M., & Fleming, M. (2015). Screening and brief intervention in the psychiatric setting. In I. Crome, L. Wu, R. Rao, & P. Crome (Eds.), *Substance use and older people* (pp. 195–211). Chichester, West Sussex, UK: John Wiley & Sons.

Smith, S., Dart, R., Katz, N., Paillard, F., Adams, E., Comer, S., ... Dworkin, R. (2013). Classification and definition of misuse, abuse, and related events in clinical trials: ACTTION systematic review and recommendations. *Pain, 154*, 2287–2296.

Suryadevara, U., Holbert, R., & Averbuch, R. (2018). Opioid use in the elderly. *Psychiatric Times, 35*(1), 15–21.

Wright, N., D'Agnone, O., Krajci, P., Littlewood, R., Alho, H., Reamer, J., ... Maremmani, I. (2015). Addressing misuse and diversion of opioid substitution medication: Guidance based on systematic evidence review and real world experience. *Journal of Public Health, 38*(3), 368–374.

Further Reading

American Psychiatric Association. (2013). *Diagnostic and statistical manual of mental disorders* (5th ed.). Washington, DC: Author.

Goldschmidt, D. (2018). *Amid deepening addiction crisis, FDA approves powerful new opioid.* Retrieved from https://www.cnn.com/2018/11/02/health/new-opioid-dsuvia-fda- approval-bn/index.html.

WellCare. (2018). *ICD-10-CM documentation and coding best practices Substances Use Disorders and DSM-5.* Retrieved from https://www.wellcare.com/~/media/PDFs/NA/Provider/NA_CARE_ICD_10_CM_Documentation_and_Coding_Best_Practices_Neoplasm_Coding_ENG_5_2018_R.ashx.

11

THE MEDICAL EXAMINER RESPONSE

Robert Stabley
San Diego County Medical Examiners Office, San Diego, California, United States

CHAPTER OUTLINE
Introduction   231
Anatomic and Physiological Factors   232
Forensic Markers of Elder Abuse   233
Injuries   234
The Autopsy Examination   237
Summary   238
References   239

Introduction

In terms of population, it has been estimated that more than 12% in North America is represented by persons over 65 years of age (Pudelek, 2002). This percentage is expected to continue to increase and nearly double by 2040. In addition, approximately 10% of elder adults in the United States have experienced some form of abuse, and only a fraction of cases are reported (Cohn, Salmon, & Stobo, 2002). The reason is multifactorial, but likely part of the problem is a lack of training and experience in evaluating incidents of abuse. For medical examiners, only a small percentage of the total caseload is represented by potential elder abuse, depending on the jurisdiction; the majority of deaths are determined not to be a result of abuse. In fact, most cases of abuse reported to Adult Protective Services (APS) are due to self-neglect (Lachs, Williams, O'Brien, Hurst, & Horwitz, 1996). Overall, the number of cases of elder abuse is most likely grossly underestimated and underreported.

Elder Abuse. https://doi.org/10.1016/B978-0-12-815779-4.00011-2

The reasons are multifactorial and probably have much to do with anatomic and physiologic as well as psychological factors that change as one gets older. Evaluation of potential or suspected elder abuse requires a high index of suspicion with correlation of scene findings, extensive interviewing of caregivers, family members, and friends. The clinical and pathologic findings are reviewed, with detailed examination of injuries to include full body radiographs and other ancillary studies such as toxicology. The major road block in evaluation of suspected elder abuse cases continues to be the fact that there is no gold standard or pathognomonic finding for determining what defines elder abuse, making it difficult to understand abuse and risk factors that contribute to it. There are findings that are certainly more suggestive of abuse but not definitive, and correlation with other aspects of the case is mandatory. Without correlation with other information, determining what is abuse continues to be problematic, even in the medical examiner's office. Some of the factors that are problematic are discussed below.

Anatomic and Physiological Factors

As one ages, changes in anatomy and physiology as well as the acquisition of diseases increases the likelihood of injury regardless of the mechanism of the injury, making it difficult to evaluate potential elder abuse cases. For instance, brain atrophy results in increased volume within the subdural space and exposes the bridging veins, making them more susceptible to injury, even with mild trauma.

Medications such as anticoagulants increase the likelihood of suffering catastrophic bleeds, especially when the bleeding is intracranial.

Cardiovascular diseases such as atherosclerosis and arteriosclerosis as a result of aging make vessels stiffer and less compliant, which results in injury even from minor trauma, especially vessels in the neck. These injuries can lead to dissection and thrombosis after injury. In the neck, these injuries can also result in emboli formation that can travel to the brain and cause devastating injuries such as ischemic strokes.

Hepatic cirrhosis combined with injuries can result in massive bleeding that can lead to exsanguination. Many clotting factors are produced in the liver. When the liver is significantly cirrhotic, there is a decrease in the amount of these clotting factors produced that leads to coagulopathy and the potential for massive bleeding. There are many causes of cirrhosis. In the United Sttaes, the most common cause is chronic ethanol abuse. Alcoholics, because of their liver disease, can have extensive bruising all over their body mimicking abuse. They are also at increased risk of head injuries including skull fractures and brain contusions as a result of susceptibility to falling frequently.

Osteoporosis increases the potential for pathologic fractures associated with falls that may be difficult to discern from abuse unless the medical history of the decedent is known, and findings consistent with osteoporosis are demonstrable during the post-mortem examination.

Dementia in all types increases the likelihood for falls and other events leading to injuries and death. In addition, depending on the type of dementia, brain atrophy can occur, leading to an increased likelihood of intracranial bleeding from blunt head trauma. The elderly might lack the judgment to avoid unsafe conditions and may depend more on their caregivers. As a result, elders are more likely to be taken advantage of or abused and neglected by a caregiver, physically, emotionally, and financially.

The skin is thinner and drier and the vessels beneath the skin are more fragile in older persons, resulting in injuries from blunt force trauma with minimal force. In females, the vaginal mucosa is atrophic and drier, making it more susceptible to injury. The anal mucosa is also more susceptible to injury.

These factors, in addition to many others, make evaluation of injuries in the elderly challenging, and it is not uncommon for investigators to assume that observed injuries are age-related instead of related to potential abuse.

Forensic Markers of Elder Abuse

There are several different types of elder abuse. Types that manifest with physical findings that can be evaluated by the medical examiner include physical abuse, sexual abuse, neglect, and self-neglect. These can be evaluated using several forensic markers that include blunt force injuries such as lacerations, abrasions, contusions, and fracture, evidence of malnutrition and dehydration, pressure ulcers, poor hygiene, burns, and other types of injuries (Gironda, Nguyen, & Mosqueda, 2016). Patterns of injury are important and may be indicative of an accidental injury but also may suggest abuse based on the location, type, and specific injury pattern. Patterned injuries such as abrasions and contusions may recapitulate the object that created the injury. For instance, rounded objects may create a "tram-tracking" appearance and other objects may show their specific pattern on the skin. Hand slaps may show finger patterns; looped cords may show the loop pattern on the skin as abrasions, contusions, and even lacerations. Injuries may be in different stages of healing, especially if multiple fractures and contusions are suspect. Strangulation should be considered as a possible scenario, especially if the abuse results in sudden death.

Based on this author's experience, the majority of injuries seen in the medical examiner's office in the elderly consist of blunt force trauma of the head and neck and extremities. Other injuries include fractures of ribs and spinal vertebrae. The effects of these injuries are compounded by comorbidities, medications, and the patient's care environment. Many elderly patients suffering injuries experience a decline in health and ultimately die without returning to baseline. The question then becomes, "how much did the injuries contribute to death?," especially if the injuries occurred months before death and the elder had multiple comorbidities.

Injuries

The majority of injuries that occur in the forensic setting related to abuse are blunt force injuries to include abrasions, contusions, bruises, lacerations, and bone fractures. Abrasions such as brush burn, scratch, graze, and road rash are created as a result of the superficial layer of skin being removed by contact of an object. The contact occurs at the site of the abrasion. These usually heal without scar formation and may be patterned, showing the characteristics of the object that caused the injury. Abrasions have a red color when they occur antemortem and are more yellow orange when they occur postmortem, such as when the body is removed from a scene.

Contusions are a result of blood vessel rupture and the accumulation of blood beneath the skin. They may also be patterned, but much more infrequently than abrasions. Visibility may be delayed and they do not always show up at the site of impact; they may occur at a distance from the site of impact. In general, contusions are difficult to date. People metabolize hemeprotein at different rates between individuals and even within the same individual. For bruising in older adults, dating is even more unreliable than in younger adults. When more than one bruise is identified and they appear to vary in age, chronic abuse should be suspected.

Lacerations are a result of tearing of the skin where the tensile strength is weakest and may occur at the site of impact or a distance away from the impact site. The hallmark of a laceration is tissue bridging where strands of collagen, blood vessels, or small nerves span the wound between the edges. Not all lacerations exhibit tissue bridging, but when visible, leave no doubt as to the fact that the injury is a laceration and a result of blunt trauma. Lacerations are also associated with fractures. Rarely, lacerations are patterned. These types of injuries may be seen combined; lacerations may have abrasions and contusions around their edges.

Fractures are a type of laceration observed in bone, although the word laceration is not commonly used when describing a bone fracture. Fractures in a person who is not ambulatory should arouse suspicion of abuse or neglect.

Injuries from falls are more likely to occur over bony prominences and in one plane or on one side of the body. Injuries not occurring over prominences or in multiple planes or on multiple sides of the body are suspicious. Injury patterns should match the history; if not, there is a problem and more investigation is required.

Injuries of the head and face should be considered suspect, especially if these are contusions and occur on the ears and neck. Contusions of the extremities are more common in accidents such as falls (Mosqueda, Burnight, & Liao, 2005). Injuries occurring on multiple surfaces of the head and face, especially within the same time frame, are suspect. Correlation with how the injury occurred, if accurate, can help greatly in the evaluation of these injuries. A focal depressed skull fracture denotes an impact site. Blunt trauma by an object would be considered in this case and could be the result of accident or homicide.

Epidural, subdural, and subarachnoid hemorrhages are considered related to trauma, although subarachnoid hemorrhage may have a pathological origin such as is the case with a ruptured saccular (berry) aneurysm. Subdural hemorrhage may also occur as an extension of a large intraparenchymal hemorrhage. In the forensic setting, the majority of subdural hemorrhages occur as a result of trauma such as falls, motor vehicle and motorcycle crashes, and pedestrians struck by motor vehicles with blunt head trauma.

Injuries of the oral mucosa, especially if the injuries involve lacerations of the frenula, should be considered highly suspicious. These are injuries not normally occurring in everyday trauma. Many of these injuries occur as a result of being punched or struck by another person or an object.

Injuries of the neck include possible strangulation and vertebral fractures. Fractures commonly occur from falls. Diseases of bone can make vertebrae more susceptible to fractures and subluxations.

Torso injuries include rib fractures and thoracic and lumbar vertebral fractures.

Injuries of the extremities can be extremely important in the evaluation of elder abuse. Injuries of the extremities that include contusions of the medial aspects of the arms and thighs are suspicious for abuse. In addition, injuries of the inner aspects of the thighs should raise suspicion of possible sexual abuse. Defensive injuries may be seen that include blunt force injuries of the forearms and hands, especially if they are on the posterior aspects. Examination of the wrist and ankles should be undertaken as a matter of standard practice to rule out binding injuries from restraints. Full body radiographs should be pursued in all cases of suspected abuse, especially the extremities. Certain types of fractures can be more indicative of elder abuse such as spiral fractures suggestive of grasping and twisting of the extremity, whereas transverse fractures would be more consistent with a reported fall.

Burns can be a sign of abuse or neglect, especially self-neglect. Burns may come in the form of thermal, chemical, and electrical. Burns in the elderly, especially in the over-65 age group, have an increased mortality (Muller, Pegg, & Rule, 2001). This is further increased when the elder has extensive comorbidities such as cardiovascular disease, diabetes, and chronic obstructive pulmonary disease. Peripheral neuropathy from diabetes may preclude a person from feeling a burn or other injury, especially on the dorsal aspects of the feet.

Ulcers are common, particularly in someone who is immobile and confined to a bed or chair or in someone who has medical disease. They are divided into venous, arterial, diabetic, and decubitus. Decubitus ulcers result from immobility and prolonged pressure over bony prominences that cause tissue ischemia and necrosis. They are staged in four levels depending on the depth of the ulcer. They are very common in cases of neglect, but their presence is not pathognomonic for neglect. However, with current management strategies, most ulcers can be prevented, although pressure ulcers can develop even with the best care.

Strangulation can occur in elder abuse and should be considered in all cases of suspected maltreatment. External findings seen in these cases might be ligature marks around the neck, fingernail abrasions, neck contusions, and petechial hemorrhages in the eyes, on the face, and in the oral cavity predominantly above the ligature. Petechial hemorrhages are a sign of asphyxia but not specific to asphyxia. They can occur in deaths from heart disease and from vigorous resuscitation. In some cases, there may be no physical findings on the neck externally. Internal findings seen at autopsy include hemorrhages of the soft tissues of the neck to include the strap muscles and fractures of the hyoid bone, thyroid cartilage (especially the flat laminae), and possibly the cricoid cartilage. Sometimes, fractures of these structures can occur during the autopsy process and should be documented as such in the autopsy report; however, if the fractures are associated with hemorrhages, they occurred antemortem and not postmortem. If the death is a result of smothering from a pillow or some other object, there may be no external or internal findings, especially if the elder is debilitated and cannot fight back.

Neglect and self-neglect can be assessed by evaluating overall body habitus, nutritional status, and hydration status. Indicators may be long, dirty, and diseased fingernails and toenails, matted hair with lice, scabies, bed bugs, poor oral dentition, diseases including cancers that are untreated, skin excoriations, skin rashes, dermatitis from exposure to urine and feces, and pressure ulcers that appear untreated. Elders that require containment devices such as diapers are at an increased risk of injury and infection from urine and feces. Intertriginal dermatitis is more prominent in immobile and obese individuals and could be a sign of neglect if it persists or worsens.

The Autopsy Examination

The autopsy examination of a decedent suspected of dying as a result of elder abuse should begin with an extensive review of the circumstances surrounding death, including a review of medical records and interviews with family and caretakers. It should also include a review of information from evaluations by APS and other investigational agencies such as police and sheriff departments and the scene review. Photographic documentation begins at the scene, if there is one.

The autopsy should include an extensive external examination to include overall body habitus and hydration status, visible therapeutic interventions, injuries, body appearance to include evaluation of the skin as well as fingernails and toenails, documenting the presence of arthropods, and postmortem changes. Photographic documentation should be performed for all injuries and other findings that are suspicious. Ulcers should be documented to include location, size, extent (depth), and the presence of partial healing and evidence of infection. Other injuries should be evaluated as to the type, size, and extent. All injuries should be correlated with internal findings if appropriate. If indicated, dissection into the soft tissue around the wrists and ankles should be performed. Dissection into questionable areas such as contusions versus lividity and avulsions should be performed. Internal examination should document natural disease, injuries, and organs that are normal. Organ weights should be included where appropriate. The brain and spinal cord should be removed and evaluated preferably with a neuropathologist. Full body radiographs should be standard practice for suspected elder abuse cases as well as full toxicology based on the local office's standard protocol. Where appropriate, a sexual assault examination should be performed. All findings should correlate with the history. For documentation purposes, pertinent negative findings are just as important as pertinent positives.

Toxicology can be extremely important especially if one suspects over- or undermedication and in more rare causes of death such as poisoning by other chemicals including heavy metals or cyanide. Medications may be used as a restraint method in elder abuse.

Summary

Elder abuse is a worldwide problem. Evaluation of elder abuse is extremely challenging and problematic even for the medical examiner when compared to evaluating child abuse and domestic violence, most likely because of the specific population considered; this population is not as healthy compared with a younger one. As a result, there is no forensic gold standard that is consistent with elder abuse, making some risk factors difficult to define. There are many confounding factors that hamper the evaluation such as changes in anatomy and physiology as one ages, disease states acquired by the elder, and medications that may contribute to further injury. In some cases, neglect may result in injury from withholding of care and medications. Many injuries are consistent with aging and some are more consistent with abuse or neglect. Accurate evaluation requires extensive training to be able to recognize potential abuse, a high index of suspicion, and correlation with circumstances surrounding death, including knowledge of the caretaker, and information from family, friends, and other caregivers. The story should explain the injury pattern. Thorough autopsy, examination is required with extensive documentation of pertinent positives and negatives. Toxicology can be of great help in the evaluation. With more training, experience, research, and willingness to consider elder abuse, evaluation of elder mistreatment should become less problematic and easier to approach.

References

Cohn, F., Salmon, M., & Stobo, J. (Eds.). (2002). *Confronting chronic neglect: The education and training of health professionals on family violence.* Washington, D.C: Institute of Medicine, The National Academies Press.

Gironda, M. W., Nguyen, A. L., & Mosqueda, L. M. (2016). Is this broken bone because of abuse? Characteristics and comorbid diagnoses in older adults with fractures. *Journal of the American Geriatrics Society, 64*(8), 1651–1655.

Lachs, M. S., Williams, C., O'Brien, S., Hurst, L., & Horwitz, R. (1996). Older adults: An 11–Year longitudinal study of adult protective service use. *Archives of Internal Medicine, 156*(4), 449–453.

Mosqueda, L., Burnight, K., & Liao, S. (2005). The life cycle of bruises in older adults. *Journal of the American Geriatrics Society, 53*(8), 1339–1343.

Muller, M. J., Pegg, S. P., & Rule, M. R. (2001). Determinants of death following burn injury. *British Journal of Surgery, 88*(4), 583–587.

Pudelek, B. (2002). Geriatric trauma: Special needs for a special population. *AACN Clinical Issues, 13*(1), 61–72.

THE CRIMINAL JUSTICE RESPONSE TO ELDER ABUSE

Paul R. Greenwood
*Former Head of Elder Abuse Prosecution Unit, San Diego District Attorney,
San Diego, CA, United States*

CHAPTER OUTLINE
Introduction   241
Embarking on the Journey: Building a
MultiDisciplinary Approach   242
From Investigation to Prosecution   246
Types of Criminal Elder Abuse   247
Preparing the Elderly Victim for
the Criminal Justice System   253
Challenges for the Future   255
References   256

Introduction

I remember the call well. It came in late December 1995. I had been in the San Diego District Attorney's (DA's) Office for just over two and a half years and was enjoying an assignment called three strikes, which allowed me to be involved in back-to-back jury trials. Unknown to me at the time, this call changed my whole career path in the DA's office. I was told to report to the DA's management office. The conversation was brief. The DA explained that he had been told by Adult Protective Services (APS) that our office and law enforcement generally were ignoring a huge problem called elder abuse. The DA had decided to create a new elder abuse unit and I was told that I was going to be the prosecutor assigned.

I asked a simple question, "What is elder abuse"? The response I received was "go talk to APS." I then inquired about a manual but was informed that I would probably be the person to end up writing one.

As I left the DA's office, I confess that I was not particularly excited about the new assignment, but I promised myself that I would do it for 2–3 years and then seek a transfer back into the real hard-core prosecution work that I had signed up for.

How wrong I was! Little did I know that within 2–3 years I would be handling high-profile media cases such as homicides, sexual assaults, and serious physical and financial abuse cases involving elderly victims.

That elder abuse assignment turned into a 22-year journey pursuing justice for these victims.

The following chapter is my opportunity to share some of the experiences and lessons that I have learned along the way. The writing style will be very different from the other authors; I am a trial lawyer and I rely on storytelling. The reader will be part of my jury.

Embarking on the Journey: Building a MultiDisciplinary Approach

In January 1996, I was given an office in the Family Protection Division (FPD) of the DA's office. It was decided that elder abuse prosecutions would be part of this energetic FPD which up to that point handled child abductions, child abuse, and domestic violence. Looking back, it was a smart move to put me there. Before long I found myself dealing with similar issues that the other FPD prosecutors encountered, for example, how to handle a recanting victim.

I walked into a fully furnished office. It was equipped with a computer, a telephone, and a yellow pad. But there was one major problem. I had no cases. All the other prosecutors were busy heading to court, but nobody was bringing me any files. Traditionally, a prosecutor relies on local law enforcement to investigate a case and then bring the file over to our office for review and possible filing. I quickly learned my first lesson. Silence is one of the biggest barriers to successful investigation and prosecution of elder abuse cases. I began to realize that if I was ever going to take on a caseload, I could no longer rely on traditional methods. For the first two and a half of my career at the DAs office, I had never been without a case. A supervisor would always hand me Manila-colored files that had been dropped off by the San Diego Police Department. Up to this point, I had only been trained to be reactive, but now, there was nothing to react to; I needed to be proactive.

Fortunately, I was able to draw on my prior experience as a lawyer. Before arriving in California, I had been a solicitor in private practice in England. I had developed a criminal defense practice and was accustomed to networking with people to build up my caseload. As I sat in my new office, I decided that if law enforcement was not coming to me, I would need to reach out to them.

For 7 months, I did not prosecute one elder abuse case. Instead I spent most of my time driving around the county meeting with APS and with law enforcement. There are over 15 different law enforcement agencies within San Diego County, and back in 1996, none of them had any designated detective handling elder abuse cases.

I decided to invite myself to attend shift changes in the early mornings and early afternoon. I would be given 5 minutes to address patrol officers, and I would make a plea for cases! As I talked to police officers and deputy sheriffs, it became apparent that there were two major reasons why I was not seeing any cases. Occasionally, an officer would tell me that their agency had indeed investigated an elder abuse case in the past but that after it was submitted to the DA, nothing ever happened. As a result, officers would be reluctant to send over any further cases.

But the chief reason was that it seemed that law enforcement was dealing with a major misconception. When I would ask why I was not seeing any cases in my office, I would often be met with the same response: "Greenwood, you don't want these cases." "Why not"? I would ask. And the answer was always the same: "Elderly people make terrible witnesses in the courtroom." So, I tried to make a deal with the officers. I promised that if they investigated a report of suspected elder abuse, they could bring that report to me and I would then work with them to see if there was a case that could be filed. I also told them to let me worry about the effectiveness of the elderly victim as a witness in the courtroom.

Slowly but surely the cases started to trickle in from all over the county, both from the urban areas and more remote rural locations. By the end of 1996, I had filed about 15 felony cases.

In those early days, I also reached out to APS. Before my assignment I had never heard of APS. I was well aware of the role that Child Protective Services played but had no clue as to the function of APS. It dawned on me that if I had not realized that APS was typically the first response to any elder abuse incident, then the general public would also be in the dark. So, I decided to work on a public advertising campaign, but that would cost money, and my office had not budgeted for such an expense.

Around the same time, I started to receive invitations to speak at various Rotary clubs around the county. I would typically get 15 minutes to address a group of Rotarians about my assignment and about what I had learned regarding crimes that were being committed against senior citizens. After one such meeting, I returned to my office as the phone was ringing. It was a Rotarian who had been at the lunch and he asked how he could help. Instinctively, I told him about my desire to establish a public service announcement whereby we could circulate the telephone number that the public could call if they suspected elder abuse. Within a week I was sitting in an advertising agency office. The agency agreed to create a pro bono campaign. Three months later, I stood at a busy intersection in downtown San Diego and watched as a massive billboard was unveiled announcing a slogan "abuse is getting old" and giving out the reporting line number of 1 (800) 510-2020.

This announcement created quite a stir in the community and particularly with our local newspaper, the San Diego Union Tribune. A reporter called me to inquire about this new crime of elder abuse. The next day a front-page article appeared and along with the 1–800 number; the newspaper also printed my direct office line.

And so it began. APS started seeing a spike in telephone reports; I was getting numerous calls, and law enforcement was also noting an increase in referrals. But it was important that when cases were referred to law enforcement, the investigation would be handled by someone who understood the dynamics of dealing with elderly victims.

An invitation came from the San Diego police chief to address his upper management. I took the opportunity to challenge the chief that if in fact he agreed that elder abuse investigations should be a priority, then he should establish such a unit. Chief David Bejarano followed through. By 1998, he created a fully staffed elder abuse investigative unit consisting of four full-time detectives and a supervising sergeant. What a difference this made! Referrals to area police stations were redirected to the investigative unit, and I started to see an increase not only in actual cases but also in the quality of the investigation. By working closely with the same detectives, we began to develop guidelines and expectations for what was needed to issue an effective case.

I then turned my attention to the medical community. I received invitations to speak to nurses and doctors at various clinics and hospitals. We would discuss their obligations as mandated reporters, and I would try to allay the concerns particularly of physicians who feared being subpoenaed to a court and having to sit around all day waiting to testify.

I also reached out to the first responder medical personnel such as EMTs, paramedics, and firefighters. That audience proved crucial. I started to hear stories of neglect, suspicious injuries, and even concerns about uninvestigated deaths of elders. It was a wake-up call. Despite the progress that had been made, I was beginning to understand that we were still missing many cases and that too few predators were being held accountable.

I then spoke to the Medical Examiner's (ME's) Office about ways in which we could try to reduce the number of situations where suspicious deaths of elders fell between the cracks. I was learning through various articles about "gray murders." I also followed the troubling criminal case from England involving Dr. Harold Shipman who was ultimately convicted of murdering 15 of his patients. The resulting inquiry identified over 200 victims, the majority of whom were elderly women.

In March 2003, the County of San Diego created one of the nation's first Elder Death Review Teams. This was a collaboration between the DA's Office, the ME, the Sheriff, and the Aging and Independence Services. We started to meet quarterly and chose to discuss the suspicious death of an elder and would ask questions such as: "Was this death preventable?" and "Could an agency have responded in a different fashion?" One major advance that emerged was an understanding that before the ME's office waived jurisdiction, the ME investigator would always check with APS to see if the decedent was in the database as a potential victim of elder abuse.

As the number of reports of suspected financial elder abuse increased, I decided that we needed to devote time to talk to financial institutions. Indeed, it seemed logical that employees of banks and credit unions should become mandated reporters. Our efforts to expand the list of mandated reporters met with considerable resistance, but ultimately, in 2007, an agreement was reached. As a result, we were able to engage with various banks and credit unions and help train their staff in ways to recognize red flags of financial elder abuse.

Another group of individuals who became mandated reporters were the clergy. Interestingly, such a development got a lukewarm reception from many people within the faith community, but at least it provided an opportunity to increase the awareness level. One of the most common indicators that elder abuse is occurring is isolation. I found that many older victims were men and women of faith, and that the perpetrator of abuse would immediately cut off the victim's relationship with the place of worship. As such, it was imperative that the faith leaders be aware of such isolation and take steps to make unannounced home visits.

From Investigation to Prosecution

Now that we had a multidisciplinary team (MDT) approach, it was inevitable that the cases would begin to arrive on my desk without me having to go and look for them. The challenge now was not so much how to deal with the silence but how to convert elder abuse allegations into provable cases that would end up with convictions.

In California, we use an age-based definition for an elder. California Penal Code section 368 defines an elder as anybody 65 years of age or older. That same code section also covers dependent adults who are defined as aged 18 through 64 with certain physical or mental limitations. Even though this chapter focuses on elder abuse, the same lessons learned apply equally to dependent adult abuse.

Not every state uses an age-based definition. Many states rely on a "vulnerable adult" definition, which in my view presents an unnecessary additional burden of proof on the prosecutor, where one of the elements of the crime to be established is that the victim was "vulnerable." This may account for why in some parts of the country, elder abuse prosecutions are rare.

One of the mistakes that I believe prosecutors make is to assume that elder abuse prosecutions are difficult. In my experience, these cases can be no more difficult than any other. Regrettably, we have fallen into the misconception—as previously discussed with law enforcement—that elderly victims make poor witnesses in the courtroom. My experience based on over 600 prosecutions is very different.

When teaching on the subject, I often refer to my favorite elderly female victim as Agnes. She is 85 years of age. She has the most infectious smile. When she walks into the courtroom and passes the jury box, she looks at the 12 jurors and smiles. By the time she sits in the witness box, four of my jurors want to adopt her as their grandmother.

The primary reason why we have convinced ourselves that older adults will be ineffective witnesses is forgetfulness. But the majority of victims who testified in my cases have not been forgetful. They tended to remember an incident and may even have documented certain details. The law typically allows a witness to refresh his or her memory, and even when some elderly victims show signs of dementia that can often enhance the case: Jurors will see for themselves how a defendant took full advantage of a victim's cognitive decline.

One of the benefits of surrounding myself with other FPD prosecutors who were experienced in presenting a domestic violence case was that I could learn quickly how to deal with a reluctant or recanting victim. Many of my cases have involved an elderly mother who was beaten up by her drug addicted, unemployed son. After the initial arrest, the mother would sometimes make a call to my office and beg me not to file charges or would call to tell me that she was "dropping the charges" or "refusing to press charges." Inevitably, the reason for the call would have been precipitated by the fact that the in-custody son had made a collect call from jail to his mother urging her to talk to the DA.

One thing that human nature has taught me is that if we allow a suspect to "get away with it" because of a victim's reluctance or fear of potential retaliation, this only emboldens the perpetrator. That is why we adopted a tough policy of not allowing victims of elder abuse to choose which cases get filed or rejected. If we make the victim the decision-maker, it actually places the victim in more danger. At arraignment, the prosecutor can make it very clear to the court and to the defendant that the fact that charges were filed was because of the prosecutor and not because of the victim (Table 12.1).

Types of Criminal Elder Abuse

Physical elder abuse can take many forms including slapping, punching, and pushing. Sometimes because of the frailty of the victim, even the slightest push can lead to serious injury. Under California law, a felony conviction does not require any actual injury; it is enough that the circumstances of the conduct are likely to produce great bodily harm or death. I wish that more states would adopt similar legislation in recognition of the "eggshell rule"—meaning that a defendant takes the victim as he finds him or her.

The typical physical abuser in my experience is the unemployed, drug- or alcohol-addicted son who is still living at home with his widowed mother. He uses an excuse such as a bad back as his reason for not working. He needs money to fund his addiction and so he steals his mother's jewelry and pawns it. When she discovers the theft, the mother confronts her son and he reacts by punching her in the face. She suffers a black eye or worse.

Mental or emotional abuse is far more difficult to document unless the perpetrator leaves a recorded message or makes written threats. However, words can be as damaging as physical contact, and continual verbal harassment can impact the elder's health.

Table 12.1 Details From California Penal Code Section 368 Crimes Against Elders, Dependent Adults, and Persons With Disabilities.

(a) The Legislature finds and declares that crimes against elders and dependent adults are deserving of special consideration and protection, not unlike the special protections provided for minor children, because elders and dependent adults may be confused, on various medications, mentally or physically impaired, or incompetent and therefore less able to protect themselves, to understand or report criminal conduct or to testify in court proceedings on their own behalf.

(b)(1) Any person who knows or reasonably should know that a person is an elder or dependent adult and who, under circumstances or conditions likely to produce great bodily harm or death, willfully causes or permits any elder or dependent adult to suffer, or inflicts thereon unjustifiable physical pain or mental suffering, or having the care or custody of any elder or dependent adult, willfully causes or permits the person or health of the elder or dependent adult to be injured, or willfully causes or permits the elder or dependent adult to be placed in a situation in which his or her person or health is endangered, is punishable by imprisonment in a county jail not exceeding 1 year, by a fine not to exceed 6000 dollars ($6000), by both fine and imprisonment, or by imprisonment in the state prison for 2, 3, or 4 years.

(c) Any person who knows or reasonably should know that a person is an elder or dependent adult and who, under circumstances or conditions other than those likely to produce great bodily harm or death, willfully causes or permits any elder or dependent adult to suffer, or inflicts thereon unjustifiable physical pain or mental suffering, or having the care or custody of any elder or dependent adult, willfully causes or permits the person or health of the elder or dependent adult to be injured or willfully causes or permits the elder or dependent adult to be placed in a situation in which his or her person or health may be endangered, is guilty of a misdemeanor. A second or subsequent violation of this subdivision is punishable by a fine not to exceed 2000 dollars ($2000), by imprisonment in a county jail not to exceed 1 year, or by both fine and imprisonment.

(g) As used in this section, "elder" means a person who is 65 years of age or older.

(h) As used in this section, "dependent adult" means a person, regardless of whether the person lives independently, who is between the ages of 18 and 64, who has physical or mental limitations which restrict his or her ability to carry out normal activities or to protect his or her rights, including, but not limited to, persons who have physical or developmental disabilities or whose physical or mental abilities have diminished because of age. "Dependent adult" includes a person between the ages of 18 and 64 who is admitted as an inpatient to a 24-hour health facility, as defined in Sections 1250, 1250.2, and 1250.3 of the Health and Safety Code.

(i) As used in this section, "caretaker" means a person who has the care, custody, or control of, or who stands in a position of trust with, an elder or a dependent adult.

Retrieved from: http://leginfo.legislature.ca.gov/faces/codes_displaySection.xhtml?sectionNum=368&lawCode=PEN.

Criminal neglect includes situations where a caregiver has willfully deprived the elderly client of, for example, medical attention, proper nourishment, or appropriate hygiene. A classic victim of elder neglect would be someone who is semicomatose, malnourished, dehydrated, or found covered with pressure sores. In many states, there is a requirement that the suspect in a neglect case is a person who has demonstrated a duty of care toward the victim. In most cases, it is imperative to obtain an expert opinion from a geriatric nurse or doctor as to the extent of the neglect before issuing the case.

Financial elder abuse is probably the fastest growing form of elder abuse. In my 22 years of prosecuting elder abuse cases, financial exploitation probably accounted for at least 65% of my total caseload.

Theft from elders takes many forms. Examples are the caregiver who steals jewelry; the unlicensed contractor who takes an excessive deposit from the unsuspecting homeowner and fails to do the work; the bank teller who misappropriates money from the elder's account; the insurance agent who sells a fraudulent annuity; the realtor who buys the house from the senior at the price well under market value; or the court appointed guardian or conservator who fleeces their ward's assets. In recent years, due to the fact that more seniors are using technology and the internet, we have seen an explosion in the various types of scams. We are all familiar with the IRS bogus call threatening to have the elder arrested if the outstanding tax obligation is not paid within a few hours. Then there is the congratulatory phone call telling the victim that he or she is the winner of a sweepstakes and that the prize will be delivered once the taxes are paid. Sometimes the caller impersonates a grandchild and convinces the victim to send bail money to effectuate the release of the grandchild. We have also noted an increase in the romance scam—where scammers use legitimate dating websites to target older widows and widowers with bogus profiles.

When APS receives a report of suspected financial elder abuse which they substantiate, the case will be cross reported to local law enforcement. But there is a danger that the initial response will be "that it is just a civil matter." It is therefore important for prosecutors to persuade law enforcement that only someone suitably qualified can make that determination. It is preferable that the police are encouraged to take the initial report and run the facts by a trained prosecutor who can then make the ultimate determination as to whether the case is merely civil.

In evaluating financial exploitation cases, I have concluded that there are three possible scenarios:

Scenario number one entails a situation where the elderly victim has no cognitive impairment. He or she is able to testify competently that the defendant took property belonging to the victim without the victim's consent.

Scenario number two involves a victim who is unable to testify because of their advanced impairment. The transaction took place at a time when the victim was unable to provide consent, and the prosecutor will bring in a doctor to lay the foundation to establish lack of consent.

Scenario number three is the most challenging. This is where the victim is marginally competent to testify although there may be some signs of short-term memory loss. The victim appears to have voluntarily transferred assets to the suspect and may even appear to understand the nature and extent of the transaction. The suspect typically describes the transfer as either a gift or a loan. In reality, the victim has been unduly influenced. The challenge for the prosecutor is to overcome the "gift or loan" defense and establish sufficient evidence to show that any valid consent was nullified by fraud, lies, and misrepresentations. This is the situation that evokes most of the "it is a civil matter" responses from law enforcement, and so further discussion is merited.

It is essential that in this scenario, we can uncover certain evidence that will point to how the exertion of undue influence removed the consensual nature of the transaction. For example, I need to know the length of the relationship between victim and suspect. The longer the friendship, the more difficult it becomes to establish theft. I am also curious as to where and how the victim and suspect met. We often discover "chance" meetings outside stores in the parking lot, or from a knock on the door encounter, or at a place of worship or a casino. Then I need to find out about the victim's spending habits before meeting the suspect. If we are able to show that a long pattern of frugality is suddenly shattered when the suspect enters the victim's life, this will enhance the theory that transactions were conducted through manipulation rather than by an exercise of free will. Moreover, we need to take a close look at what the victim's money is being spent on. It is an old saying but still true: we must follow the money. That is why having a forensic accountant on your MDT is such an asset. We should be able to unearth expenditures that are clearly designed to benefit the suspect and not the victim. For example, we may identify purchases of a new car, vacation trips, gym membership, or clothes from a luxury store—all made without the victim's specific knowledge.

At the very heart of this scenario is the ability of the suspect to successfully persuade the victim to part with assets by using a combination of deception and charm. That is why we need to engage in a thorough victim interview. We want to find out what the suspect revealed to the victim about himself or herself. Did the suspect use an affinity ruse by pretending to be from the same area where the victim grew up? Or did the suspect fabricate an identity or profession with which the victim was totally impressed?

We also need to be able to show that the victim portrays characteristics that suggest that he or she is susceptible to undue influence. If possible, the victim should be evaluated by a geriatric mental health professional. Having such a professional on the elder abuse MDT is key to understanding how consent is removed through undue influence.

If we are to have an impact as prosecutors in stemming this tide of financial abuse, then we need to aggressively tackle the issue of consent head on. It is important that prosecutors and investigators know whether their state has any such jury instruction. California has a rarely used jury instruction that I have relied on in arguing lack of consent.

A California judge in a criminal trial can read the following instruction to the jurors:

To consent to a transaction a person (victim) must

1. Act freely and voluntarily and not under the influence of threats, force, or duress and
2. Have knowledge of the true nature of the act or transaction involved and
3. Possess the mental capacity to make an intelligent choice whether or not to do something proposed by another person (suspect).

The judge will then add the following comment: "consent requires a free will and positive cooperation in act or attitude."

There is a general agreement among scholars, researchers, and investigators that elder financial abuse is having a devastating impact on the lives of many victims. It sometimes leads to an early death caused by depression, suicide, or by giving up the will to live. What we don't know is the extent of the losses. Various published articles have cited losses at between $2 billion and $37 billion a year just in the United States alone (National Council on Aging, n.d.).

And then there is the hidden crime of sexual abuse of elders. In the past couple of years, several national media organizations have cast a spotlight on this crime, particularly in regard to the failure by traditional law enforcement to uncover, investigate, and prosecute alleged rapes in long-term care facilities. The profile of a "typical" case is that of an elderly female resident suffering from advanced dementia who is sexually assaulted by a male employee with access to the victim's room.

Such assaults can remain hidden because of the victim's inability to report the crime or to appreciate the nature of the nonconsensual act. Sometimes the victim may be too afraid to report the abuser out of fear of retaliation or the victim's cry for help is misinterpreted as delusional by an uncaring facility that is more concerned about its public image.

What these media articles have uncovered is a desperate need for every jurisdiction to reevaluate whether there are appropriate checks and balances in place to identify and respond to allegations of suspected sexual elder abuse. In September 2013, the San Diego Union Tribune newspaper published a series of hard-hitting articles entitled "Crimes go Uninvestigated in Care Homes." As a result, the County Board of Supervisors met with the DA and myself and agreed to locate additional funds so that our elder abuse prosecution unit could be expanded to also focus on uncovering hidden crimes including sexual assaults. For the next 3 years I worked with our local office of the California Attorney General and with the state agency of the Department of Social Services (DSS) that has jurisdiction over assisted living facilities in our county. We developed a protocol whereby DSS e-mailed my unit and the Attorney General's office fresh reports of alleged abuse in any one of the over 680 assisted living facilities in San Diego County. This traditionally is one of the biggest problems—getting the information first hand and within hours of the initial report being made. Too often a facility can try to delay reporting a suspected sexual assault by a staff member even though such a delay is a direct violation of their mandated reporting duties. By the time law enforcement is notified any opportunity to seize incriminating evidence is gone. The victim may have been bathed, her nightclothes may have been washed or discarded, bedding removed, and the suspect may have disappeared.

Just as with elder financial exploitation, consent will likely be a common defense. So, it is vital that investigators and prosecutors understand early in the investigation whether the victim lacks the ability to consent to sexual activity. It is important that hospitals, Sexual Assault Response Teams (SARTs), and law enforcement establish an understanding regarding obtaining implied consent for a SART exam where the victim is considered unable to provide consent. Is there a conservator or guardian appointed by a court or is there someone with Power of Attorney? What happens if there is no such back up? The worst possible outcome would be for a SART examiner or investigator to obtain the victim's consent via a signature only to later discover that the victim was unable to appreciate the significance of the document.

Preparing the Elderly Victim for the Criminal Justice System

It can be intimidating at any age to receive a subpoena demanding attendance at a court house to testify in a criminal matter. That uneasiness can then extend to the actual courtroom where the victim has to sit within a few yards of the defendant. That is why a prepared prosecutor and a victim advocate can help reduce fears, misconceptions, and reluctance on the part of an elderly victim and embolden the victim to become an effective and powerful witness.

Some important factors are

Logistics: Find out early in the case whether the senior has special needs for transportation. The prosecutor, through victim witness services, may need to provide wheelchair assistance, oxygen, or an escort. The elder may require special hearing or optical devices for his or her court appearance.

Medical concerns: Questions to ask might include: Is the senior taking medication that could affect the ability to testify? Does the elderly witness cope better in the morning or afternoon? What is the elder's state of health? Is the elder being treated medically for anything and by whom? It may turn out that the elder is physically incapable of coming to court, thereby necessitating a request for the court to come to the senior's bedside. The fact that a defendant is in custody should not preclude the possibility of conducting a hearing at the victim's bedside provided proper arrangements are made with the presiding judge ahead of time. Alternatively, it may be possible to set up a two-way video conferencing system from the victim's bedside which will still allow the defendant and defense counsel to "confront" the victim from the courtroom.

Personal concerns: The elder may have a hearing deficiency or vision problem that may impact the credibility of his or her testimony. Knowing this beforehand will allow prosecutors to prepare their questions accordingly. Hearing or visual deficiencies may also impact a person's effectiveness during testimony. A victim who cannot hear out of one ear or at a certain distance, or who has trouble seeing except directly in front, will need the prosecutor to be on his or her "good side" during questioning. Knowing this information beforehand helps an astute prosecutor be prepared to adjust accordingly.

The victim may also have a problem with incontinence that could affect their willingness to attend. Such issues need to be addressed before the court date to alleviate concerns.

Comfort of the senior at court: Invariably, witnesses are kept waiting at court. Standing in hallways or sitting on hard benches for hours on end is difficult for even young people; imagine the discomfort for "old" bones. It is vital that prosecutors provide seniors with a hospitable and friendly environment in which to wait. Therefore, every effort should be made to establish a waiting area exclusively for seniors, consisting of a room with comfortable sofas, a television, soft lighting, reading materials, and crossword puzzles.

One of the reasons that seniors are targeted is that many suspects rely on the fact that by the time the crime is detected, investigated, and an arrest is made, the victim may have already died.

So, prosecutors need to find ways to preserve the testimony of an elderly victim in a way that will withstand a motion to suppress made by defense counsel. In 2004, the United States Supreme Court ruled in Crawford versus Washington that the Sixth Amendment (the confrontation clause) requires that the defendant has had a prior opportunity to cross-examine the victim before "testimonial" evidence can be introduced from the now unavailable victim. Crawford's impact on prosecution of crimes against elders who are unavailable for cross-examination is especially problematic. While many physical abuse cases can still be proved beyond a reasonable doubt even in the absence of the victim, the victim's testimony is often crucial when prosecuting a financial abuse case under scenarios one and three as described above. Direct testimony may be the only way to establish that the defendant did not have the victim's consent at the time of the transfer of assets from the victim to the defendant.

Crawford's influence extends to the timeline by which a prosecutor presents a victim's testimony. Grand jury proceedings are discouraged as cross-examination by defense attorneys is excluded; and therefore victim Grand Jury testimony cannot later be introduced at trial if the victim becomes unavailable. It is therefore incumbent on the prosecution to ensure that a preliminary hearing takes place as soon as is practical and that the victim is exposed to cross-examination at that hearing. Requests for a delay in setting a preliminary hearing should normally be vigorously opposed. And when setting the preliminary hearing, consideration should be given as to whether the victim's testimony should be preserved through videotaping. It is one thing to read the victim's preliminary hearing testimony at trial; it is a whole different experience for a jury to watch the prior testimony as it unfolds via a video recording.

Challenges for the Future

As the elderly population continues to grow, all the indications are that the crime of elder abuse will become one of this country's biggest social issues in the next 30 years. Despite the fact that some jurisdictions have made significant advances in responding to this crime, unfortunately the majority of states have failed to grasp the need for greater resources and training to combat the escalation in the various types of elder abuse. APS are stretched to the breaking point. We need to secure massive additional funding to provide for more front-line case workers to deal with the ever increasing referrals. It is shocking to compare the ratio of Child Protective Services workers with that of APS. Such an imbalance needs to be addressed.

We also should examine ways in which our court system can become more user friendly to elder victims. Consideration should be given to adopting elder courts that handle both civil and criminal matters involving allegations of elder abuse. Judges who preside over such cases would be trained in making sure that access to justice is available for seniors—such as streamlining procedures for obtaining restraining orders and designing courtrooms with senior impairment issues and disabilities in mind.

An emerging concern involves the abuse of power by certain court appointed guardians and conservators. Probate courts should receive special training for their staff to keep an eye on how fiduciaries account for their time and spending of the ward's assets.

Police and Sheriff agencies need to ensure that their officers and deputies are exposed to elder abuse issues both at entry level through the academy and throughout their career. We must ensure that the response of "it is just a civil matter" or "victim declines prosecution" is gradually eradicated from law enforcement's vocabulary.

State prosecutor associations must offer annual trainings to equip their prosecutors, investigators, and victim advocates with skills on how to present various types of elder abuse cases. We also need to examine ways that crimes that occur in long-term care facilities are more quickly identified, investigated, and prosecuted. Greater cooperation between state agencies that license these facilities, the State Ombudsman's offices, and law enforcement agencies is urgently needed. We cannot continue to turn a blind eye to such crimes that have gone unpunished.

Finally, on a federal level, we need to find solutions to the ever-growing problem of Internet and telephone scams that reach across state and international borders. Surely, we can establish task forces in major urban areas involving the various federal agencies such as Department of Justice, US Postal Inspectors, Federal Bureau of Investigation, Secret Service, and state and local law enforcement agencies.

We have all heard the quote that talks about how we measure a community—by the way we care for the young, the elderly, and the defenseless. So, how do we measure a country? There is so much more that we can do to protect our elders, and one immediate solution is to learn how to aggressively pursue the predators through our criminal justice system.

References

California Penal Code. (n.d.). Retrieved from http://leginfo.legislature.ca.gov/faces/codes_displaySection.xhtml?sectionNum=368&lawCode=PEN.

National Council on Aging. (n.d.). Elder abuse facts. Retrieved from www.ncoa.org/public-policy-action/elder-justice/elder-abuse-facts/.

INDEX

Note: 'Page numbers followed by "t" indicate tables, "f" indicate figures'.

Abandonment, 178–179
Abbreviated Injury Scale (AIS), 129t
Abrasions, 27, 28f, 121, 234
Abusive sexual contact, 109
Accidental injury, 31–32, 233–234
Adult Protective Services (APS), 8–9, 44–45, 166, 192–193, 202, 208, 231
Adverse Childhood Experiences (ACEs) scores, 59
Advocacy, 101
Aggression, verbal, 171–172
Aging and victimization
  declining mental function, 21
  diminished capacity, 21
  financial abuse, 22
  positive lifestyle, 21
  proactive approach, 21
  signs of, 21
  vulnerability, 21
Aging population
  accidental death and suicide, 12
  cognitive decline and dementia, 12
  health care, 11–12
  multicultural competence, 12
  socioeconomics, 12
Alcohol-Related Problems Survey, 225–226
Alcohol use disorder
  binge drinking alcohol, 216
  consumption limit, 216
  "functional alcoholics", 216–217
  homemade alcohol, 216–217
  ICD-10 codes, 219t
  sedative effects, 217

Alcohol Use Disorders Identification Test (AUDIT), 225–226
Alzheimer's dementia (AD)
  apolipoprotein E gene (ApoE) mutation, 62–63
  brain tissue atrophy, 61–62
  classic, 63–64
  difficulties, 61–62
  early-onset, 62–63
  maltreatment, 61–62
  severe, 78–79
  signs and symptoms, 63
  tau protein accumulations, 61–62
American Association of Retired Persons (AARP) movement, 100–101
Amnestic mild cognitive impairment, 60
  case study, 57
  clinical evaluation, 59
  diagnosis, 61
Anal excoriation, 28
Anosognosia, 72
Anticoagulants, 27–28
Antipsychotics, chemical restraint, 224
Asphyxia, 25
Assisted living caregivers, 96–97
Assisted living facilities, 23, 76–77
Atrophy, 141–142
Attachment loss, 167–168
Attachment theory, 167
Autopsy examination
  dissection, 237–238
  external examination, 237–238
  internal examination, 237–238

medical records and interviews, 237
photographic documentation, 237–238
sexual assault examination, 237–238
toxicology, 238

"Baby battering", 2
Barbiturates, 217
Behavioral variant frontotemporal dementia (bvFTD), 68
Benzodiazepines, chemical restraint, 224
Benzodiazepine use disorder, 217–218
Binge drinking alcohol, 216
Black's Law Dictionary, 8–9
Blunt force injuries, 233–234
  abrasions, 234
  contusions, 234–235
  fractures, 234
  lacerations, 234–235
Brain's development, 90–91
Brief Abuse Screen for the Elderly (BASE), 36, 175
Bruise, 121–122
Bruising, 24–25, 27, 27f, 32
Burns, 236
  classification, 124, 125f
  first-degree burn, 125f
  partial thickness burn, 126f
  second and third-degree, 126f
  thickness and injury, 126f

Canadian Elder Abuse Suspicion Index, 36
Cardiovascular diseases, 232

Caregiver Abuse Screen for the Elderly (CASE), 36
Caregiver burden, 97
Caregiver neglect, 29
Caregiver Psychological Elder Abuse Behavior Scale (CPEABS), 175–176
Centers for Medicare and Medicaid services, 78
Chemical restraint
  agitation, 224
  definition, 224
  pharmacologic intervention, 224
Child abuse, 9
Child Protective Services (CPS), 9, 243
Codeine, 221t
Cognition, 58t
Cognitive impairment, 58t.
  See also Mild cognitive impairment (MCI)
Collaborative approach, 184
Collagen synthesis, 118
Comorbidity Alcohol Risk Evaluation Tool (CARET), 225–226
Conflict Tactic Scale (CTS), 35, 176–177
Contextual Theory of Abuse, 164–165
Contraction, wound, 118–119
Contusion, 121–123, 234–235
Coordinated Community Response Teams (CCRT), 131
Crime scene investigator (CSI), 187
Criminal abuse, 165
Criminal defense practice, 243
Criminal justice response
  age-based definition, 246
  criminal elder abuse
    criminal neglect, 248–249
    financial elder abuse, 249–251
    jurisdiction, 252
    mental/emotional abuse, 247

physical elder abuse, 247
    sexual abuse and assaults, 251–252
  domestic violence case, 246–247
  elder abuse prosecutions, 246
  elderly victim preparation, 253–254
  future challenges, 255–256
  multidisciplinary team (MDT) approach, 242–245
  victim's cognitive decline, 246
  victim's reluctance, 247
Criminal law, 8
Criminal liability, 37–38
Cultural awareness
  African American communities, 40–41
  American Indian/Alaska Native (AI/AN) elders, 41
  Asian American elders, 39
  demographic changes, 38
  elderly prisoners, 44
  immigrant populations, 41–42
  immigrants with green cards, 39
  intervention and advocacy
    assistance sources, 46–49
    eligibility and service requirements, 44–45
    forensic documentation, 44–45
    Older Americans Act (OAA), 45–46
  Latino elders, 40
  LGBTQ elders, 42–43
  nonphysical abuse, 39–40
  physical abuse, 39–40
  rural communities, 39
  seeking behavior, 39–40
  unphysical abuse, 39–40
Cultural norms change, 14
Cyclical violence, 98–99
Cytokines, 120

Death certificate, 207
Death investigation
  community

death certificate, 207
  family members and caregivers, 208
  law enforcement, 207
  physical examination, 207–208
  scene investigation, 207–208
  trauma and injury, 207
health-care facility
  documentation, 205
  emergency department (ED), 204
  emergency medical technicians (EMTs), 204
  laboratory studies, 205
  medical record, 204–205
  osteoporosis, 206
  trauma risk, 206
Death investigation system. *See* Medicolegal death investigation (MLDI)
Decubitus ulcers, 236
Defensive injuries, 236
Dementia, 233
  Alzheimer's dementia. *See* Alzheimer's dementia (AD)
  assisted living facilities, 76–77
  brain changes, 56
  care transitions, 76
  case study, 57–60
  definition, 58t
  dementia with Lewy bodies (DLB), 69–70
  frontotemporal dementia. *See* Frontotemporal dementia (FTD)
  mild stage, 71–73
  mixed, 71
  moderate stage, 73–75
  nursing homes, 77–78
  severe stage, 75–76
  sexual assault and rape, 152, 153f
  types, 62t
  vascular dementia. *See* Vascular dementia (VaD)

Dementia with Lewy bodies (DLB)
parasomnia, 69–70
Parkinson disease, 70
signs ans symptoms, 69–70
visual hallucinations, 69–70
Department of Social Services (DSS), 252
Dermis, 110
Dextromethorphan (DXM), 222
Diazepam, 217
Diphenhydramine, 222
Disrespect, 14
Distrust, 166–167
Diversion, 223
Doxylamine, 222
Dyspareunia pain, 141–142
Dysthymic mental state, 168

Ecchymosis and ecchymotic spread, 123
Elastin, 118–119
Elder abuse
Adult Protective Services (APS), 9
"aging in place", 10–11
awareness and legislation, 4t–5t
"baby battering", 2
community and cultural norms, 14
criminal justice response. See Criminal justice response
cultural awareness. See Cultural awareness
death investigation. See Death investigation
definition and difficulties, 3–6
dementia. See Dementia
documentation
challenges, 34–35
and reporting, 37–38
short questionnaires and scales, 34–35
tools and measures, 35–37
written tools, 35
Elder Justice Act, 2
and family law, 7–9
family violence, 2

financial crimes, 13
forensic markers, 15
"granny battering", 2
"hidden problem", 2
homicide, 1
incidence and prevalence, 12–15
institutional abuse. See Institutional abuse
interpersonal violence. See Interpersonal violence
low income, 13
markers and injuries, 2–3
medical and legal implications, 15
multidisciplinary collaboration. See Multidisciplinary collaboration
multifaceted nature, 6–7
observable injury vs. suspected abuse
accidental injury and inflicted injury, 31–32
challenges in Identification, 32–33
fear of disclosure, 33–34
physical decline, 30
physical abuse. See Physical abuse
psychological abuse. See Psychological abuse
right to privacy, 10
right to self-determination, 10
risk and vulnerability
aging and victimization, 21–22
case study, 50
comprehensive geriatric assessment, 19–20
diseases and disorders mimics abuse, 24–29
institutional abuse, 22–24
lifestyle and social choices, 19–20
neglect and self-neglect, 29–30
risk factors, 19–20
risk factors, 13

sexual assault and rape. See Sexual assault and rape
social and economic change, 13–14
substance use and misuse. See Substance use and misuse
Elder Abuse Decision Support System (EADSS), 177
Elder Abuse Prevention Unit (EAPU), 29–30
Elder Abuse Suspicion Index (EASI), 174–175
Elder Assessment Instrument (EAI), 35, 175
Elder Justice Act, 2, 29, 44–45
Elderly Indicators of Abuse (E-IOA) scale, 36
Elder Mistreatment Response Programs, 46
Elder protective services (EPS), 8
Elder Psychological Abuse Scale (EPAS), 175–176
Electronic health record (EHR), 101
Emergency medical service (EMS) protocols, 24
Emergency medical technicians (EMTs), 204
Emotional abuse (EA), 87, 163–164, 247
Employee and staff programs, 103
Employment practices, 93
Epidermal cells, 117
Epidermis, 110
Epithelialization, 117

Faith-based programs, 46
Family law, 7–9
Family Protection Division (FPD), 242
Fecal incontinence, 151–152
Federal and international laws, 8–9
Fentanyl, 218–219, 221t
Fibroblast growth factor, 120
Fibroblasts, 117–118
Fibronectin, 117
Fibroplasia, 117–118

Field triage decision schema, 127–129, 128f
Financial abuse, 7, 40–41, 249–251
Financial abuse specialist teams (FAST), 48
Financial crimes, 13
Financial feasibility, 11
Financial service industry, 102–103
Fluid production, 111–112
Forensic markers
  hand slaps, 233–234
  injuries
    blunt force injuries, 233–234
    burns, 236
    extremities, 236
    from falls, 235
    neck, 235
    oral mucosa, 235
    patterned, 233–234
    petechial hemorrhages, 236–237
    strangulation, 236–237
    subarachnoid hemorrhage, 235
    torso injuries, 235
    ulcers, 236
  neglect and self-neglect, 237
  strangulation, 233–234
Forensic nurse death investigator (FNDI), 201–202
Forensic nurse examiner (FNE), 188
  case example, 196–197
  cognitive deficit, 190–191
  law enforcement, 191
  photography, 191–192
  training and education, 190
  victim of elder abuse, 191
  written report, 191–192
Fractured bone, 2–3
Fractures, 235
Frontotemporal dementia (FTD)
  behavioral variant, 68
  case study, 68–69
  mean age, 67–68

nonfluent primary progressive aphasia, 68
semantic variant primary progressive aphasia, 68
Functional changes, 141–142

Generational violence, 90
Genital injury, 150–152
Genital injury scale, 151–152
Granulation formation, 116
Green House Project, 102
Guardianship, 8–9

Health Insurance Portability and Accountability Act (HIPAA) guidelines, 192
Healthy sexual relationship, 144–145
Hemiparesis, 65
Hemiplegia, 65
Hepatic cirrhosis, 232–233
"Home", 10–11
Homemade alcohol, 216–217
HwalekeSengstock Elder Abuse Screening Test (HeS/ EAST), 35, 174
Hydrocodone, 221t
Hydromorphone, 221t
Hypodermis, 110

Incisional wounds, 117
Inflammation, 115
Inflicted injury, 31–32
Informed consent, 189
Injury Severity Scores, 112–114
Institutional abuse
  "active senior communities", 22
  cost and payment, 22–23
  decubiti, 23–24
  emergency departments, 24
  out-of-home options, 22
  prehospital providers, 24
  risk factors and consequences, 23–24
  round-the-clock care, 22
  unlicensed assistive personnel, 23

Integument system, 109–110, 113f
Intentional injury, 108, 132f
  assessment barriers, 129–130
  bruising studies, 129–130
  with comorbidities, 132
  neglect, 133–134, 133f
Intermittent caregivers, 97
International Covenant on Economic, Social and Cultural Rights, 10
International Network for Prevention of Elder Abuse, 49
Interpersonal violence
  elders growth projections, 86
  incidence and prevalence, 86
  interprofessional providers, 85–86
  risk factors
    age-related physiologic changes, 87
    clinical gaps, 89–90
    emergency departments and hospitalization, 87
    emotional and psychological abuse, 87
    generational violence, 90
    health-care access, 88–89
    living environments, 87–88
    maltreatment, 89
    quality of life, 87
    self-reported abuse, 88
    underidentification and underreporting, 90
    vulnerabilities, 86–87, 90
  victims of elder abuse, 86
Intimate partner violence (IPV), 24
15-Item paper-and-pencil test, 35

Jagged open wound, 26f

Ketamine
  chemical restraint, 224
  dementia, 224–225
  medical record, 225

Laceration, 234–235
  blunt forces, 121
  hand, 121f
  knee, 122f
Langerhan lines, 151–152
Law enforcement
  crime scene investigator
      (CSI), 187
  investigator, 187–188
  medicolegal death
      investigation (MLDI),
      202–203
  responding officer
    crime scene, 185–186
    human dignity,
      185–186
    medical intervention, 185
    medical needs, 185
Librium, 217
Lichen sclerosus, 28
Logistics, 253
Loneliness, 6–7
Long-acting benzodiazepines,
  218
Loperamide, 222
Lymphocytes, 115–116

Macrophages, 115–116
Maturation phase, 119
Medical examiner response
  anatomic and physiological
      factors, 232–233
  autopsy examination,
      237–238
  clinical and pathologic
      findings, 232
  forensic markers. *See* Forensic
      markers
Medication diversion, 223
Medicolegal death investigation
  (MLDI)
  case example, 208–209
  components, 202–203
  death investigation systems,
      200
  death investigator, 200

elder death investigation. *See*
    Death investigation
forensic pathologist, 200
reportable deaths, 200, 201t
Memory, definition, 58t
Memory loss. *See also* Dementia
  allostatic load, 59
  cognitive impairment, 58t. *See
    also* Mild cognitive
    impairment (MCI)
  comprehensive physical
    examination, 58
  definition, 58t
  laboratory tests, 58
Mental Status Exam, 173–174
Mental stress, 171–172
Meprobamate, 217
Michigan Alcoholism Screening
    InstrumenteGeriatric
    Version (MAST-G),
    225–226
Mild cognitive impairment
    (MCI)
  amnestic, 60
    case study, 57
    clinical evaluation, 59
    diagnosis, 61
  definition, 58t, 60
  nonamnestic, 60
    case study, 57–58
    clinical evaluation, 60
    diagnosis, 61
  screening tools, 60–61
Mini Mental Status Exam
    (MMSE) score, 36–37,
    60–61, 174–175
Mistreatment, 3
Modified Conflict Tactics Scale
    (m-CTS), 176–177
Montreal Cognitive Assessment
    (MoCA), 60–61
Multidisciplinary collaboration
  case example, 195–197
  forensic nurse examiner
    (FNE), 190–192
  information sharing, 195
  justice system

adult protective services
    (APS), 192–193
  district attorneys office, 194
  prosecuting attorney,
    193–194
law enforcement. *See* Law
    enforcement
medical provider and
    physician
  admission, 190
  emergency department, 189
  informed consent, 189
  laboratory analysis,
    189–190
  radiological studies,
    189–190
  victim, 188–189
multidisciplinary team, 184
Multidisciplinary team (MDT)
  approach, 242–245

Narcotics, 218–220
National Academies of Sciences
    (NAS), 165–166
National Center on Elder Abuse
    (NCEA), 6, 13, 44–46,
    163–164
National Institute on Drug
    Abuse (NIDA), 225–226
National Intimate Partner and
    Sexual Violence Survey, 13
National Resource Center on
    LGBT Aging (NRCLA), 48
Neglect, 29–30
  definition, 109
  elder death investigation, 209
Neuron development, 90–91
Neutrophils, 115–116
Nonamnestic mild cognitive
    impairment, 60
  case study, 57–58
  clinical evaluation, 60
  diagnosis, 61
Noncompliance, 33–34
Nonfluent primary progressive
    aphasia frontotemporal
    dementia, 68

Occlusive and semiocclusive dressings, 117
Older Adult Mistreatment Assessment, 176
Older Adult Psychological Abuse Measure (OAPAM), 176
Older Americans Act (OAA), 45–46
Omnibus Budget and Reconciliation Act, 44–45
Open wounds, 25, 26f–27f
Opioid use disorder
  drug-drug interactions, 220
  ICD-10-CM codes, 219t
  opioids, 221t
  symptoms, 220
  synthetic opiates, 218–219
  withdrawal effects, 220
Oral mucosal injuries, 235
Osteoporosis, 206, 233
Over-the-counter (OTC) medications
  preparations, 222
  symptoms and illnesses, 221–222
Overtreatment, 93
Oxycodone, 221t
OxyContin, 218–219

Parent-child dynamics, 91
Parkinson disease, 70
Patterned injuries, 233–234
Periorbital eye trauma, 25, 26f
Perpetrated abusive behaviors, 168
Perpetrators, 130
Petechial hemorrhages, 236–237
Phencyclidine (PCP), 222
Physical abuse
  case study, 15–16
  criminal justice response, 247
  cultural awareness, 39–40
  definition, 109
  institutional setting, 23–24
  intentional injury. See Intentional injury

manifestations, 108
vulnerability, 6–7
and wound identification. See Skin injury
Physically abusive behaviors (PhAB), 176–177
Plasmin, 117
Plasminogen, 115
Platelet-derived growth factor (PDGF), 120
Polypharmacy, 213–214
Polysubstance use, 217
Poor mental and physical health, 19–20
Posterior gluteal bruising, 25, 26f
Posttraumatic stress disorder (PTSD), 70–71
Potentially harmful behavior (PHB), 176–177
Prescription medications, 93, 202–203
Pressure ulcers, 236
Prison Rape Elimination Act (PREA), 44
Procollagen, 118
Proliferation, 118
Prosecuting attorney, 193–194
Pseudoephedrine, 222
Psychological abuse (PA), 13, 19–20
  abandonment, 178–179
  assessment and evaluation tools, 173–177
  case study, 179–180
  developmental factors, 166–168
  education, 24
  emotional abuse (EA), 163–164
  family caregiver, 170
  forensic and medical analysis, 164–165
  impact and consequences, 168–169, 169t
  institutional neglect and abuse, 23–24
  interpersonal violence, 87
  isolation and social abuse, 172–173

life space, 166
nonfamily caregivers, 170–171
prevalence data, 163–164
signs and symptoms, 163–164
sociocultural contexts and relational factors, 165–166
verbal abuse, 171–172
violence and relationships, 96–97
Psychologically abusive behaviors (PsAB), 176–177

Rape, 141
Reportable deaths, 200, 201t
Round open red wound, accidental trauma, 27f

Secretory glands, 111
Self-neglect, 29–30
Self-reported abuse, 88
Semantic variant primary progressive aphasia, 68
Senile purpura, 27–28
Serial and cyclical violence, 98–99
Sex offenders, 147
Sexual abuse, 109
Sexual assault and rape
  aging, 143–144
  autopsy examination, 237–238
  Baby Boomers, 144
  capacity and competence, 153–154
  case study, 145–146, 152–154
  criminal justice response, 251–252
  definition, 141
  dementia, 152, 153f
  eyewitness and forensic laboratory evaluation, 148–149
  fulminant hepatitis B infection, 154–155
  genitalia and aging, 141–142

genital injury, 150–152
Greatest Generation, 144
healthy sexual relationship,
144–145
lifelong consequences, 140
mimics, 28
morbidity and mortality, 140
sex offenders, 147
sexual crimes, 146–147
sexually transmitted disease,
142–143, 149–150
sexual predators, 147
signs and indicators, 146–147
Silent Generation, 144
trauma, 155–157
violent crime, 140
Sexual Assault Response Teams
(SARTs), 252
Sexually transmitted disease,
142–143
Sexual predators, 147
Sexual violence, 141
Short-acting benzodiazepines,
218
Shorter version Michigan
Alcoholism Screening
InstrumenteGeriatric
Version (SMAST-G),
225–226
Skin
accessory structures, 110–111
aging impact, 111–112
color, 109–110
dermis, 110
discharge, 111
drainage, 111
epidermis, 110
functions, 109–110
glands, 111
hair and the hair follicle,
109–110
hypodermis, 110
sensory receptor, 109–110
Skin injury
Abbreviated Injury Scale
(AIS), 129t
abrasion, 121
avulsion, 127
bruise, 121–122

burn, 124
depth and coagulation
zones, 129f
ecchymosis and ecchymotic
spread, 123
epithelialization, 117
erythema, 127
fibroplasia, 117–118
field triage decision schema,
127–129, 128f
healing phases, 119–121
hematoma, 127
inflammation
cellular aspect, 115–116
coagulation process, 115
leg infection, 116f
vasodilation, 115
laceration, 121, 121f–122f
maturation phase, 119
petechiae, 123–124, 124f
proliferation, 116, 118
purpura, 124
subdermal hematoma,
123, 123f
vasoconstriction, 115
Social isolation, 6–7, 172–173
Social Security Act, 9
Social Work Evaluation, 174–175
Sociocultural norms, 19–20
Solar damage, 32
Solar purpura, 27–28
Steroid medications, 27–28
Stigmatization, 167–168
Strangulation, 233–234
Subarachnoid hemorrhage, 235
Subconjunctival hemorrhage,
25, 25f
Subdural hemorrhage, 235
Substance Abuse and Mental
Health Services
Administration, 214
Substance use and misuse
alcohol use and polysubstance
use disorder, 216–217
assessment, 225–226
benzodiazepine use disorder,
217–218
care plan, 225–226
case study, 227

chemical restraint, 224–225
cognitive impairment, 214
comorbidities, 213–214
demographics, 213–214
DSM-5 diagnostics, 215t
education, 226
ICD-10-CM codes, 219t
incidence, 213–214
medication diversion, 223
opioid use disorder, 218–220
over-the-counter
medications, 221–222
polypharmacy, 213–214
screening and treatment,
225–226
severity level, 214
Sufentanil, 221t
Superficial wounds, 117

Tax retirement income and
pensions, 12
Thinning integument, 120–121
T lymphocytes, 115–116
Topical estrogens, 141–142
Transforming growth factor-β,
120
Trauma
case-control study, 112–114
Injury Severity Score, 112–114
mortality rates, 112–114
red flags, 112–114
"Triangle of violence", 3–6
Tropocollagen, 118
Tumor necrosis factor-α, 120

Ulcers, 236
Unintentional elder abuse,
99–100
Unintentional injury, 131, 131f
Unlicensed assistive
personnel, 23

Vascular dementia (VaD)
case study, 65–67
clotted arterioles, 64–65
comorbid diseases, 64–65
head injury, 64–67
hypertension, 64–65
signs, 65

Vascular dementia (VaD)
(*Continued*)
    strangulation, 64–65
Vasoconstriction, 115
Vasodilation, 115
Verbal abuse, 171–172
Verbal intimidation, 172
Victim assistance advocate, 194
Violence and relationships.
    See also Interpersonal
        violence
    burden and fatigue, 97–99
    caregiver role change, 91–93
    care provider, 95–97
    cyclical violence, 98–99
    health-care providers,
        93–97
    power and privilege, 90–91

prevention
    advocacy, 101
    American Association of
        Retired Persons (AARP)
        movement, 100–101
    assisted living and
        supportive living
        environments, 102
    baby boomers, 100–101
    community service
        organizations, 101–102
    elder care industry, 103
    life care planners, 102–103
    screenings, 101
    smart homes and smart
        devices, 102
    training and education, 102

    unintentional elder abuse,
        99–100
Vulnerability Abuse Screening
    Scale (VASS), 36, 175
Vulnerable adult, 246

Washerwoman syndrome,
    111–112
World Elder Abuse Awareness
    Day, 49
Wound healing
    epithelialization, 117
    fibroplasia, 117–118
    inflammation, 115
    maturation phase, 119
    proliferation, 116, 118
    vasoconstriction, 115

9780128157794